The Guide To
Real Estate Exchanging

Other works by Jack Cummings

Nonfiction

The Complete Guide to Real Estate Financing

The Complete Handbook of How to Farm Real Estate Listings and Sales

Building Your Wealth Through Creative Real Estate Investing

Cashless Investing in Real Estate

Successful Real Estate Investing for the Single Person

$1,000 Down Can Make You Rich

The Real Estate Financing Manual

The Cummings Exchange Letter

The Business Traveler's Survival Guide

Fiction

Lauderdale Run

The Venture

The Ultimate Game

The Guide To
Real Estate Exchanging

Jack Cummings

John Wiley & Sons, Inc.

New York • Chichester • Brisbane • Toronto • Singapore

To Miss Bronte—the only girl for me

Copyright © 1991 by Jack Cummings

Published by John Wiley & Sons, Inc.

Library of Congress Cataloging-in-Publication Data

Cummings, Jack, 1940-
    The guide to real estate exchanging / by Jack Cummings.
        p. cm.
        Includes bibliographical references.
    ISBN 0-471-53328-9 (alk. paper). --ISBN 0-471-53327-0 (pbk.: alk. paper)
    1. Real property. Exchange of. I. Title.
    HD1395.C86 1991
    333.33--dc20

                                    90-24546

Printed in the United States of America

91 92 10 9 8 7 6 5 4 3 2 1

Contents

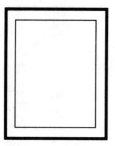 **Acknowledgments**

For any book of this magnitude, other people must be supportive of the effort. For this book there are several such people who need to be recognized. Most important would be my wife, who by now understands that there is nothing personal between my computer and me and who plans around my deadlines as one would prepare for a hurricane.

Then there are the "insiders" of the real estate game I have been associated with over the past 25 years. There are far too many to list, and it isn't their names that are really important, but the lessons they have taught me. I am still learning, too.

For the tax laws and other IRS information contained in this book, I owe a special thanks to Robert Chalnick and Bob Ricci at Millward & Co. Certified Public Accountants in Fort Lauderdale, Florida, for their research and assistance in making sure that the information provided is current.

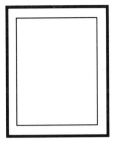

Introduction

If you or anyone you know has ever wondered what it takes to win at the real estate game, you are holding the answer in your hand. This book opens the door to the last loophole left in real estate investing—exchange and barter. This book is your guide to the world of building wealth through real estate.

Of course, your real question at this moment is: Is this book worth the price? Will you or whomever you might present it to profit from it? In short, should you chuck this book back on the shelf and look for another, or should you buy this book?

Answer: Buy this book.

Here's why. This book represents a love affair between me and all real estate investors, novices or advanced "insiders." This book is written for **you**—an investor who wants to become an insider or, if you already are, to get the edge on the other insiders. This book is your key to the door on which opportunity frequently knocks. Get ready to open that door. Buy this book.

Prior to writing this book, I wrote down the following goals, which have been my guideposts from start to finish.

My Goals as Writer

1. Write a book that is entertaining to read.
2. Build the reader's knowledge, step by step, so that by the end of the book even the most creative of techniques will be smooth and easygoing.
3. Provide a book in which any single chapter is more than worth the price of the whole book.

Sure, real estate investing is serious business, but that doesn't mean you can't have fun learning about it. With that in mind, you will find this book to be different, refreshing, and most rewarding. The material flows in an easy progression of examples and techniques that are designed to take you from the most basic element of **what it takes to win at the real estate game,** to very advanced money-making ideas and techniques—which, by the time you get to them, will seem a natural extension of your growing self-confidence and ability.

In the very first chapter you discover why **chaos** creates opportunity and how to stop butting your head against brick walls.

Do you know who the real enemies of the buyer and seller are? There are six, and Chapter 1 lists them and tells you how to deal with them and **beat them.**

Ever wonder about the **Greener-Grass Theory?** It is the fundamental reason that most exchanges work. It is so simple, yet so profound, that it is often overlooked as a primary technique. Not anymore—not by you, at least.

The book shifts gear in Chapter 2 and gets down to some of the detailed rules and regulations that govern the use of **installment sales,** the 1034 **house-for-house exchange,** and the last loophole of all, **the 1031 tax-free exchange.** Unlike other treatments of these subjects, Chapter 2 takes you through a warm-up, then outlines each subject with easy-to-understand examples. Most important, this book not only gives you the rules, examples, and potential problems, but it shows you how to finesse and maneuver the technique so that you can quickly attain your own investment goals. In Chapter 14, "Nine Creative Techniques That Are Magic to Exchanges," I give you all the building blocks you can use to mix and match in hundreds of different ways with other techniques to create your own rainbow of "insider's tools."

Glance through the table of contents. Notice the **10 keys to establishing proper goals** in Chapter 1; those 10 keys will get you started on the right foot and headed in the right direction.

With the right kind of goals you can now build your investment bank with your comfort zone that turns into a gold mine. Chapter 4 takes you through each step to show you how to set up your own comfort zone, develop your team members, and to show you whom you should know in your community, and how to meet them so that they know you.

Ever wonder how to get the most out of your real estate broker? Chapter 9 gives you the keys to dealing with the professional agent. Learn the five steps to getting **maximum benefits from your real estate agent,** learn the three key factors in dealing with the pros, discover the **seven deal-breaking factors** and how to overcome them.

The 25 things you need to know as a seller, including how to negotiate the offer and counteroffer, are all a part of Chapter 9 as you develop into a smoothly running investing machine. You are discovering how to get and keep the edge.

Here are subjects never before put into print: barter, the deal maker and sweetener; **Zanders,** the fantastic running game that allows many exchanges to be made and completed in less than half an hour; barter scrip, the money you actually print (legally) and spend to build your wealth.

No other book about real estate investing has ever provided you with such a complete opportunity to discover and master the world of real estate exchange and barter, and in Chapter 11 presents a step-by-step procedure for starting your own exchange club. There's no better way to prove to everyone that you are a true insider.

"Nine Creative Techniques," Chapter 14, contains a wealth of information; any one of the nine can make the difference between winning or losing your next real estate transaction.

Eleven pitfalls and how to deal with them are found in Chapter 15. Each is a potential deal killer, and each is broken down to show you not only how to deal with the problem when it comes your way, but how to avoid **ever** having to deal with it.

All real estate investments make it to the closing table. This is also where many transactions blow apart. Chapter 16 shows you how to get through the closing, what you can do when one of the seven **preclosing problems** comes up, and how to follow up after the closing.

Chapter 17, "Taking Positive Steps for Positive Gains," is designed for you to achieve the following:

- Become a real estate insider
- Build your knowledge of real estate investment techniques
- Understand and be able to use real estate exchange and barter to **maximize your real estate investments**
- Have more confidence in your investment ability
- Have greater profit from more real estate deals
- Become financially independent
- Make a greater connection between financial success and happiness

You have the world ahead of you. Buy this book and start now to take control of your future. This is your roadmap to financial success.

The Insider's Guide to Real Estate Exchanges

What It Takes to Win at the Real Estate Game

The game of real estate investing is played by many different people. Some, like David Delgotto, win accidentally. He purchased a five-acre tract of land in the middle of Florida that was a swampy pine- and cypress-wooded expanse that fate and the luck of the draw destined to be next to Disneyworld. Other players, like Craig Voight, win because they do their homework; he is one of the most astute pencil pushers and due-diligence guys in the game. When he wins it is because he knew he would right from the very moment he acquired the property. Your goal is to be more like Craig Voight and less like Dave.

Playing the game of real estate investing is like any other game. The more of an insider you are, the less risk you have in what others presume to be "taking chances."

The Importance of Insider's Tools

Acquiring the insider's tools is a key part to becoming a member of the elite group of men and women who make their living, build their fortunes, and live an exciting, fun-filled life of financial independence. After all, the greater your understanding of the tools—how to use them, when to use them, and why they work—the more you will become expert and proficient in anything you do. Proficiency in the game of real estate investing is measured by your success at making a profit. The bigger the profit the greater the success you will be.

Profits, income, and financial independence are not a natural progression of your knowledge. The ability to use the tools of the real estate insider will not ensure your success anymore than knowing how to use carpenter's tools will permit you to turn out master woodwork. But dedication, practice, and getting a few mistakes under your belt will.

Options That Move You Closer to Your Goals

Make this the first and last consideration of everything you do in your investing experience: learn everything you can; the techniques, the methods to overcome problems, and the mistakes you can avoid by following the advice of others who have been down the path before. Then apply the techniques and use the tools to move yourself in the direction you want to go. Recognize the opportunities knocking at your door. Expect that you will encounter roadblocks and that you will not be able to overcome them all, at least not at first. Recognize right now that you will have as a primary priority your dedication to your goals and will not be sidetracked by trying to overcome roadblocks that open up the door to nowhere. When you encounter a brick wall it may be a blessing that causes you to sit back and decide if that is the goal you really want to obtain.

Put Uncle Sam on Your Side for a Change

In any form of investing—whether stocks, racehorses, stamps, art, commodities, or real estate—insiders know that the more tricks you can use properly and legally to make the Internal Revenue codes work in your favor, the greater your success and profit will be. By having more factors in your favor you lower your risk in any specific investment.

Warning! Not all CPA's are experts on real estate investing. Find a good accountant who represents successful investors. Putting your act together to become as successful as you can is not as easy as falling off a log. No single book, course, or tape can turn you into an overnight whiz in real estate investing. Even the best and most experienced make mistakes from time to time, and they learn from those mistakes. So will you. You can not expect to learn everything about everything, and some things, such as the tax code, are complicated and constantly changing, which cause CPA's to go gray and lose their hair at a young age. Plan on spending some time (and not as much money as you might think) with a good accountant to learn the tricks of the trade.

These tricks are not sleight-of-hand maneuvers; they follow the tax code to provide the best opportunity for you to achieve your goal more quickly and profitably. These tricks are what is referred to as loopholes in the code.

Discover the Last Loophole: The Real Estate Exchange

When it comes to getting the edge over competition, it should be clear that dealing from a position of strength will be far better than having to fight your way to the closing table with only a slim margin for success. Because real estate is a very flexible form of investing and covers many different kinds of investment opportunities, a wide blanket of Internal Revenue regulations affects the ultimate outcome of your investment.

The tax code of the United States is complex and can be very intimidating. The enforcers of the Internal Revenue Code, agents of the Internal Revenue Service, are the supreme intimidators. I have seen grown men cringe at the prospect of an audit. But take heart, I want to set your mind at rest.

Important! Do not fear the IRS. Do not be intimidated by the tax code. Learn to use it to your own advantage. The insiders do.

How to Become an Insider

Having been a Realtor and real estate investor for over 25 years, I have found that with very few exceptions real estate exchanges are kept under the control of real estate brokers.

National, statewide, and local Board of Realtor exchange groups exist today to the full and complete exclusion of the private investor, who is an "outsider."

I admit that I participated in the task of keeping the group exclusive to members of the real estate profession for reasons that I now recognize were wrong and narrow-minded. There are valid arguments against allowing non-Realtors or unlicensed members in a professional association, but as you will discover in this book, there is no valid reason for the investor to be excluded from becoming an insider in real estate exchanges.

Rediscover the Oldest Game in Town—Exchange

Exchange is the foundation of all economics. We generally relate economics to a monetary society and dollar transactions. Yet the opportunity to swap goods, services, and property in exchange for something else needed, wanted, or taken as an accommodation to the transaction is the start of everything and is today a viable tool that is used by nations, banks, and insider real estate investors. There are many forms of doing exchanges that involve real estate, and many reasons why the transaction works and is beneficial to all the participants. Take a look at a basic example of a real estate transaction where an exchange occurs.

The Rental Exchange

> Brad wants to move to a better apartment because his wife Susan is soon to have a baby, but he does not have the $1,500 security and last month's rent to give the new landlord. Because Brad is handy with a paintbrush, he goes to the owner of the apartment building and agrees to paint and fix up the building, working nights and weekends at a fair rate of payment to be applied against the required $1,500 to move in. In fact, Brad goes one step further: he negotiates to provide services to total $3,000 so that an additional $1,500 can apply against future rent.

This is a simple example of an exchange of a future service for an immediate gain. Of course, Brad could have worked on the side, saved up the money, and handed over the needed security and last month's rent, but this was his way of making ends meet and getting ahead now, without having to wait for it.

I have given this example first because it appears on the surface to have nothing to do with the IRS, the tax code, or getting Uncle Sam on your side. But take another look.

Why Benefits Are the Key

The benefits are often greater than the value. Brad knew that if he looked around he would find an apartment owner who would **want** to have his building improved to the value Brad would be willing to offer as "sweat equity." In this example, the $3,000 improvement is greater than $3,000 of hard cash, from the apartment owner's point of view, because of the following benefits.

Benefits to the Apartment Owner

1. Labor worth $3,000.
2. A vacant apartment now rented.
3. Apartment owner does not have to escrow the security because it is waived in exchange for the work.
4. If the work is solely to the apartment Brad will be living in, the owner may not have to report it as income.
5. The owner's building is being improved, which may help him rent other vacant apartments or increase rent in those already rented.
6. The owner did not have to reach into his pocket and come up with the $3,000 to have this all happen.

Obtaining Added Value Without Paying for It

Whenever you can give the other party added benefits at no added cost to you, you open up opportunities to give him a total package of benefits that have the original value they wanted at a reduced cost to you. This concept may help you close a transaction that has eluded you for any of a number of reasons. Unlike Brad's "sweat equity" offer (to provide a value of labor in exchange for the requirement to post security, pay the last month's rent, and get other credit for rent to be paid), your deal might contain some other form of exchange or barter. Instead of sweat equity, actual labor, your next deal may include a computer you are never going to use, landscaping skills, or a lot in Ohio you bought five years ago.

How the Loophole Works

There was a time not so very long ago when tax code loopholes made real estate investing very attractive as a tax shelter. In this kind of game, the wealthy investor was not risking much when he put up capital to buy into a shopping center or apartment building (two of the types of real estate the syndicators of tax shelters liked to buy). The reason for the reduced or nonexistent risk was the credits the investor got that reduced the future tax he would have to pay on his total earned income from all sources. These tax credits came to the investor in the form of losses or paper write-off of the depreciation of capital assets. Depreciation regulations allowed the investor to deduct, over a relatively short time, the total value of improvements (everything except the cost or value of the land, in the case of most real estate investments). In the properly structured tax-shelter deal, the deductions (accounting losses) could quickly exceed the total capital invested. While a transaction might look like a loser on paper, the investor was putting money in his pocket because he was not paying tax on his other income, which he would have had to pay were it not for the tax-shelter investment. At the height of tax-shelter investing, the tax code taxed the top earnings of the very wealthy at tax rates double or more the rates currently in use. Because another provision in the tax code at the time gave the investor a major exclusion (60 percent) of the amount of a gain, any future recovery of a gain by a sale would receive additional shelter against taxation. Therefore, the gravy in the tax-shelter game was if the property actually made money or went up in value.

Changes in the Tax Code That Make Exchanges Valuable

A series of changes in the tax code put an end to the old tax-shelter game by reducing the amount of depreciation on improvements and removing the 60 percent exclusion on a previously qualified capital gain. The high tax rates were softened, thus reducing the need to look for ways to beat the IRS. The tax code changes were designed to close loopholes that according to the proponents of the changes were siphoning away treasury funds that would have been paid on earned income.

As Usual, Government Plans Go Awry

In a shortsighted move, the changes to the tax code resulted in a disaster to the real estate market. Not only did it cause real estate to lose its glamour as an investment, it doomed many tax shelters that survived only because of the expanding market. The failure of hundreds and thousands of such investments in turn put a blanket over the whole real estate market.

How Tax Code Changes Have Affected the S&L Failures

Once real estate was off the glamour list, and with investors finding themselves holding properties that had been purchased at artificially high prices or with high carrying costs that could not be deducted any longer, there was a snowball effect. An avalanche started that reached all the way back to the lenders who were now having to foreclose their loans and take back bad properties, or properties developers could not sell or lease up because of the general decline in various markets.

Why Chaos Creates Opportunity

With one loophole after another being closed, an opportunity came for those who knew how to use an old tool that had been around for a long time. It is called Internal Revenue Code (IRC) Section 1031, and is often called the tax-free exchange.

The Last Loophole Revisited

The tax-free exchange, when used properly, allows the investor to go from one real estate investment to the next without having to pay the tax on any gain. This aspect was always attractive, even in the good old days of the 60 percent exclusion on capital gains. I mention this because as of this writing, there is continued talk in government circles of revising the current capital gains law back to something like what it was in those good old days. Do not overlook the tax-free exchange in any situation, circumstance, or tax bracket. It worked then, it works now, and it will work in the future. It is based on the simple principle that no tax to pay is better than any tax to pay.

What Happens When You Don't Have to Pay Tax

Assume that your tax rate on your earned income was 28 percent and you just sold, for $65,000, a vacant lot for which you paid $5,000 ten years earlier. At the closing of the sale you pay $5,000 commission to the selling broker and walk out of the lawyer's office with a cashier's check for $60,000. Can you go out and buy another investment for $60,000? Sure—but be ready to pay the tax on your $55,000 gain.

At a tax rate of 28 percent your income tax for the gain on the sale of the lot would be $15,400. Your net reinvestment capital is now $44,600.

On the other hand . . . if you had set up and properly used a tax-free exchange (IRC Section 1031), you would be able to plough the full $60,000 into another investment. And you would never pay the $15,400 tax. This is exactly the same as getting a loan that you never have to pay back and that has a zero interest rate charged against it. Not bad, not bad at all.

Learn the Insider's Game and Its Special Rules

real estate exchanges have always been considered an insider's game, because of the complexity of making exchanges and the opportunity for many brokers to deal with their own property. Investors who have participated in exchanges have usually been brought to the exchange by a broker rather than the other way around—and even the most sophisticated real estate investor, who may know about exchanges and sometimes use them, rarely uses them to the maximum benefit possible.

The paradox in this insider's game is that most of the insiders and the members of the real estate profession do not know how to properly use this fantastic investment tool.

Dealing with the Professional Paradox

While most states have educational requirements and exams a person must pass to be licensed as a real estate salesman or broker, these people learn virtually **zero** about exchanges. Worse, I know of no formal education offered outside the "insider groups" to teach the techniques of real estate exchanging. Even the few books that have been written on the subject seem to tackle the concept of tax-free exchanges as a broker's tool rather than an investment tool. While this is good for the true insiders, it does nothing for the investor who continually finds the door slammed shut in his face as he tries to make deals that would benefit not only himself but often the other party as well. Wake up! real estate exchanges are a benefit to all real estate investors, not something to avoid.

Why This Book Is for All Real Estate Investors

In my early real estate sales years I quickly saw exchanges as a fantastic tool for the investor. It didn't matter if you used the tax-free aspect of the exchange or not. But I was an insider and believed that as an insider, the only way to keep exchanges a broker's tool was to exclude the nonprofessional from the exchange mechanisms. The whole industry should have seen the light earlier, but they didn't. This book is the first to be dedicated to the investor.

This is your guide to becoming an insider. The broker and salesman will benefit greatly by learning the techniques explained in this book for use in his own investing as well as in helping his clients attain their goals.

In over 25 years of extending my own services to prospective buyers and sellers, I have always maintained that if I could help "them" attain or move closer to their goals, my own goals and monetary reward would follow. Both events took place. They will for you too.

Investors will discover, in later chapters of this book, how to get the most out of real estate professionals to expand their opportunities. In turn, brokers and salesmen should hope for clients to come to them, this book tucked under their arm, with the opening phrase, "I need a good salesman who will work with me, so that together we can develop a team to help me acquire property and later sell that real estate."

At last. Now the average investor can become an insider and not only learn but also be able to use and profit from the exchange techniques kept secret by the professionals all these years.

To begin your quest to obtain a full and rounded real estate investment education, it is important that you understand several elements about what it takes to become a successful real estate investor.

Dispelling Myths About Real Estate Investing

Most people connected with the real estate industry, whether buyers, sellers, or brokers, have a misconception as to who the "enemy" is when buying or selling. This, as you will shortly see, can cause a major blunder in formulating investment strategies for both buying and selling property. Both buying and selling should be coordinated as part of a plan designed to take the investor down a path toward a specific goal. It is not necessary for a particular purchase or sale to actually achieve the final goal; instead each successive move should be a part of the plan to reach the desired goal.

Stop Butting Your Head Against Brick Walls

Every plan should also accept that an occasional step backward may be necessary or may occur through some unforeseen circumstances. Do not spend a lot of time trying to overcome brick walls or dig under roadblocks. Often, it is much easier to stop for a moment, take a look at your plan, and then revise it to open new pathways around those roadblocks and brick walls.

Your ability to devise and then implement your plan will depend on your complete understanding of whom or what you must battle along the way. To the novice as well as the professional, the enemy is usually viewed as the other party in the transaction! Buyers view sellers as the clog in the road, and sellers see buyers as necessary but still formidable enemies. Brokers often see both buyer and seller as antagonists, and their lawyers and accountants as specific traps to be avoided at all cost.

In the real world of buying and selling property there are techniques to aid you in reducing risk and help you attain your desired goals. They are not just manipulations of numbers, nor are they only opportunities available to you through the use of loopholes. I am speaking about the totality of experience that allows you to deal with every stage of the investment game . . . and, most of all, with the other player.

Who Are the Other Players in the Investment Game?

Each partner in the investment game anticipates the player on the other team who wants to win just as much and just as badly as he does. Preparation for the game, knowledge of how it is played, learning all the tricks, knowing when to go for the close, and understanding how and when to make the final move are very important. The other players and the other team are not necessarily your enemies. Imagine that the real estate investment game is like building a tunnel through a mountain with two construction teams working from either side. It is not a race to see who gets to the middle first. The game's successful conclusion is that each side satisfies its objectives and moves closer to its own goal. Like the tunnel diggers, buyers and sellers start out a mountain apart. Yet the parties can work harmoniously together for the satisfaction of both.

Your Enemies

The real danger still lurks in the darkness. Take a look at the real enemies.

The Real Enemies of the Buyer and Seller

- Time
- The IRS
- Preconceived notions
- Lack of goals
- Unopened doors
- Themselves

Nowhere in the list of archenemies does "the other party" appear. Take a quick look at each of the six items listed.

Time

Time is the factor on which everything depends. It becomes critical in any investment situation because if you take too much of it, someone else steps in and removes the opportunity you might have had to either buy or sell your property. Try to rush things, and mistakes are easily made. But time is key to the art of negotiation, even though the proper use of time as a negotiating factor is hard to pinpoint, because time is relative to each deal and to each side of the transaction.

Good salespeople know that time is the Number 1 closing factor in any deal. Both buyers and sellers need time to make a decision. But too much time causes the deal to cool down, and once momentum is lost the salesman can feel a sale going out the window.

Savvy investors recognize that to use time properly is to act in such a way that momentum is not lost, and that having an intermediary who understands this is a plus in any deal. This works for both sides . . . the buyer and seller.

Arbitrators use time to bring about solutions to very complex matters by sitting down at the bargaining table until the matter is resolved. "We will take all the time we need to end this matter once and for all." What this means is "No one leaves the room until everyone agrees." Time becomes the pressure to meld the deal into a firm agreement. The sooner you realize that time can be **used** as a tool, the better you will function in the real world. Time is, does, and ends. Make the best use of it . . . you cannot replace it.

How much time the buyer or the seller has to complete a transaction is usually a critical factor, not only for the party with the time problem but for the other party as well. For example, a seller who is behind in his mortgage payments, with a lender about to foreclose, does not have the leisure to enter into a prolonged marketing program to sell his property. The prospective buyer must recognize the seller's problem and act within the maximum time frame available, rather than hold out for a drop in the price. Deals are lost so quickly that would-be buyers rationalize, in a modern form of Zen, that the deal must not have been meant to be. That is not what you should do. You want to recognize opportunity and act on it before others do.

A buyer who must find another property within 45 days to satisfy the requirements of a previous 1031 tax-free exchange is under similar pressures to complete the transaction. Are you the possible "other party"? If you are and can take advantage of the time pressure on the first party, you can utilize the age-old concept of deal making: "He that has time doth win every time."

In real estate, **time** is the great equalizer. Give me enough **time** and I can pay just about any price. Let me have enough **time** and with prudent investing and normally increasing values, **time** will make me a millionaire. Give me sufficient **time** and I will show you how to do the same.

The IRS

No investment plan can proceed with any assurance of success without taking into consideration the tax consequences. Each person must approach this enemy with the understanding that what has worked for another person may not work for them, owing to the nature of their tax responsibilities now and potential ones in the future.

Part of your investment team should include a person who can advise you on the impact of your tax liabilities on your overall investment plan. Do not simply ask questions of your CPA about a specific investment without letting the tax adviser know how you would like the investment to further your investment goals.

The key to the tax code is not to presume that it simply works against you. The tax code and its regulations are impersonal. They are applied to everyone—and yet provisions within the code mitigate the impact of other aspects of the code.

The use of loopholes to mitigate your future tax liabilities are critical elements, but so, too, is proper planning to make the most of opportunities which come up when someone else has a time problem with respect to their own tax liability.

Use the IRS Code, Don't Fear It

It can work for you, if you let it. The Internal Revenue Code, Section 1031, is one loophole you can use. But it is not the only reason to use an exchange, and it is not the only edge the IRS will give you. Look for these edges and learn how to use the code to give yourself even a small benefit, which you can pass on to the buyer or seller in your next transaction.

Preconceived Notions

It doesn't make any difference what they are, any preconceived notion can get in your way. When you become inflexible, you defeat yourself long before you approach the close of the transaction.

Preconceived Notions You Should Avoid

- Always buy a fixer-upper, 'cause that's the only place you can make money in real estate.
- Never pioneer in slum areas.
- Don't buy vacant land.
- If you cannot get 15 percent cash on cash, don't buy.
- Flat roofs are a no-no.

The key here is to realize that there is no specific rule of thumb. "Always," "never," and "don't" are relative terms. What may work in one specific circumstance for one person may not work under the same circumstances for another person, owing to his "element" that changes the whole chemistry of the transaction. Real estate is so fragile that the slightest change in the totality of the deal can bring about dramatic changes in the end results.

Smart investors make every effort to follow their plan, but do so with an open mind. Nothing should be so set that a change in any governing factor cannot be integrated into that investment plan. Things do change, both within and outside your control. Adapt to those changes by ridding yourself of preconceived ideas that are inflexible. Use every change to modify your goals, and take the time to redesign your plan.

Lack of Goals

Or worse, no goals at all. (I will touch on this aspect again and again in this book.) This is one of the most important factors in any investing, but even more so in real estate. **You should discover the importance of goals.** The reason for this is that real estate is a basic of life. Unless you plan on being a street person, you must live somewhere, owning, renting, or living with someone who owns or rents.

If you rent or own you are making an investment into real estate which should be part of your master plan, and without well designed goals your master plan will be an ever-changing path to frustration and disappointment. Learn the way out of this black closet by reviewing the ten keys to establishing proper investment goals.

The 10 Keys to Establish Proper Goals

1. Know what you are capable of doing.
2. Understand your limitations.
3. Discuss your future plans with all persons concerned.
4. Pick a long-range goal beyond your current ability.
5. Establish short-range goals to expand your current ability (both financial and personal).
6. Establish timetables to reach the intermediate levels.
7. Implement the plan.
8. Check status of your timetable along the way.
9. Be sure all your team members know what you expect of them.
10. Anticipate the need for changes en route to your final goal.

Unopened Doors

There is nothing more frustrating than the feeling, "If I had only known that!" Unless, however, you are already in possession of every fact and have at your disposal every option available when you start making decisions, you will need to accept this frustration. The alternative is to fail to act or make decisions because you fear making the wrong decision. Many people are paralyzed by this very sensation and are unaware that making no decision is often worse than making a poor decision.

How to Make Decisions That Let You Win

You simply need to do the best you can and become acquainted with the facts that are important to the situation. If your goals are clear and you have been honest with yourself as to your abilities, you are ahead of most people.

The very fact that you are reading this book indicates that you want to take charge of your own destiny. You are already taking steps to expand your self-confidence and improve your ability to recognize opportunities.

real estate has a major advantage over other forms of investment. It is location-oriented. I don't mean just the cliché that property is dependent on location, location, location, although that is true. What I mean is that real estate is an absolute item that has use and value relative to where it is located. This is the single factor that distinguishes real estate from every other item in which you can invest.

It's Easy to Become a Local Expert

What happens in your hometown is a microcosm of the real estate industry. Some properties are going up in value and some are going down. Sure, national statistics and trends will have some effect on your local real estate market, but the effect in your town may be greatly different from the effect in another area of the country. Your opportunity to succeed will be dependent on your ability to recognize the opportunities that knock at your own door; you need not be concerned with things that are going on a thousand miles away.

The 7 Steps to Becoming an Expert

1. Get to know your backyard (area where you plan to invest).
2. Attend city council meetings, planning and zoning meetings, and other government and community events.
3. Get to know the town and county planners, and have them fill you in on future plans for roads, schools, hospitals, and other buildings.
4. Start to look at different kinds of property to acquaint yourself with values.
5. Pick an area of town and a type of property you feel is best suited to help you achieve your goals.
6. Get to know that area of town and that kind of property like the palm of your hand.
7. Continue to learn and expand.

Why Risk Is Reduced to Nearly Zero

As you become your own local expert, you will discover that things that seemed risky before are now obvious. Your self-confidence will grow. You are on your way to being a success!

Themselves

You are your own worst enemy. You know it. You have looked yourself in the mirror a thousand times and thought it. Well, it's true. You will procrastinate, even kid yourself into believing that there is a good reason not to do something when deep down you know you should. Why? Because you and I are like everyone else. We both hate to be rejected, have our friends laugh at us, be told we were wrong, lose face, or fail. Because of these things you, I, and everyone else finds defensive moves to protect ourselves in the event we do fail, in case our friends do laugh at us.

It is the defensive steps we take that get in our way. Ironic but true. Both you and I can do and say the wrong thing, and later, on reflection, we relive the moment to perfection, doing and saying exactly the right thing.

To thine own self be true. It is uncanny how, knowing that it would be unproductive to start an argument before negotiations even begin when coming face to face with the other party, arguments are so easily started.

There is no ultimate solution to how you handle yourself. This is a problem you have already had to face and no doubt will face again in the future. My only suggestion is to reflect on each occasion in the past when **you** have gotten in the way of **you.** Think about how the situation developed and who or what you blamed for the circumstances, rather than owning up to the fact that **you** were the problem all the time, and strive to remove **you** as your future obstacle.

Become an Exchanger, Not Just an Investor

I welcome any investor who is discovering this new tool: exchanges are exciting, and have their place in any investor's bag of tricks. The art and finesse of making exchanges work can be attributed to four fundamentals. These are:

The 4 Fundamentals of Why Exchanges Work
1. The Tax-Free Benefits
2. The Greener-Grass Theory
3. Saving Face
4. An Accommodation Move

To provide you with all the information necessary to prepare you for exchanges in the real world, this book will expand on each of these four fundamentals.

1. The Tax-Free Benefits

The most important is the tax-free benefit, but the other three factors may come into play in every exchange—even those where the monetary savings from the tax-free benefits are substantial, or when there is no savings at all.

2. The Greener-Grass Theory

Basic, but valid, is the fact that there are property owners who would rather own what you have than what they have. I call this the Greener-Grass Theory because many people view things on the other side of the fence as more attractive.

Later on I will show you how to recognize this as a primary motivation in some people, and how you can use your own "greener grass" to make those deals come together.

3. Saving Face

The investor who overpaid, or bought at the top of the market then milked the property, or let it run down because of his inability to manage it may never get back what he paid. Selling a property for less than you paid for it is contrary to the "rule of the bartender"; as we all know, losing is tantamount to failure, and no one wants to fail.

I have seen people on the verge of foreclosure and at the point when they were risking all their invested capital in a specific property turn down deals that would have bailed them out, just to put some cash in their pocket above their delinquent loans and debts. Why? Because **they** had become their own worst enemy. They let a preconceived idea get in their way.

Enter the exchange. No values need be indicated, thus there is no direct evidence that a seller is disposing of his property for less than he paid.

Phil's Preforeclosure Exchange
Phil is like many people who buy at the top of a market: he saddled himself with a mort-

gage that took all his free cash to pay each month, only to discover himself out of work a few years later. Mortgage owed was $150,000 with monthly payments of $1,500 principal, taxes, and interest. The real market value on the property is $200,000. Phil had paid $250,000 four years earlier.

You come along and offer Phil the following:

- A free and clear residential lot in a beautiful North Carolina ski area.
- One year's free rent in the same home.
- You will take over all mortgage debt and obligations.

You can calculate what this means to you in expense and arrive at a value that may be closer to the $200,000 value, due to what you have in the lot in North Carolina. You will have to pay $22,500 in mortgage payments (the three past due and the next 12), plus deed over the lot in North Carolina. But you do not have to show values.

Phil has to accept, reject, or counter the offer on the basis of how it solves his own problem. The offer carries no obvious "failure" stigma—and who knows, a free and clear lot and a year of breather time living in his "own home" might be just the thing to let Phil get back on his feet.

☞ **Key Words:** Deal in Benefits Rather Than Money

International transactions look at things this way: oil for butter, aircraft for rice, computers for ships. The need on one side is balanced by the benefit offered. Each side of the transaction gets something, and even if it is not exactly what was sought, the need is satisfied. If rice is not available, will wheat do? It might, if you agree to take less of what you originally wanted, or can give a bit more of what they want.

4. An Accommodation Move

In many real estate exchanges, the other side doesn't want the subject property at all, but the exchange is made because it helps move things in the right direction. Some of these "accommodation" exchanges involve a relatively small percentage of exchange. The property taken may be put aside for some future transaction, passed on to the broker as all or part of the commission, or put up for resale as soon as possible.

Alex owns five time-share weeks in Orlando. The facility is a nice one but in the past five years of ownership Alex has been to Disneyworld only once, and that was the first year he owned these units. The weeks are free and clear, sold originally for $8,000 each. Alex obtained these weeks in an exchange and has decided to move them out of his portfolio.

In the normal course of his investing activities, Alex finds a small office building he would like to acquire. The property is offered for sale at $500,000. Alex starts to negotiate to buy the building and begins by offering $425,000 cash to the existing mortgage of $350,000, provided the seller holds a second mortgage of $35,000.

The seller rejects this, and after several counteroffers by each party the negotiations stand with the seller agreeing to take $475,000 and hold a second mortgage of $25,000 if Alex pays the balance of $100,000. Alex knows that the broker expects to receive a commission of $28,500 from the seller. Keeping this in mind, Alex makes the following counteroffer: $75,000 cash, the seller to hold a second mortgage of $25,000, and four time-share weeks in

Orlando. He attaches the sales brochure he originally received from the project, which indicates the weeks originally sold for $8,000 each week. At that price, the time-share weeks would be worth a total of $32,000.

The seller has the option now to take the deal as it is and keep the time-share weeks himself. Or he can go to the broker and suggest that to have a signed contract right now, all the broker has to agree to do is take the four time-share weeks as his commission. At the "previously sold" price of $8,000 per week this is an overpayment of commission to the broker and gives the broker an opportunity to leverage out of them at a future time. Of course, the broker can say no or attempt to bargain for part cash and part of the weeks. However, if the broker is "exchange-oriented," he will take the weeks as his commission and Alex will accomplish his goal of acquiring the office building and at the same time removing four of the time-share weeks from his portfolio.

Why Big Deals Absorb More Accommodation

In a multimillion-dollar sale there may be sufficient equity to support a major exchange, even though the property traded is not wanted by the accepting party. This occurs for a number of good reasons, usually in a situation where the party giving up the property must use this equity to make the transaction work for him, and/or where the property has obvious value and may be more salable in the current market than the other property.

Take for example a large shopping center, with several years of mismanagement, over 30 percent vacancy, a declining prospect for lease renewals, and a seller very anxious to sell. The market for this kind of real estate is very limited.

A smart broker handling the marketing program for this property might look around for other potential uses, or users. Finding such a situation, a person who may not be looking to acquire such a property might be "sold" on the idea of putting the vacant space to another use or to profit through better management ability. An inducement might be to suggest that the "buyer" exchange a property being held for development to the center owner.

The center owner who sees the major goal satisfied—the sale of the center—may agree to accept a substantial portion of the transaction in other property that must later be sold or exchanged.

Tax-Free Deals Are Not the Only Way to Go

The tax-free aspect may or may not enter into these exchanges. This is very important, because some exchangers become so involved that they overlook the obvious: the motivations causing a "seller" to dispose of his property may be so strong that he will grasp at any reasonable offer without respect to tax consequences.

Exchanges Maximize Your Investment Return

Exchanges have the advantage of leveraging your investment capital, with the end result of maximizing your investment yield or return. This occurs in several ways. The tax-free exchange (the 1031 exchange) eliminates the need to pay tax on the gain, giving the investor those funds to reinvest.

- Increased reinvestment potential due to the tax-free provisions. In this type of exchange there is a qualified 1031 exchange, and at least one party is able to avoid paying the income tax that would otherwise have been due on the gain, which maximizes reinvestment of capital.

- In an exchange from one income property into another income property with a greater yield potential, the tax-free portion of the exchange would be additional gravy and not the main motivation to do the exchange. An example of this kind of exchange might be the deal that results with the 30 percent vacant center mentioned earlier. If the would-be buyer exchanges a vacant tract of land on which he planned to build his own office complex and is now able to use the vacant space in the center as office space, the combination of conversion of non-income-producing property for an income-generating investment, needed personal space, and zero tax on any profit from the vacant land most certainly increases the investment yield.

Exchanges Let You Build Equity Fast

In a normal investment scenario you would look for a property you wanted, acquire it, either improve its value or wait for it to increase, put it on the market, sell it, start looking for another investment, and start the whole game over again. By introducing the exchange into the picture you eliminate putting your property on the market and having to wait for a buyer. Removing these two elements from your investment strategy increases your control over your future 1,000 percent. What you do is to become an aggressive seller by finding a "taker" for your property. In doing this you cut the time between your transactions. Time **is** money.

Time Is the Root of All Profit and Loss

The reality of real estate is that no matter how good the property or how fairly it is priced, it will rarely sell immediately. The irony is that if it does sell immediately, your first doubt as buyer is that you offered too much, and as seller that you let it go too cheap. A time vs. value consideration comes into play in every situation. You cannot make a comparison between different properties or different times, so what happened to you last year or last month has little to do with what is going to happen the next time. In some markets—when money is tight, when there is talk about layoffs at the plant, or when a general downturn in the economy has spilled over to the real estate market and is drying up the buyers—a property just will not sell, even at a bargain price.

Real Estate Is Not Like Other Investments

Unlike stocks and bonds and other universal commodities, with which it makes no difference where you are when you buy the investment (because it doesn't have to be wherever you are), real estate is so local that the buyer has to come to the property. While it is true that internationals are buying properties thousands of miles from their bases, these are rare instances and unique to specific properties.

By moving ahead of the market and making the decision "I will exchange and not sell," you can take your justifiably valued property and enter the buyer's side of the game without having to be a seller first.

How to Build Your Fortune But Never Sell Anything

A client of mine who taught me a great deal about exchanges rarely sold anything. But he did dispose of a lot of property through exchanges.

August Urbanek, who was at one time one of the nation's premier apartment builders and owners, also dabbled in office buildings, shopping centers, and single-family homes. He took his game seriously (still does in fact), and knew how to use the tax-free exchange to great advantage.

You Can Still Get Cash When You Exchange

Mr. Urbanek owns such prime property that it is not unusual for buyers to approach him, even though his property has not been offered for sale. Often, when the situation was right, that is to say, when a prospective buyer was offering a very attractive price, Mr. Urbanek would simply tell the buyer to put it in writing, with a check to bind the deal.

Once this had happened, his lawyer would draft an exchange proposal which binds the cash buyer to the deal and allows Mr. Urbanek to go into the real estate market and negotiate for other investments as though he was "buying for cash" instead of making an exchange, ultimately using the buyer's cash as though it were his own.

The end result of this kind of transaction would be a sale and exchange that, if properly documented, would meet the conditions of a deferred tax-free exchange for Mr. Urbanek, and he would acquire what he wanted using the money put up by the other party, who has ended up with Urbanek's original property. The technique is simple, but the rules governing this kind of exchange must be carefully attended to. In Chapter 2 you will find a detailed account of the rules and regulations for exchanges.

An Introduction to Building "Legs" for Exchanges

A leg, in real estate exchange terminology, is a third or additional party introduced to the exchange to form a triangular transaction. In this kind of deal each party obtains a property—but not one on one. In the above transaction, a third party came into the picture who had something that one of the other two needed or wanted. In this case, Urbanek needed cash to give to the seller of the property he wanted to end up with. In many transactions there are three or more parties, or property-and-cash, or mortgages, with the final result that everyone gets something out of the deal to solve a problem or meet a need.

Later in this book I will explain the details of how you build "legs" to provide a wide base for your exchanges. The idea is to give yourself more options and more profit avenues to follow. If you own a home that you want to dispose of so that you can undertake another investment, and can develop two or three "potential exchanges" from persons who would like to own your home in exchange for their property, you have additional directions open to you. Even if you do not want any of the properties offered to you, possibly one or more of them could be attractive to the owner of the property you **do** want. Having a shopping list of property (yours and other properties offered to you in exchange) can be a fast way to get something better for you than what you own.

Discover the Importance of "Takers"

Building legs begins with finding **takers** for your property. This means a person who would like to own what you have. At this point it is not so important what that person has to offer; the critical element is simply that this person does want to own your property. Look at the Ross Exchange.

The Ross Exchange

Ross owns a nice single-family home in San Diego that he has used as a rental. He now wants to upgrade to a larger investment. The value of the home is $175,000 and Ross has paid off all but $50,000 of the first mortgage. His equity is $125,000 ($175,000 less the mortgage of $50,000).

Ross runs an ad for an exchange in the local newspaper and is contacted by the owners of a vacant lot, a warehouse, and a 25-unit apartment building. While Ross is not interested in any of these items, he now has four properties to use in his quest for his desired investment, because each of the three property owners will ultimately **take** the Ross house and substitute their own property in the final exchange.

Matching "Takers" with "Havers"

So far all Ross has is a list of "takers"; what he needs to find is someone who has what he wants. The "haver" can be anyone out there who is the owner of a property Ross will take. It could very well be a property Ross would look for as if he were a "buyer." Once he found it, Ross would offer his "takers" as well as his own property as a shopping list for the owner of the property Ross really wants. Somewhere along the way matches are made because the primary goals of all parties are met. This is how legs are built.

How Increased Benefits Increase Value

Anytime you can add a benefit to a property you own, you increase the value of that property. If you can exchange an already established value for something that gives you more benefits, you are multiplying your wealth. Exchanges can do both.

Increasing the Bottom Line

The "bottom line," which in financial terms is the amount of cash the investor has to spend at the end of the year after all expenses and taxes are paid, is the key in almost every financial investment. In any income-producing property or one that will have a future income potential, the value becomes dependent on the yield the investor can expect from the property. An apartment building that has gross rents of $45,000 per year and total operating expenses of $15,000 per year will have a net operating income (called NOI) of $30,000 per year. This is a pretax calculation and does not take into consideration any debt interest, which must be calculated to get to the bottom line.

The major deduction that mitigates your tax bite when you own real estate is the depreciation of your capital asset. This is the area the IRS likes to play around with, and in the tax reform of 1986 it was depreciation that was greatly reduced. Nonetheless, for most properties depreciation is a paper expense only, and has the final result of keeping dollars in the pocket. It does this by reducing the amount of income tax you would otherwise have to pay. In this way, if your NOI was $30,000 and your overall tax bracket (including this income and other income from other sources) was 25 percent, you would have to pay $7,500 in tax on that sum ($30,000 x .25 = $7,500).

Because this is an apartment building, you are allowed to depreciate the furniture, fixtures, and all items which are part of the building, but not the land. If the total depreciation for this year were $20,000, you would be allowed to deduct this from the NOI, giving $10,000 net income ($30,000 less $20,000). The $10,000 is the bottom line. The plus factor in the calculation of income tax on the bottom line is the fact that a reduced adjusted gross income may lower your overall tax rate. Moving down $20,000 in the rate scale could drop your tax rate from 25 percent to 20 percent. This calculation would depend on your other income, of course, but with a sizable reduction a reduced tax rate could be expected. The tax calculation as it relates to the apartment income is now 20 percent of $10,000, or $2,000, instead of $7,500 had there been no depreciation at all. This savings of $5,500 becomes spendable income after tax, and is the fundamental benefit that is called **tax-sheltered income.**

Complex tables show different depreciation rates for the specific items and improvements in the building. You need to discuss these with your accountant. Ten different investors may decide to set up 10 different depreciation schedules, depending on their own plans, because there is only one maximum rate you can take. However, it is possible that because of other circumstances you may not want to take the maximum depreciation available and may instead seek a longer, more level, form of depreciation, or even a schedule that weights the depreciation to later years. Pushing your depreciation to later years may be beneficial if you are going through a rebuilding program to turn around a property that will not produce its maximum income for several years.

How Exchanges Affect Depreciation

If you take an accelerated rate of depreciation or own a property long enough, you can run out of depreciation that you have been using to decrease your income tax. The time it takes for this to happen will depend on many factors. If your property has several different depreciable items, such as furniture and mechanical items, which can be depreciated faster than the bricks and mortar, you may discover that after 10 years you have lost the major benefit you were getting from depreciation. The loss of this "paper" deduction is exacerbated because the income has been increasing, either to keep pace with the cost of living or as a result of your good management. The net result is a widening gap between income and tax shelter available. The bottom line, while still increasing from added income, no longer has as much buffer for you to use. Review the following example where NOI increases but depreciation drops off.

Dealing with Declining Depreciation and Growing Taxable Income

Tax Year	NOI	Depreciation	Taxable Income
1980	$30,000	$26,000	$ 4,000
1990	$40,000	$15,000	$25,000
1995	$45,000	$ 5,000	$40,000

Declining depreciation does not make the property less desirable or affect value. And with proper planning you and your CPA can level out your schedule of depreciation to your benefit. Savvy investors seek to maximize all their benefits.

The 3 Ways to Increase Your Tax-Shelter Benefits

1. Make new or replace old improvements.
2. Sell and buy another property.
3. Exchange into a greater base.

When you build or replace something old you have a new cost base, which gets added to your book value and can increase your depreciation. If you add 10 units to your existing apartment building, for example, the cost of this addition, as well as the cost of all the furniture and appointments needed to complete the addition, will be added to your basis for depreciation. If you borrow all the funds needed to make this addition you can add tax shelter without any out-of-pocket cost. This can be an ideal way to improve your investment potential and is a valid way to go when the circumstances permit. However, investments that can upgrade the building are frequently accomplished through continual "repairs," which is an operational expense and a direct deduction the year spent.

You can sell your old property and take the proceeds and buy another, but we have already seen how income tax on the gain can affect that. But as bad as income tax is, the gain on the sale of an asset that has been depreciated is worse.

Understanding the Give-and-Take of Depreciation

When you depreciate your property, you reduce your income by the "paper expense" equal to the depreciation allowed for that year. Take Bruss, for example. He has owned an apartment building for 10 years at an original cost basis of $260,000. His total depreciation (for all items) during the 10-year period was $110,000, which gave him a book value (or "adjusted cost basis," as accountants call it) of $150,000 ($260,000 less $110,000).

Now, 10 years later, Bruss decides he wants to sell this property, but discovers that everything he gets above his adjusted cost basis will be considered earned income. If he were to sell for $400,000 he would have a gain of $250,000. Under the current tax considerations this gain would be added to his other income and become a part of his total adjusted gross income. His accountant told him that a lump sum such as this would push Bruss into the maximum tax bracket, unless he had some carry-over losses to offset this sudden income. Even with a tax rate of only 25 percent, Bruss would have to pay an income tax of $62,500 on his gain.

To see more clearly the effect of the depreciation, take a look at the same situation if he sold the property for the $260,000 he originally paid: he would have a gain of $110,000. This shows up as the actual amount of depreciation taken over 10 years, and assumes no appreciation in the value of the property. This $110,000 would be added to his adjusted gross income. If the rate were the same as in the earlier calculation, 25 percent, his tax would be $27,500 . . . paying back Uncle Sam for the tax shelter he got over the 10-year term.

Exchanges, when properly executed, allow you to solve the problem of decreased depreciation (reduced tax shelter) without having to take the penalty and pay the income tax on the gain. By not having to pay the income tax you get that added input to increase your equity in the "new" investment.

How Bruss Increases His Depreciation

Bruss has depreciated his apartment complex down to a base of $150,000. Yet the market value would be an easy $400,000. He owes only $75,000 on his old mortgage and has a good $325,000 of equity. He begins to look for another income property to acquire and locates several apartment complexes, any one of which he would like to own.

The best for him is a 50-unit building with a very attractive price for the local market, $1,100,000. Bruss offers to make a direct exchange for the 50 units, giving his own smaller apartment complex as down payment. There is a first mortgage of only $450,000 on the 50 units, so Bruss has several ways to go to close this transaction. Three options are:

1. Refinance and put a new first mortgage on the property to give cash back to the owner.
2. Assume the existing mortgage and get the seller to hold secondary financing.
3. Refinance only a portion of the total investment and get the seller to hold the balance.

In each of these situations Bruss does not have to come up with additional capital in order to close the transaction. Even if the owner of the 50 units does not want Bruss's property, there would be the option of finding a buyer for the Bruss apartments and still completing a valid 1031 tax-free exchange giving the owner of the 50 units the proceeds of the sale and allowing Bruss to complete his exchange. If Bruss uses his equity from his old units and finances the balance, he will have a total debt of $725,000 on the new units. The land value under the 50 units is estimated to be $150,000. The advantage to Bruss is multifold, but from a tax-shelter point of view here is what happens.

New Property Value

Start with old base	$150,000
Less mortgage given up	-75,000

Plus mortgage taken over	+ 725,000
	————
New basis	$800,000
Less value of land in new property	-150,000
	————
Net basis for depreciation	$650,000

The amount of $650,000 is the new base from which Bruss can obtain tax shelter through depreciation. He arrived at this point using the 1031 exchange to move his equity into another investment without having to pay the income tax on the gain.

In some circumstances an investor might want to actually sell and then purchase the second property, rather than use the exchange method. If, for example, Bruss had a substantial loss or other tax deduction that he could use to offset all or part of any gain from the sale, he would be advised to consider the alternative route to improve his future depreciation. If Bruss was not concerned about paying an income tax on the gain from a sale, his new base would be the purchase price of $1,100,000, and the amount of future tax shelter through depreciation would be the purchase price less the $150,000 allocated land value. The total depreciable asset of $950,000 is a substantial increase over that obtained in the exchange.

How Exchanges Increase the Bottom Line

Tax shelter has the bottom-line effect of increasing the amount of cash available after all expenses and tax have been paid. The mortgage effect of real estate income property is that someone else is paying off your debt. The phrase "use other people's money" is often abbreviated to "using OPM," as a way to ultimate success and financial independence in real estate investing. The tax reform of 1986 hit another blow at the real estate investor that can be softened to some degree by using the tax-free exchange to increase the spendable income now, and help build equity faster.

Bruss exchanged one property where the tax shelter and the amount of debt that could be paid off by OPM was smaller than he felt he could handle, and ended up with an obligation to pay off a $750,000 loan. If Bruss is a good manager of rental property (or can hire a good one), and has done his homework in finding a sound property with good rental potential, he will eventually let OPM retire this added debt. When this loan is paid off, and assuming that normal investment appreciation will occur, his future value will be above what the original price was, with the added plus factor that he no longer owes that $750,000 loan.

Discover the Hidden Benefits of Real Estate Ownership

Each type of real estate investment has some extra benefit that may not be obvious to the outsider. Some of the benefits come from your opportunity to take additional legal tax deductions due to your participation in ownership and management of your real estate. These specific deductions will depend on your involvement and the kind of real estate owned. Hotel owners are able to get some of the best "outside deductions," such as travel and entertainment, by using their own facilities as the foundation for this kind of expense. Having extra accommodations for guests or a place to get away to from time to time is a benefit for all property owners of rental units. With sizable properties there is the added benefit of having a staff working for you, plus a multitude of perks, from samples of cleaning supplies to management conventions and seminars around the world.

Every investor should have a session with a good accountant to discuss the many legal ways to make your investment in real estate pay off in every possible way.

Reduce Stress

Ever wake up in the middle of the night unable to go back to sleep because you are worried about something having to do with money—a bill you cannot pay, or a problem that could be solved if you had enough money? Or ever found yourself living on the edge, always having to collect next month's rent just to cover this month's expenses? Join the club. There are many outsiders who have not discovered that investing in real estate need not be the stressful situation some people make it. While real estate exchanges and other creative investing techniques in themselves do not reduce stress, the overall ability to plan your own future with confidence will.

Build a Portfolio of Investment Skills

Every investor must have a comfort zone. This is the geographic and technical base from which you operate and where you become an expert. The funny part about this is that you will become an expert very soon after you begin to apply the information in this book to your investment life. What you don't know can bring you to financial ruin as quickly as making decisions armed with only part of the information. Becoming an insider in the real estate investment circle will be easy, but the success you expect will require many hours of work and diligence. Before you know it, you will discover that people are bringing you properties and your position as an insider is secure.

Expand Your Market a Thousandfold

real estate salesmen know that the listing is the key. If they have a property people want they are assured a commission, because a deal will be just around the corner. It is much the same with investors, except that in the conventional market success depends on profit, and getting a profit most often requires some kind of leverage upward. The "stick-in-the-mud" investor thinks that means he must sell, take his profit, and then invest in something else. A "super investor," such as you are soon to be, knows that flexibility does not mean being a blade of grass that bends in the wind; it means becoming a field of grass.

Any Exchange That Moves You Closer to Your Goal Is a Good Exchange

Keep this thought in mind as you roam through the world of investing: try to become that field of grass, to absorb as much knowledge as you can. Work at becoming the local expert in your own comfort zone of investing by becoming involved in what is going on around you. Attend city meetings, meet local officials on all levels who have control over your life and investment area. Avoid the urge to fight back at what first seems to be injustice in your neighborhood—later you may discover you were wrong.

Advance yourself into an exciting world of real estate, where you can find financial independence . . . if you are ready, willing, and able to work hard at playing the game.

2

Real Estate Exchanges: Dealing with the IRS

Your Not-So-Silent Partner

You have a partner in everything you do, the government of the United States. With very few exceptions, this partner gets a share of your investments and the money you earn, and collects from you one way or the other. The enforcement of the government's rights to its share of you centers on the institution called the IRS (Internal Revenue Service).

A Brief History of the IRS

When the Internal Revenue Service first came into being in 1913, Congressman Cordell Hull, speaking in a debate in the United States Congress, said, "That system [IRS], unequal as it is indefensible, is the mightiest engine of oppression imposed upon an honest yeomanry since the feudal ages." He could have just as well been talking about the IRS of today. It carries a very big stick, which it uses in a very intimidating way. Contrary to the fundamental laws of the land, in the eyes of the IRS you are guilty if they say so and you must prove your innocence.

Events Leading Up to the Current Tax Laws

Even though the IRS did not come into being until 1913, the United States government did have rights of taxation that affected its citizens prior to that date. Up until the War of 1812, all federal revenue was generated by taxes on distilled spirits, carriages, refined sugar, tobacco and snuff, property sold at auctions, corporate bonds, and slaves. Owing to the high cost of war, the nation's first "sales tax" was levied on gold, silverware, jewelry, and watches. This tax and all income taxes were repealed in 1817, and the government relied on tariffs on imported goods to provide sufficient revenue to operate the government.

To pay for the Civil War, Congress in 1862 enacted the first income-tax law, which was the forerunner of the 1913 law. That required people earning up to $10,000 per year (a most handsome sum of money at that time) to pay 3 percent to the government. Wars were cheaper to fight in those days.

How to Avoid Tax on Your Investments

If you had a brother-in-law who was going to get a piece of everything you possessed, earned, owned, gave away, left after you died, or had if you were caught selling drugs, you would want to know as much as possible about how you could keep more and give your brother-in-law less . . . wouldn't you?

What if there were some loopholes that would allow you to avoid giving some of your wealth to your brother-in-law? Would you want to know what they are? Would you use them?

You Can Reduce or Eliminate Tax

The best part about understanding the IRS codes is that with forethought you can substantially reduce or, in many instances, fully eliminate the amount of tax you owe. Careful forethought and a sound investment plan will enable you to build your financial independence faster.

This is not unpatriotic. The laws that allow you to reduce your tax liability are there for a reason. They are not mistakes or provisions that have escaped the scrutiny of IRS agents. They are legal avenues that you should take advantage of.

You go into a store to buy one hundred gallons of paint and see two different displays of the same paint. One shelf has a price of $25 per gallon, and the other shelf has a sign that says, "Free plus a $5-per-gallon rebate." Is there any doubt which rack you would select from? The tax laws are like that. You have the same income, the same deductions, only two different displays. You can pay the tax if you choose to or you can use the rules to avoid paying the tax.

The problem with the Internal Revenue Service is that its rules and regulations are not quite as simple as that sign for free paint. The Internal Revenue Code undergoes constant revision. Even when a rule and its regulations are put down in black and white, their applicability can be interpreted differently, depending on circumstances.

The Importance of Being Ready for the Audit

Real estate investing is one of the areas where the same regulation can be viewed in different ways, depending on circumstance, namely the event, the intent, and the end results. These three elements are the basis on which the IRS audits taxpayers and on which they defend themselves.

Each real estate transaction is an event unlike any other. Even if the same parties were to accomplish two nearly similar transactions with almost the same end results, there could be substantial differences that would cause the IRS to approach one case differently from the other. Because an audit often occurs well after the event, the original intent is often clouded by the ultimate results, and the IRS generally looks at what actually happened, not at what you said was going to happen.

This chapter is designed to provide a solid look at the basics of accountability to the IRS for most real estate transactions.

You will be able to come back to this chapter at any time later to review the steps you need to follow or to copy the forms you can use to calculate the different stages of your transactions for tax purposes. While it is possible that there will be no changes at all in any of the rules and regulations contained in this chapter, it would be advisable to doublecheck with your CPA or accountant. Your local library should have a copy of *The Law of Federal Income Taxation*, published by Callaghan & Company, which, if you get a fully up-to-date version, will be a good place to check what changes in tax law may have occurred.

This chapter is divided into four subsections:

1. Conventional sales
2. Installment sales
3. 1034 residential sales and exchanges
4. Tax-free 1031 exchanges

Each section will give you a solid foundation on the taxation regulations and will explain how you can easily calculate the values on which you will be taxed. The Appendix contains the tax tables 1990, which show the tax rates that apply to your circumstances.

Keep in mind that this chapter and, for that matter, this book, is not the final authority on real estate taxation and real estate exchanges. This book is written for real estate investors or professionals who want to maximize their opportunities by investing in real estate. Laws change, and it will be up to you to keep abreast of developments so you can adapt your investment strategies appropriately and maintain your edge in the real estate game.

1. Conventional Sales—The Foundation

In a conventional sale there are several elements that you must know in order to calculate the potential tax liability of that transaction. Look at a simple straightforward transaction to begin this review of conventional sales.

> For the past twelve years Albert has owned a vacant lot, which he thought would be a good investment. He was right because he paid $5,000 for the lot and now has a contract offering him $105,000. Albert will have to pay a total of $11,500 for real estate commissions and other costs to close the transaction and transfer title to the buyer. The sale is for cash and Albert needs to know what amount of taxable gain will be added to his earned income.

What You Need to Know to Calculate Tax Liability

- Basis and adjusted basis (current book value of property)
- Sale price (amount shown on contract)
- Selling expenses (commissions and other direct expenses tied to the closing of the transaction)

How to Find Taxable Gain

a.	Mortgage seller is relieved of	$ 0
b.	Cash or other boot seller gets	105,000
1.	Sale price	$105,000
2.	**Less** expenses of sale	11,500
3.	Amount realized on sale	$ 93,500
4.	**Less** basis (current adjusted basis)	5,000
5.	Taxable gain	$ 88,500

If there were no other deductions on this transaction, $88,500 would be added to Albert's taxable income. Without reviewing Albert's completed year-end tax return you cannot determine the precise tax Albert would have to pay. It should be clear, however, that in the absence of substantial personal and/or business deductions, this amount of gain could push Albert's income into a much higher tax bracket.

The elements needed to complete the above calculations are **basis** and **adjusted basis.** These amounts are key for calculating gain or loss on the disposition of property and for determining other accounting figures such as depreciation, bad debt, and casualty-loss deductions.

When a property is purchased the original basis is the actual cost of the property. In the above case, Albert paid $5,000 for the property. As long at that $5,000 did not also include an expense that Albert took as a deduction against his income tax, the $5,000 would be the original basis. Basis is also frequently called the "book value" of a property. This value can remain the same, or it can go up or down over the term of ownership.

Because the basis is the foundation of so many calculations, the importance of care in keeping track of this amount cannot be overstated.

Establishing the Original Basis

Cost basis. In most instances this is the format for determining the original basis. The buyer adds up the property cost: what was paid and the total of any mortgage assumed, plus commissions and other expenses connected with the purchase that are not deductible against income in the year of the acquisition.

Fair market value as basis. There may be times when a cost approach will not be possible or would distort the real value of the property. In the event of exchanges, inherited property, transfers, and other acquisitions where no clear payment can be calculated, the **fair market value** will be considered the foundation for the exchange. In the event of 1031 and 1034 exchanges, further adjustments must be accomplished to end up with the adjusted basis that the new owner would establish as his basis.

How Basis Is Increased

Basis is increased when you make improvements on the property or have expenditures chargeable to a capital account. Expenses that increase the basis include not only improvements but also purchase commissions, legal cost for defending or perfecting title, title insurance, and recording fees as well as capitalized expenses in buying, building, or developing an asset that have a useful life of over one year from the cost of the asset. Real estate taxes in the year of acquisition are counted as a part of the overall basis if the buyer assumes the seller's obligation to pay that tax. With minor exceptions, current expenses that are deductible against income may not be added to basis.

To help yourself avoid overlooking any adjustment to your basis, use the following annual-adjustments-to-basis form. If you are not sure of the depreciation figure, let your accountant fill that part in. Read also the next section. Not all real estate can be depreciated. For example, your residence is not a depreciable item except for parts of the residence where you may maintain an office or have other business activities. In Albert's case there is no depreciation nor are there any improvements, as his investment is vacant land.

Annual Adjustments to Basis

1. Basis at beginning of the year $_____
2. Improvements made (not repairs or maintenance)

_____   _____

_____   _____

_____   _____

_____   _____

_____   _____

_____   _____

_____   _____

Total $_____
Less depreciation taken   _____
New basis $_____

Calculating Depreciation

Depreciation is the accounting calculation that results in an expense that is deductible for calculations of income tax due. Depreciation taken each year is directly subtracted from your basis. Because the depreciation is an expense and deductible from income, it becomes an important factor in real estate investing. It is a "paper" expense that reduces taxes. Reducing taxes increases the investor's spendable income. With this in mind it should be obvious that if you compare two properties that both throw off a cash flow of $50,000, if one had an annual depreciation of $40,000 (thus a taxable income of only $10,000) and the other property had no depreciation at all, the property with only $10,000 in taxable income would be the one with the greater spendable income.

As depreciation reduces the book value or basis of a property, when that property is sold the gain from the sale is increased by the total amount of depreciation previously taken, and all the benefit gained in advance deductions from income are now taxed. Even if the investor doesn't take advantage of a **tax-free exchange** or **installment sale** (see following sections) to mitigate his tax consequences, the overall effect of the depreciation deduction is advantageous to him.

Calculations of depreciation have become rather cumbersome over the years. To avoid getting into complex and boring details that may confuse you more than help you, I recommend that your team member CPA or accountant tackle that part of your annual clean-up.

Important! Because there are different levels of depreciation and because you can accelerate some aspects of the rate at which you depreciate an item, your accountant should be aware of your overall goals. If you plan to sell in a few years, or if you are building up long-term equity and plan on exchanging down the road, then make sure your CPA knows this. It can greatly affect how he sets up your depreciation schedules.

2. Installment Sales

In a kinder and gentler way, the IRS has actually devised a logical method to protect the tax-payer from a situation where a sale is made but the taxpayer does not get enough money from the proceeds of the sale to pay the tax.

Rather than put the taxpayer in the embarrassing situation of having to go to jail for not paying the tax, the IRS developed the provision called **installment sale.**

An installment sale is where the seller receives the proceeds of the sale over more than one year and is allowed to pay tax due on the percentage of the gain actually received instead of all at once.

Good tax planning can take advantage of the installment sale by reducing the gain that would be realized in the year of the sale.

What If You Have a Capital Loss

Important! If the taxpayer has a capital loss available in the year of the sale it would be advisable to review the amount of loss and to determine if the installment sale would be advantageous to take. Should a capital loss occur and be available in a subsequent year, a review should be made to determine whether the installment sale should be continued or an election out of the installment reporting should be taken.

In the example given of a conventional sale, where Albert sold a lot for $105,000 and ended up with a $88,500 gain, he might have benefited from an installment sale.

Assume that Albert took back a first mortgage in the amount of $85,000 and received cash at closing of $20,000. His installment-sales calculations would be accomplished on this installment sales calculation form.

Installment Sales Calculation

   1. Sale price $105,000

      Less expenses of sale   11,500

      Less basis in property   5,000

   2. Gain on sale $ 88,500

   3. Mortgage the seller is relieved of $ 0

   4. Adjusted basis at day of closing $ 5,000

   5. Amount existing mortgage exceeds basis $ 0

      (Line 3 less Line 4)

      (if Line 4 is more than Line 3 enter 0)

   6. Contract price (combination of following) $105,000

      a. Cash, boot, or mortgages $105,000

      b. Mortgage over basis $ 0

   7. Calculate gross profit ratio. Divide Line 2, the

      gain on the sale, by Line 6, the contract price   .842857

   8. Express as percentage (Line 7 x 100)   84.2857%

   9. Mortgage held by seller $ 85,000

  10. Total received at closing $ 20,000

      (combination of following)

      a. Cash and boot $ 20,000

      b. Mortgage over basis $ 0

  11. Gain received at closing $ 16,857

      (Line 10 total x Line 7)

  12. Amount of mortgage held by seller that $ 71,642

      represents gain (x Line 9 x Line 7)

Review of this installment sale will show that of the $20,000 that Albert got at the closing, he had to pay out $11,500 for closing costs and other closing related expenses. His net cash intake therefore would have been $8,500. If he had to pay all the tax the year of the sale, he would have to go out of pocket to pay the taxes on the gain he received ($16,857.15).

Had the buyer paid all the expenses of the closing, the calculations would have shown a contract price of $93,500 ($105,000 less expenses of $11,500). This would result in a gross gain ratio of 94.6524 percent ($88,500 divided by $93,500). Assuming the buyer gave Albert only $8,500 down ($20,000 less 11,500 expenses), the gain would have been only $8,045.45. The total gain remains the same, however, as the calculations for selling expenses differ in an installment sale in that they are not deducted from the sale price to calculate **sale proceeds** but are, in effect, calculated as a separate amount—as if it had been added to the basis to arrive at the gain.

What Is Mortgage Over Basis?

In the calculations for Line 10, the term **mortgage over basis** occurs. While Albert had no existing mortgage, therefore no need to calculate this amount, many transactions will have existing mortgages that are assumed or taken subject to by the buyer at the closing of the transaction. Had Albert taken out a loan several years prior to the sale in the amount of $40,000, the entire transaction would have changed. As for the mortgage over basis, Albert's tax basis in the property is only $5,000, which means that the IRS will calculate that Albert has a $35,000 mortgage-over-basis situation and now must treat this excess as **earned income** in the year of the sale. Remember, Albert had use of the $40,000 for the period following the loan without paying tax on that money. Now he must pay the piper. Look at the installment sale taking into account these changes: the net price is $93,500; the seller assumes an existing mortgage of $40,000; Albert gives him another $45,000 second mortgage; and the buyer comes up with $8,500 and pays all closing costs.

Installment Sale Calculation

1.	Sale price	$93,500
	Less expenses of sale	0
	Less basis in property	5,000
2.	Gain on sale	$88,500
3.	Mortgage the seller is relieved of	$40,000
4.	Adjusted basis at day of closing	$ 5,000
5.	Amount existing mortgage exceeds basis	$35,000
	(Line 3 less Line 2)	
	(if Line 4 is more than Line 3 enter 0)	
6.	Contract price (combination of following)	$88,500
	a. Cash, boot, or mortgages	$53,500
	b. Mortgage over basis	$35,000
7.	Calculate gross profit ratio. Divide Line 2, the	
	gain on the sale, by Line 6, the contract price	1.
8.	Expressed as percentage (Line 7 x 100)	100%
9.	Mortgage held by seller	$45,000
10.	Total received at closing	$43,500
	(combination of following)	
	a. Cash and boot	$ 8,500
	b. Mortgage over basis	$35,000
11.	Gain received at closing	$43,500
	(Line 10 x Line 7)	
12.	Amount of mortgage held by seller that	$43,500
	represents gain (Line 9 x Line 7)	

Review of Installment Sales

Some special circumstances to consider when you use the installment sale concern the basic rules of qualification.

Qualifying for an Installment Sale

To qualify for the installment sale method you must adhere to just one rule: you must have a sales contract that provides for at least one payment to be received after the close of the tax year in which the disposition occurs. This rule differs greatly from that of earlier tax years, when the installment sale criteria required the seller to receive no more than 30 percent down and spread the payments over a minimum of two additional installments.

Special Factors to Watch Out For

Your idea and the IRS's idea of what you have received generally differ. In the case of the installment sale, the seller is deemed to have received several "payments" even though no actual money was delivered to his hands in the year of the sale.

Mortgage over basis. You have already seen how this works. The seller got the money sometime ago, and is now required to pay the tax on it.

Secondary financing that is payable on demand. The IRS will contend that payment was actually received in the year of the sale if the seller is holding a mortgage that is payable on the **seller's** demand, or in certain cases where the debt is readily tradable.

To ensure that the seller does not have a potential problem with this "constructive receipt" concept, it is a good idea to make sure that the mortgage sets out regular terms and conditions and does not have security other than the person's signature and the property as collateral.

In the past the use of installment sales was much more complicated. The 30–percent–down rule was frequently miscalculated, and taxpayers who had anticipated that they had properly qualified for an installment sale were often shocked to discover—two years later, when the IRS got around to an audit—that they had not properly filed. They now owed $12 million in back taxes.

The use of installment sales accounting can save you money and is an ideal method of spreading a taxable gain over several years. In the event you can find no other way to plan for the use of the proceeds of a potential sale, such as a tax-free exchange, by careful scheduling you can move the closing date so that you can get all your funds in a matter of weeks and still accomplish the magic of spreading, to some degree at least, your tax liability.

3. The 1034 Exchange—House for House

This form of tax-free exchange enables a property owner to exchange one residence for another and to avoid tax on all the gain that does not exceed the adjusted sales price of the old residence. The end result of this exchange permits you to move the equity in a home that has substantially appreciated to another home (or apartment) without being taxed on the gain. To understand this miniloophole, review some of the definitions used in the rules and regulations.

Definitions Used in 1034 Exchanges

"Old residence." This is the property you would sell, exchange, or otherwise dispose of which was used by you as a primary residence prior to the time that you elect to make the exchange of your taxable gain (if any) to the new residence. Validation of residence is clearly that property which was your tax residence to distinguish one living residence from another, in the event you owned several such properties.

"New residence." This is the new property that you now claim to be your legal or tax residence. You may have acquired this property up to two years prior to the date you sell (close on and pass title of) the old residence, or you may acquire a new residence up to two years after you sell your old residence. Because of this, it is possible that you already own a property you will move into as your primary residence and are using that property for some other purpose. It could be a second home, or one used occasionally by you and rented out when you are not there.

Both new and old residences may include a houseboat, a house trailer, a home, an apartment, and stock in a cooperative apartment that contains living quarters.

"Adjusted sale price." To calculate the gain (if any) in the sale of the old residence, the sale price shall be adjusted to deduct from it certain work done to the old residence to assist in its sale. This important computation is quite often overlooked at the time. To qualify as a deduction to the sale price, the fix-up expenses must meet these conditions:

1. They must be not otherwise deductible in computing taxable income. This enables you to deduct such items such as repairs, decorating, painting, clean-up, and other expenses that can improve the looks of a property but that would not add to the basis (such as adding a garage to the property).

2. They cannot be selling expenses, such as fees paid to an attorney to secure an abstract or to review title.

3. The work must have been done during the 90-day period that ended when you entered into a contract to sell the subject property. Note that this date is the day the agreement between you and the buyer (or exchanger) is a valid contract. This date is different from the sale date, which is the date the property is actually deeded to the buyer.

4. In addition to the above expenses, the normal selling expenses are also deducted from the sale price, as in all usual sales procedures. These expenses are "selling expenses" and differ from the above expenses, which are unique to the 1034 exchange.

"Sale date." The actual date when the old property is deeded to another party. This date is different from the contract date on which the fix-up expenses are based. The sale date establishes the exact year and day from which you count the 24 months prior to and 24 months after to acquire and utilize the 1034 exchange.

"Time period." The time period for most owners is 24 months prior to and/or after the sale date. There are several exceptions to this. These exceptions involve people who, after selling their home, reside outside the United States or who are in the U.S. military. If either of these two events applies to you, review the extended time periods with your accountant to see exactly how much extra time you may have to utilize the 1034. The maximum allowed at the time of this writing is eight years after the sale date, but these items are subject to emergency measures in event of war or other international crises that cause Congress to give special perks to the military.

"Time and manner of making the election." The election under Section 1034 shall be made with the filing of your income tax return for the taxable year during which the disposition of your old residence occurs.

Laurens 1034 Exchange Example

Laurens decided to sell his apartment, which cost him $150,000 seven years ago. In seven years he has made substantial improvements to the apartment at a cost of $35,000. In anticipation of the sale his broker suggests that he do some minor fix-up, painting, and decorating, to make the apartment justify its present asking price of $375,000. Laurens starts the work on March 3, 1991, and completes it on April 10. The work is paid for as it is being done and costs $4,000.

On June 1, 1990, Laurens enters into a contract to sell the property for $360,000, closes on the title on August 1 of the same year, and pays a brokerage commission of $15,000. No other closing costs are attributed to Laurens.

A year earlier, Laurens had purchased another apartment as an investment. He now decides to move into that apartment as his personal residence. That apartment cost him $295,000. In the year of the sale of his old residence, he decided to take advantage of Internal Revenue Code Section 1034.

The Laurens transaction is illustrated using the 1034 residence-for-residence exchange form. Because the new residence costs less than the money received for the old residence, not all of the realized gain ($160,000 shown on Line 13) is transferred to the new residence. Because of this, Laurens will have a taxable gain in the year of this allocation. That amount, shown on Line 16, is the "gain recognized." Without other qualification or offsetting deductions, it would be taxable.

Keep in mind that if Laurens had sold his old residence with an installment sale (shown earlier in this chapter), the gain shown on Line 16 could be spread over several years and not fully realized in the year of this allocation. Separate calculations would be needed to ascertain the taxable gain in that event. The recognized gain would be divided by the total contract price to arrive at the fractional percentage, which when multiplied by the down payment or future principal payments gives the gain received during any tax year.

Notice that in the calculations for the Laurens exchange no depreciation is shown on Line 7. Had Laurens maintained an office in his home and taken depreciation, that would have reduced the basis of the property. This depreciation calculation is needed even if the office is no longer in the residence. However, if the office remains a part of the property, Laurens will have to exclude the percentage of the value of the property that relates to the office. If, for example, the office value were 15 percent of the total, the transaction, from the 1034 point of view, would be divided into two separate calculations. The office portion of the sale would not qualify for 1034 treatment. If there is to be an office in the new residence, that property can be divided into two separate transactions as well, and each is viewed differently: the residence as a 1034 and the office as a 1031 transaction.

1034 Residence-for-Residence Exchange

Adjusted sale price of old property

1.	Sale price of old residence	$360,000
2.	**Less** fix-up cost	4,000
3.	**Less** selling expenses	15,000
4.	Adjusted sale price	$340,000

Basis, old residence

5.	Original cost	$150,000
6.	**Plus** improvements made	35,000
7.	**Less** depreciation taken	0
8.	Basis of the old residence	$185,000

Realized gain

9.	Sale price of old residence, Line 1	$360,000
10.	**Less** selling expenses	15,000
11.	Amount realized in the sale	$345,000
12.	**Less** basis of old residence, Line 8	185,000
13.	Realized gain on old residence	$160,000

If new residence cost is less than Line 4

14.	Adjusted sale price of old residence, Line 4	$341,000
15.	**Less** cost of new residence	295,000
16.	Gain recognized (taxable) from sale	$ 46,000
17.	Total realized gain, Line 13	$160,000
18.	**Less** Line 16	46,000
19.	Gain not allocated to new property	$114,000
20.	Cost of new residence, Line 15	$295,000
21.	**Less** gain not allocated, Line 19	114,000

22. New basis of the new property $181,000

If new residence cost is more than Line 4
23. Cost of new residence $
24. **Less** Line 13 (gain of old residence)

               _____

25. Basis of the new residence $
               =========

In the following example the details are the same, except that Laurens purchases a new home at a cost of $425,000.

1034 Residence-for-Residence Exchange

Adjusted sale price of old property
1.	Sale price of old residence	$360,000
2.	**Less** fix-up cost	4,000
3.	**Less** selling expenses	15,000
4.	Adjusted sale price	$340,000

Basis, old residence
5.	Original cost	$150,000
6.	**Plus** improvements made	35,000
7.	**Less** depreciation taken	0
8.	Basis of old residence	$185,000

Realized gain
9.	Sale price of old residence, Line 1	$360,000
10.	**Less** selling expenses	15,000
11.	Amount realized in the sale	$345,000
12.	**Less** basis of old residence, Line 8	185,000
13.	Realized gain on old residence	$160,000

If new residence cost is less than Line 4
14. Adjusted sale price of old residence, Line 4 $
15. **Less** cost of new residence

16.	Gain recognized (taxable) from sale	$
		=========
17.	Total realized gain, Line 13	$
18.	**Less** Line 16	
		_____
19.	Gain not allocated to new property	$
		=========
20.	Cost of new residence, Line 15	$
21.	**Less** gain not allocated, Line 19	
		_____
22.	New basis of the new property	$

If new residence cost is more than Line 4

23.	Cost of new residence	$425,000
24.	**Less** Line 13 (gain of old residence)	160,000
		_____
25.	Basis of the new residence	$265,000
		=========

4. The 1031 Tax-Free Exchange

"Never have so many given so little to so few." A possible quote from Donald Trump describing real estate tax-free exchanges, a powerful tax break that allows you to build equity and appreciation above your basis and to trade up to bigger and more profitable events and never pay the tax on any gain.

Using the System to Beat the Odds

Insiders know the power of working with the system. Investors who use the system rather than buck it have made big bucks going with the flow rather than fighting the tide. You see, only the mavericks think the way to make their mark in the world is to do something unique, to do something that people will stand up and cheer about. If you want people to cheer and to look up at you, stand on the edge of a skyscraper, 20 floors up, and threaten to jump.

The millionaires know better. Donald Trump will tell you, Ted Turner will tell you, and David Rockefeller knew all along, as did his father and his brothers, that the beauty of the American way is it gives you the way around its own roadblocks. Ray Kroc hamburgers knows all about using the loopholes. When are you going to find out? When will you start to build your fortune by doing the unexpected—the obvious?

I say "obvious" because making money is exactly that. Watching what is going on, following trends, and making decisions based on time and place—not much more than that. Time and place. If you are a good student of the past and can read a map, then the time and the place are not such a risk after all. Learning to follow the obvious is hard work: it requires effort and patience. It puts **you** on the line. You, not anyone else. That's something people are frightened to tackle.

Getting Around Roadblocks

That's what loopholes are all about. You need to know what they are, where they are, and combine them with good timing and all the advantages thrown at you. Use them to the hilt. There is nothing wrong with that. You owe it to yourself to try to get the most out of tax advantages, loopholes, little-known escape provisions, new laws, the repeal of old laws, and knowing what is going on. That is using the system to beat the system.

Why Section 1031: The Best Loophole Left

One of the best loopholes left to the real estate investor is the tax-free exchange. The Section 1034 exchange allows you to sell or exchange your residence and transfer your equity to another one, without paying tax on a capital gain.

The Section 1031 tax-free exchange allows you to continue to dispose of property in such a way that you can constantly move up, building wealth, gaining equity, and never paying the tax.

There is no faster way to build wealth in real estate investing than by using the 1031 exchange. It should be one of your primary tools in your bag of investment tricks.

Logic and Human Nature Save Taxes

It is not magic, however, that makes this tool work. It is human nature. It is using the logic of the law in your favor to compound the building of your equity. We are talking about using money to build money. Money that you would have had to pay out to your not-so-silent partner, the IRS. Tax money. Show me a man who knows how he can save a $100,000 in taxes and I'll show you a true insider in real estate investing.

What 1031 Means to You

Section 1031 provides that no gain or loss is taxable when properties qualify for this kind of exchange. The primary qualification is that the property exchanged be of "like kind" and that this like kind of property be held for productive use in trade or business, or for investment. The IRS also states that the qualifying property **does not include** property that is stock-in-trade or other property held primarily for sale, stocks, bonds, notes, or other securities or evidences of indebtedness or interest in other forms of ownership or action.

As of this writing, the bottom line is that the 1031 exchange provisions allow you to build equity that you can use to acquire other property and never have to pay any tax on the gain. **You choose, you are in control.**

Internal Revenue Code, Section 1031, is often called the **tax-free exchange.** This provision is not limited to real estate; in fact, many transactions under the 1031 provisions to avoid payment of tax are non-real-estate exchanges.

While the specific language of the code states that no gain or loss is recognized (taxable) if certain qualifying property is exchanged solely for "like kind" property, the definition of "like kind" has been greatly misunderstood and debated. Many knowledgeable and informed people make mistakes on this issue, partly because of the complexity of the law itself.

To make the law more manageable from the IRS's point of view, as well as to make it easier for investors to utilize the law in tax and investment planning, recently changes in the interpretation of some of the elements that made the 1031 both cumbersome as well as complex have been made. The IRS has also tightened up several of the loopholes in the law.

Rules and Regulations of Section 1031

What Kind of Property Qualifies?

The property being exchanged must be currently held for productive use in trade or business or be held for investment. It is generally assumed that the term "held for productive use in trade or business" means "used in trade or business"; this applies to equipment and other items that are a part of business or trade functions. This is distinguished from property that would be inventory or "stock" held for resale rather than investment.

The property can be real estate or other property that can be held for productive use in trade or business such as trucks, cars, ships, aircraft, tractors, and so on. If any of these items are of investment quality, they also qualify under the investment side of the code description. Do not be limited in your thinking about the scope of the 1031—it is more inclusive than you might at first imagine.

What "Held for Investment" Means

The definition of "held for investment" has evolved over time through judicial interpretation to be any property that was held by the taxpayer for the intent of investment at the time of the exchange. While it is possible that the original intent of ownership was not investment, the IRS accepts changed circumstances can cause original intent to vary. You should be aware, however, that because IRS audits frequently come several years after the fact, intent can be clouded. Let's say, for example, you had purchased a lot with the obvious intent to build a new home for yourself, plans made ready to go, only to discover that you could not afford the new construction, nor could you get financing. This causes you to change your mind about building a home, so you exchange the lot for equity in an office building. Several years later, the IRS may pick up on the building plans and other money you spent clearly for the purpose of creating a residence for yourself and challenge your 1031 exchange, particularly if you avoided sizable taxes that would have been due otherwise.

The definition of what property will qualify as like-kind held for investment is at this moment very broad. The nature of investment property must be clearly evident, however, at the instant the exchange is contemplated. Case examples have shown that very creative exchanges have qualified as like-kind property.

If you own a farm for investment and want to exchange it for a shopping center to be held for investment, those properties will be considered like-kind. A single-family home that was once your residence (or not) but which you now rent out for income and continue to own as an investment and now exchange for a medical office building also qualifies as like-kind property.

If you exchange your five-unit apartment building for a 10-unit one there is no complication in these being like-kind properties. Even if you live in one unit (one-fifth of the value of the five units), the other four-fifths will still qualify for 1031. If you occupy as your residence one of the apartments in the new building that will be treated as a separate exchange under the provisions of the Section 1034 (discussed earlier), that part of the exchange is potentially also tax-free.

The IRS is attempting to tighten the rules on what is like-kind, so be sure that you check first to see if there have been any new regulations that make your farm in California suddenly not like-kind for a farm in Florida.

"Related Parties" Can Cause Trouble

No exchange will qualify as a 1031 if the property was acquired in an exchange with a related party who later disposed of it before 24 months following the exchange. Exceptions to this rule are when property is disposed of due to the death of either party or in certain involuntary conversions such as by court order or current domain. This two-year limitation can be extended by the IRS, giving the taxpayer a longer exposure to IRS review. Because of this, any transaction between related parties (not just blood relations, as it can be business relations as well) should be approached very carefully.

Foreign Property Is Excluded

To qualify for Section 1031, property must be located within the United States. The wording of the section does not specify whether this includes United States possessions as well as states. This provision dates from 1990, so watch for case histories to provide guidance on this issue. In the past there were no restrictions as to location if the property was deemed to be of like kind.

Leaseholds

If a property is a "leasehold"—the owner of the leasehold is the tenant on the property—then the leasehold must have a minimum of 30 years remaining at the date of the transaction. Obviously to be safe one would want to ensure that sufficient time remained on the leasehold to allow for delays in closing or the need to renegotiate with other parties.

Natural Resources

With natural resources the matter is very complicated, depending not only on what kind of "ownership" is held but also on whether state law specifies that rights to the natural resource are of "like kind." If you own, or plan to exchange for rights, royalties to gas, oil, coal, or other minerals, review your state's laws and IRS cases within that state prior to attempting any 1031 exchange.

What Is "Boot"?

Boot is part of the exchange that is not like-kind property. It is taxable. It can be cash, stock, or anything that has a presumed value; it can also include things that you obtain from being relieved of an obligation. In calculating the "boot" you receive in an exchange, you can balance different obligations against each other. Look at the following form.

Checklist to Calculate Boot Received

1. Mortgage you are relieved of $_____
2   **Less** debt on the property you assume   _____
3. **Less** cash you paid to the other party   _____
4. **Less** value of other boot you gave   _____
                                              _____
5. Boot against which netting is permitted $_____
    (cannot be less than 0)
6. **Plus** value of other boot you received   _____
7. **Plus** cash you received   _____
                                              _____
8. Boot received $_____
                                              ==========

Finding Boot

Grant owned a strip store worth $250,000 with a first mortgage of $105,000, which gave him $145,000 equity. Grant's basis in this strip store is $80,000. He exchanges this for an office building owned by Alex. The price of Alex's building is $300,000 and there is a first mortgage of $110,000.

To balance the $200,000 equity that Alex has in the office building, Grant agrees to add $20,000 cash and to give Alex a $25,000 late-model car.

Checklist to Calculate Boot Received

		Grant	Alex
1.	Mortgage you are relieved of (net mortgage relief)	$105,000	$110,000
2.	**Less** debt on the property you assume	110,000	105,000
3.	**Less** cash you paid to the other party	20,000	0
4.	**Less** value of other boot you gave	25,000	0
5.	Boot against which netting is permitted (cannot be less than 0)	$ 0	$ 5,000
6.	**Plus** value of other boot you received	0	25,000
7.	**Plus** cash you received	0	20,000
8.	Boot received	$ 0	$ 50,000
		==========	==========

In this transaction Grant gets no boot, and Alex receives $50,000. In general, boot is the part of the exchange that is taxable; it can include what is called "net mortgage relief," which is the difference between the greater mortgage you give up to the smaller mortgage you assume (Line 1 less Line 2).

Non-1031 Property That Can Be Included

A 1031 exchange can include both kinds of property. If you are exchanging one qualifying 1031 property for another like-kind property, the fact that part of the exchange is a nonqualifying property does not void the exchange. For example, if you include your residence in an exchange of an investment property to acquire another investment property, the portion that is investment-for-investment will be treated as a 1031 exchange, providing all the other tests meet the criteria.

Placing Mortgages Prior to the Exchange

You can place mortgages just prior to the exchange. Tax court has held that the assumption of a liability by a taxpayer in a like-kind exchange will be recognized, even though the liability was placed on the property immediately before the exchange.

However, the IRS is apt to audit any exchange to determine that you did not attempt to do something for the sole purpose of evading tax. If your proposed exchange anticipates that there will be a last-moment refinancing that allows one party to waltz away with untaxable cash, then batten down the hatches for the storm is about to strike.

Combining 1031 and Installment Sales

Exchanges that qualify for 1031 provisions can also utilize the installment-sale form of reporting gain. This allows you to get cash, but spread over a period of time—eliminating the necessity to pay tax on the total amount in the year of the transaction.

An example: In a normal and qualifying 1031 exchange, you transfer a building with a basis of $40,000, and a fair market value of $200,000 for a building with a value of $60,000. The other party agrees to give you a note for the balance of $140,000, which will be payable over 10 years in annual payments, plus a reasonable and allowable (by the IRS) interest.

Using the provisions of both Section 1031 and the installment-sale revision act of 1980, there would be no recognized payment in the year of the transaction, and no tax due from you. This is because the receipt of like-kind property is not deemed to be a payment. In this transaction, the total contract price would be $140,000, since the qualifying property is excluded from the computations. The gross profit is also $140,000, since the realized gain of $160,000 is reduced to take account of the $20,000 ($60,000 building received less $40,000 basis of the property surrendered) not recognized because of the provisions of the 1031. The gross profit ratio is 100 percent, but since no actual payment is considered received in the year of the sale, no gain is recognized during that year.

In the past, the installment-sale provisions required that the "seller" receive no more than 30 percent of the sale price in the year of the sale. This provision is no longer a part of the law, and installment sales simply require that an additional payment of principal occur in another tax year.

Many exchanges use the mortgage-balance technique to balance the equity between the parties. This happens anytime one of the parties to the transaction takes back or holds a mortgage on the property he is giving up. This mortgage taken back can be treated in the installment-sale provisions of the code, and money not received in the installment-sale calculations is not taxed until it is received.

Special warnings! Secondary paper on other property is boot. If you take back a $50,000 mortgage, it can be treated as an installment sale. However, if the other party gives you a $50,000 note owed to him by a third party, you have just received boot, as that is not part of an installment-sale calculation.

Dealers Must Take Care with Investments

Dealers must distinguish between investment property and an identical property owned as inventory. You can be a real estate developer selling vacant lots and still own a lot that was acquired for the specific purpose of investment. But you must be able to show some evidence that this specific lot was not just a part of your inventory that did not get sold. Remember, the IRS is looking with a watchful eye at what you have done in the past.

Property Acquired to Exchange Is Disqualified to One Party

Property that is acquired for the sole purpose of exchanging is subject to being disqualified.

An example: Jack owns exactly what you want and the only way you can get Jack's property is to go out and buy what he wants. Jack can, if other circumstances warrant, qualify for the 1031 exchange, but as you are exchanging property acquired specifically for the exchange with Jack, you will not qualify.

Nonqualifying Property

The following properties are specified by the IRS as nonqualifying properties under the provisions of Section 1031. Try not to laugh when you reach Number 7:

1. Stock in trade or other property held primarily for sale
2. Stocks, bonds, or notes
3. Other securities or evidence of debt or interest
4. Partnership interests
5. Certificates of trust or beneficial interests
6. Choses in action (legal right to recover personal property or money by legal action)
7. Livestock of different sexes

Remember that some of the above items may be transferred without recognition of gain under other provisions of the Internal Revenue Code. To find out what other provisions may allow you to make "un-taxable exchanges" for any of the seven items above, I suggest a prolonged visit with your CPA or tax lawyer. Be prepared to explain all the details of the proposed exchange and what you want to accomplish the most: save tax or make the exchange.

Qualifying Personal Property

- Any mechanical apparatus (including electronic) devoted to business is like-kind to similar mechanical apparatus.
- Gold coins of two different countries, which are not used as a circulating medium of exchange and whose value is based on their gold content, qualify as like-kind. Gold and silver are not like-kind.
- Loan portfolios between banks are like-kind.
- Contracts of professional sports players (football, baseball, etc.) are like-kind property if exchanged for other players in the same sport.

Allocation of Basis in Multiasset Exchanges

When you acquire by exchange several different properties at the same time, the allocation of basis is critical. For example, you have an adjusted basis in a building of $100,000 and it has a fair market value of $160,000. You exchange this property in a qualified like-kind exchange for two qualifying properties: Property A, which has a value of $120,000, and Property B, which has a value of $40,000. The IRS requires that you allocate the basis on the same ratio that the exchange establishes.

New basis = adjusted old basis x $\dfrac{\textbf{value new property}}{\textbf{fair market value of old property}}$

Thus, the new basis in the two different properties is:

Property A: $75,000   **Property B: $25,000**

Avoid Recapture of Depreciation

The IRS allows you to take accelerated depreciation of capital improvements of income or investment properties. As has been mentioned earlier, depreciation is a paper expense which becomes a deduction from income and therefore reduces tax liability. When you use an accelerated method it is possible that you will exceed the "allowable" rate when you sell or exchange. When this happens you will recapture this excess depreciation as a "paper income" and will have a tax liability on income you don't actually get at the time of closing.

You can avoid this by making sure that you do not take accelerated depreciation as allowed by the IRS. If you have already done this, you may want to rethink the idea of making a 1031 exchange and to look at other ways to avoid or postpone the tax consequence or the actual reporting requirements for the transaction.

Other nontaxable events such as an option to sell or exchange where the actual event took place after you had made up for excessive depreciation could provide an alternative way to have your cake and eat it.

Before I continue with some specific techniques of using exchanges as a long-term plan, review the basic exchanges and the forms you can use to keep track of your exchange, your future tax consequences, and final basis.

Fifi's Basic 1031 Exchange Example

Fifi has owned a small office building for over 15 years, ever since she had it constructed as a place for her hair salon. Now retired, she has rented it out to two doctors who have spent a fortune to remodel it for their specific needs. When she bought the land and built the original building her total investment was $50,000. Fifi has depreciated the improvements for these past 15 years, to the extent that her book value of land and improvements is only $21,000. Today the rent is $44,000 per year plus all expenses of tax, insurance, and maintenance, and the property has a market value of $400,000. Fifi has no mortgage on the property, so it is free and clear of all debt.

With a book value of only $21,000 and a market value of $400,000, Fifi is faced with a gain (in the event of a sale) of $379,000. Even if she were able to average out at the moderate tax rate of 25 percent, a sale would create a tax liability of $94,750. The actual tax responsibility could be higher, depending on her other income and allowable deductions.

What Fifi really wants is to acquire a real shopping center so that she can retire and travel around France with her boyfriend.

She has found a nice center owned by Julian, which is available for $1,400,000, and the broker representing the seller has told Fifi that the seller may consider taking something free and clear in exchange. There is an existing first mortgage on the center of $675,000.

Fifi offers the center owner her free-and-clear office building worth $400,000 for the equity in the center. She asks the sellers to hold a second mortgage of $325,000 so that the deal is simple and she does not have to come up with any cash. Fifi doesn't bat an eyelash (she's read my other books).

In this transaction Fifi has met the primary qualifications for a 1031 exchange. The property she is exchanging and the property to be received are clearly held for investment.

This transaction would go through several steps to balance the equity between the two parties. The beginning situation is shown below:

Fifi has:			**Julian has:**		
Medical offices:	Value	$400,000	Shopping center:	Value	$1,400,000
Mortgage		0	Mortgage		675,000
Equity		$400,000	Equity		$ 725,000

Because Fifi has suggested that Julian hold a second mortgage for $325,000 to balance the equity, the deal would now balance as shown below:

Fifi has:			**Julian has:**		
Medical offices:	Value	$400,000	Shopping center:	Value	$1,400,000
Mortgage		0	Existing mortgage		675,000
			Second mortgage		325,000
Equity		$400,000	Equity		$ 400,000

Follow this example through a series of computations to discover taxable circumstances, if they exist, to find the new basis in the exchanged property.

Fifi's 1031 Exchange Tax Calculations

1.	Mortgage you are relieved of	$	0
2.	**Less** debt on the property you assume		1,000,000
3.	**Less** cash you paid to the other party		0
4.	**Less** value of other boot you gave		0
5.	Boot against which netting is permitted (cannot be less than 0)	$	0
6.	**Plus** value of other boot you received		0
7.	**Plus** cash you received		0
8.	Boot received	$	0
			===========

Computation of realized gain

9.	Value of 1031 qualified property you receive		$1,400,000
10.	**Plus** qualified deferred installments		0
11.	**Plus** value of boot you receive		0
12.	**Plus** cash received		0
13.	**Plus** existing debt on your old property		0
14.	Total consideration you received		$1,400,000
15.	**Less** adjusted basis of property you give		21,000
16.	**Less** cash you pay to other party at closing		0
17.	**Less** mortgages you assume at closing		1,000,000
18.	Gain or loss realized	$	379,000
19.	Gain recognized and taxable (lesser of Lines 8 and 18)	$	0
20.	Gain not taxed because of the exchange (subtract Line 19 from greater, Line 8 or 18)	$	379,000
			===========

Fifi would want to know what her new basis would be in the center so she would use the following form.

Calculation to Find New Basis

1. Adjusted basis of property given up in exchange $ 21,000
2. **Plus** adjusted basis of boot given up   0

    Total of basis for properties given up $ 1,000

Add the following

3. Cash paid to the other party $ 0
4. Mortgages you assume on new property $1,000,000
5. Gain recognized (Line 19 of tax calculations 1031) $ 0

    Subtotal $1,021,000
6. **Less** cash you received   0
7. **Less** other taxable boot you received   0
8. **Less** loss recognized   0

9. Basis of all property received $1,021,000
10. **Less** value of boot received   0

11. New basis of 1031 qualified property $1,021,000
                                                            ==========

Fifi's exchange is rather simple to follow, and is not unlike many exchanges that take place. Fifi has a substantial gain, due to the appreciation of her building and the reduction of the original basis through depreciation. Her equity has a real value to someone interested in taking on a smaller property that does not require as much effort to manage. Take a look, however, at a more complicated exchange—and view the consequences from both sides.

The Burns and Able Exchange

Burns has owned a 25-unit apartment house for four years. He meets Able, who has a beautiful waterfront site that Burns decides he would like to own so that he can construct a 240-unit apartment building. Review the basic information about each property shown on the following worksheet. Using the exchange worksheet you can complete the balance board.

I have adjusted the different amounts to provide a clear picture of the events as they unfold.

Exchange Worksheet

	Burns	Able
Kind of property	25 apt. units	Waterfront site
Value for exchange	$950,000	$1,300,000
Existing financing	$175,000	$ 288,000
Original purchase price	$600,000	$ 400,000
Additions made	$ 55,000	$ 0
Allowable selling cost	$ 80,000	$ 108,000
Depreciation taken	$230,000	$ 0
Mortgage held back to balance	$ 0	$ 0
Will pay this amount of cash	$ 0	$ 0
Will give this other boot	$ 0	$ 0
Basis in boot	$ 0	$ 0
Will give this other property	$ 0	$ 0
Basis in this other property	$ 0	$ 0
Will give this amount of paper	$ 0	$ 0
Basis in paper	$ 0	$ 0

Two-Party Balance Board

	First Party: Burns	Second Party: Able
Value of property given	$950,000	$1,300,000
Less existing mortgage	175,000	288,000
Equity	$775,000	$1,012,000

Burns makes the first move by making the offer to Able. If Able will hold a second mortgage for $237,000, there will be a balance of the equities. See the balance board below.

	First Party: Burns	Second Party: Able
Value of property given	$950,000	$1,300,000
Less existing mortgage	175,000	288,000
Equity	$775,000	$1,012,000
Less balance of mortgage		237,000
Second equity	$775,000	$ 775,000

Able rejects this, and after a lot of going back and forth the deal ends up as follows: Able will hold a second mortgage of $100,000. Burns will give to Able a sailboat worth $50,000, which Burns has on his books, with an adjusted basis of $60,000 and a first mortgage which Burns is owed by another party with a face amount of $112,000. To balance off the equity, Able will pay Burns $25,000 cash.

	First Party: Burns	**Second Party: Able**
Value of property given	$950,000	$1,300,000
Less existing mortgage	175,000	288,000
Equity to be transferred	$775,000	$1,012,000
Less balance mortgage		100,000
Second equity	$775,000	$ 912,000
Add the following		
Pays cash	$ 0	$ 25,000
Gives paper	$112,000	$ 0
Gives boot	$ 50,000	$ 0
Equity adjustment	$937,000	$ 937,000
Subtract the following		
Gets cash	$ 25,000	$ 0
Gets paper	$ 0	$ 112,000
Gets boot	$ 0	$ 50,000
Gets second equity transferred	$912,000	$ 775,000
Balance	$ 0	$ 0

The worksheet is brought up to date:

Revised Exchange Worksheet

	Burns	**Able**
Kind of property	25 apt. units	Waterfront site
Value for exchange	$950,000	$1,300,000
Existing financing	$175,000	$ 288,000
Original purchase price	$600,000	$ 400,000
Additions made	$ 55,000	$ 0
Allowable selling cost	$ 80,000	$ 108,000
Depreciation taken	$230,000	$ 0

Mortgage held back to balance	$ 0	$ 100,000
Will pay this amount of cash	$ 0	$ 25,000
Will give this other boot	$ 50,000	$ 0
Basis in boot	$ 60,000	$ 0
Will give this other property	$ 0	$ 0
Basis in other property	$ 0	$ 0
Will give this amount of paper	$112,000	$ 0
Basis in paper	$112,000	$ 0

Using the revised exchange worksheet, find the adjusted basis using the following form.

Find Adjusted Basis in Old Property

	Burns	Able
Original purchase price	$600,000	$400,000
Plus additions	55,000	0
Plus allowed closing costs	80,000	108,000
Subtotal	$735,000	$508,000
Less depreciation to closing	230,000	0
Adjusted basis	$505,000	$508,000
(Line 15 of 1031 tax calculations)		

Continue the 1031 exchange calculations by completing the tax calculation form shown below.

1031 Exchange Tax Calculations

	Burns	Able
1. Mortgage you are relieved of	$ 175,000	$ 288,000
2. **Less** debt on the property you assume	388,000	175,000
3. **Less** cash you paid to the other party	0	25,000
4. **Less** value of other boot you gave	162,000	0
5. Boot against which netting is permitted (Line 1 less Lines 2, 3, and 4) (cannot be less than 0)	$ 0	$ 88,000
6. **Plus** value of other boot you received	0	162,000
7. **Plus** cash you received	25,000	0

8. Boot received	$ 25,000	$ 250,000
	============	==========

Computation of realized gain

9. Value of 1031 qualified property you receive	$1,300,000	$ 950,000
10. **Plus** qualified deferred installments	0	100,000
11. **Plus** value of boot you receive	0	162,000
12. **Plus** cash received	25,000	0
13. **Plus** existing debt on your old property	175,000	288,000
14. Total consideration you received	$1,500,000	$1,500,000
15. **Less** adjusted basis of property you give	505,000	508,000
16. **Less** cash you pay to other party at closing	0	25,000
17. **Less** mortgages you assume at closing	388,000	175,000
18. Gain or loss realized	$ 607,000	$ 792,000
19. Gain recognized and taxable (lesser of Line 8 and 18)	$ 25,000	$ 250,000
	============	==========
20. Gain not taxed because of the exchange (subtract Line 19 from greater of Lines 8 and 18)	$ 582,000	$ 542,000

Calculation to Find New Basis

	Burns	Able
1. Adjusted basis of property given up in exchange (see calculation of adjusted basis shown earlier)	$ 505,000	$ 508,000
2. **Plus** adjusted basis of boot given up	172,00	0
Total of basis for properties given up	$ 677,000	$ 508,000
Add the following		
3. Cash you paid to the other party	$ 0	$ 25,000
4. Mortgages you assume on the new property	$ 388,000	$ 175,000
5. Gain recognized	$ 25,000	$ 250,000
Subtotal	$1,090,000	$ 958,000
Subtract from subtotal the following		
6. **Less** cash you received	25,000	0
7. **Less** other taxable boot you received	0	0
8. **Less** loss recognized on boot you gave	10,000	0

9. Basis of all property received	$ 993,000	$ 958,000
10. **Less** value of boot received (boat and paper)	0	162,000
11. Basis of 1031 qualified property	$ 993,000	$ 796,000

Note 1. Lines 2 and 17 in "1031 Exchange Tax Calculations" and Line 4 in the above "Calculation to Find New Basis" show the total amount of mortgages you assume on the new property. This amount takes into consideration the total new debt you undertake to repay. If the other party is going to hold a purchase money mortgage on this property, that mortgage will be included in the amount on Line 4, even though the other party is relieved of a lesser amount, which is the existing financing on the property prior to placement of the purchase money mortgage.

Note 2. See the next form. Burns has a loss in the value of the boat, which is part of the boot property. While a loss on a qualified 1031 property cannot be used in adjustments of basis or gain, loss on a nonqualified property can be. In the tax calculations this loss is automatically picked up through the deduction of basis, which in Burns's case is $10,000 more than the value of the boot given.

Deferred and Starker Exchanges

Often referred to as "Starker" exchanges after a case historic for tax law governing real estate exchanges, the IRS promulgated rules and regulations to make tax planning much easier with respect to deferred or delayed exchanges and multiparty exchanges.

A common multiparty exchange is where Party A wishes to dispose of property using the provisions of 1031. A Party B is found who wants to acquire A's property (B is a taker for A's property). B has nothing to exchange with A, but B is willing to accommodate A by acquiring a property (through purchase or exchange), which is then transferred to A as a like-kind exchange.

This kind of multiparty exchange often requires one event occurs anticipation of another; the actual transaction is not fully completed when the first step is closed.

Intent—A Critical Element

The details of multiparty and deferred exchanges differ greatly. In deferred exchanges it is important that the contract reflect the intent of the parties to structure a qualified exchange and that the qualifying party(s) do not receive nonqualifying property, even for an instant, as they progress through the transaction to the final transfer of properties in the like-kind exchange. The rules allow the party seeking 1031 protection to find a property he wants to end up with, and, in fact, even negotiate for the property—provided he does so as an **agent** for a second party. Another party, such as the Realtor or a lawyer, can also act as the second party's agent.

Bob owns a duplex and wants to exchange his equity for a rental property with more units. Sam is a ready, willing, and able buyer of Bob's duplex. Bob and Sam enter into an agreement whereby Sam will pay an agreed amount of money to acquire another property to exchange with Bob for his equity. Bob looks around and finds a 10-unit apartment complex he likes, which can be acquired using the money Sam has pledged for this purpose. Bob negotiates a contract in Sam's name and the three-way deal closes. The critical step is that not once does Bob have any control over Sam's money to do anything other than have that money acquire the like-kind property. If Bob has, even for a split second, control that could direct the money to any other use, the transaction will not qualify as a 1031 exchange for Bob. The other two parties to the transaction do not qualify for 1031 treatment, because the second transaction is a straight purchase agreement. If Sam made a qualified 1031 like-kind exchange using property for the 10-unit apartment and then exchanged it to Bob, it might (depending on the other requirements that need to be met) qualify as a 1031 exchange as well.

Cash in Starker Exchanges

The ultimate delivery of cash does not invalidate the delayed 1031 exchange. The agreement has a provision that in the event a like-kind property is not found, at a future date cash in lieu of the like-kind property can be transferred. If cash is so transferred, it will be treated as boot. If the full intent of the like-kind exchange is met and no cash is transferred, then the 1031 exchange would remain intact as intended.

For example, if Bob's plan to exchange his duplex for the 10-unit apartment complex, using Sam's money, runs into a snag, Bob could end up with a smaller complex and cash boot, or, failing to locate an exchange property at all, complete the transaction directly with Sam for his cash.

This factor becomes important if Bob actually deeds his duplex to Sam prior to finding a replacement like-kind exchange. In this event Bob would want to know that Sam's money is securely in place to be used for the acquisition of the like-kind property that Bob hopes to end up with. At the same time, for the 1031 to be valid Bob must not have use or control of the funds, except as agent for Sam. As the time lapse between transfer to Sam and closing on Bob can close on the new property as long as six months following the date Bob actually transfers title of the duplex to Sam. If several weeks following the transfer to Sam, Bob finds and negotiates (in Sam's name) a contract on a like-kind property, certain time periods must be carefully followed.

Time Periods Necessary in Starker Exchanges

All the time provisions that govern the delayed 1031 exchange begin on the date that the qualifying property is transferred. It is important that you recognize I used the word "transferred" and not "agreement to transfer." If Bob goes to contract with Sam on January 1, and on March 1 the duplex is transferred to Sam and an escrow established for the ultimate purpose of acquiring a like-kind property for Bob, the start date for the delayed exchanges is March 1.

Identification of Replacement Property

Current requirements give you 45 days after the date on which you transfer your property to identify the property which you will receive as like-kind property at a future date.

If the closing of the transaction with title transfer of your property to the other party occurred on March 1, you would have until April 14 to properly identify the property you are to receive.

Identification of the property or properties to be received must be unambiguous. It should be a written document signed by you (the ultimate recipient of the property) and delivered prior to the end of the identification period to a person involved in the exchange other than you (or a related party of yours). Generally, you sign a form or send a letter which contains a legal description of the property you are to receive as a function of the escrow agreement for this delayed exchange. The letter or form should be sent to the person who controls the escrow funds.

Importance of Closing Date

You have a period of up to 180 days following the transfer of your property to take title to the new like-kind property. This 180 days is in addition to the 45 days of the identification period.

Warning! There is a trap in this sequence: a final limitation stating that in no event shall you take title later than the due date for the filing of your tax return for the year of the exchange. The due date includes possible extensions allowable to you.

The date trap is not a problem, provided that you keep track of the time needed, and that you are not caught short by filing earlier than needed. Also, if your fiscal year end is other than December 31, you can mistake the deadline by looking at the calendar year.

Use a Qualified Exchange Trust

With the advent of the delayed exchange have come new proposals to change Section 1031, to regulate more effectively the methods of making this exchange so that tax planners can provide better long-term advice to their clients. Some law firms and most title insurance and escrow closing companies are developing procedures that set up the necessary documentation and paperwork to ensure that the escrow agreement between the parties is properly attended to and that there is no invalidation of the exchange because of sloppy contracts, improper filing of identification, or closing of titles. If you are planning to enter into a delayed exchange agreement I recommend that you contact one of these professionals in your area to set up the escrow agreement and to maintain that agreement throughout the exchange.

Avoid Do-It-Yourself Escrow Agreements

I have reviewed several recent publications that described in great detail the escrow documents needed when dealing with delayed exchanges. While one or more of these "boilerplate" agreements may work fine for your case, I would suggest that you not trust a preprinted form when dealing with something as tender to the wallet as having your delayed exchange blown simply because you didn't cross all your t's. Use your lawyer or find a qualified title or escrow company to set it up correctly.

The sample agreements I have included in this book are to acquaint you with agreements in general so that you will become more fluent with contract language. You should not use them as contracts since laws of your state may conflict with one or more conditions in the samples provided.

3

Balancing Equities in Exchanges

The Fundamentals of Equaling Equities Between Parties

"Look, I'll give you seven of these beautiful mangoes for twelve of your green coconuts."

"Not good enough. I want two mangoes for each coconut. Do we have a deal?"

"No, but I'll give you one mango for each coconut."

"One and a half. Make it one and a half and it's a deal."

"Okay. It's a deal."

Barter, exchange, swaps, and trades of all kinds make up the most basic form of any economic foundation in any community. Exchanges are not limited to tangible items; they can include services and promises for property, or services to be delivered in the future. Remember, the possibilities of exchanging something you own for something you want are limitless. It is a viable way for you to build your fortune, because it works. Let your mind explore the creative ways in which you can get into exchanges. Take the following example of a professional who uses his expertise as an exchange commodity.

A Lawyer Offers Future Legal Services

A lawyer with time on his hands decided to offer future legal services to a local builder as a down payment for a home. The builder knew he could use these services at some future date, so he took the deal. This shows you that people will take in exchange anything that they may have to pay real money to get. If they can at the same time unload something they do not want or are trying to sell, so much the better for everyone.

Once you begin to examine your portfolio of items and services, it is likely that you will find some way to soften the real cost of your next real estate transaction by including a barter exchange.

Arnaldo's Gem Deal

Arnaldo has been in the gemstone business for most of his life and he is very good at buying and selling gemstones of all kinds. Introducing him into the world of real estate exchange was a natural progression of events. The first transaction I did with him was when I traded a few acres of land in Florida for a quantity of gemstones of equal value. I was not sure what I

56

was going to do with the gemstones, but they were more divisible than the land and with a little work on my part I believed I could increase the value of the stones by having a jeweler set them in rings, brooches, earrings, and bracelets. Arnaldo had more gems than he needed for his normal trade and wanted something he could walk on, and because he exchanged his gems at retail he already had a profit built into his deal.

The exchange worked out well for both of us. Arnaldo got his terra firma and went on to do many other real estate exchanges. Using the gems, now converted into jewelry, I ended up with increased value and now owned more dividable items to use for other exchanges.

Finding the Right Kind of Balance

In the strategy of making offers and getting deals accepted, you must find the right formula to balance the equity of the exchange. There are two separate kinds of balance you need to establish.

The first balance is the amount of exchange equity the transaction can absorb. Sometimes you may want to make a full and complete exchange, giving the other property owner full payment for his property. This would be the case if you gave land worth $55,000 to another party who had $55,000 worth of equity in the property you wanted. But, in the final draft of the agreement, your original offer may end up as only a partial exchange. This occurs because of the circumstances of the transaction. It could be that the other party needed to get some cash out of the exchange to pay off other debts. Or, in an accommodation to your offer, the other party may agree to accept something he would not buy, want, or take in other circumstances. Also, the exchange is sometimes just an event that moves you closer to your goal.

The second balance is the actual mathematical balance of equity and boot to equalize the values you plan on offering. Review the Lido Beach transaction below.

Lido Beach for Ft. Lauderdale

John owned a beautiful home in the Lido Beach area of Florida's Gulf Coast. The home was on the market for nearly a year and John was growing tired of dealing with the slow market. Worse, he had taken a job in Ft. Lauderdale, was over 200 miles away from Lido Beach, and the added cost of maintaining two homes was more than he could comfortably handle at the time.

After a couple of weeks I found an exchange partner willing to take John's Lido Beach home. A match was made, and a direct exchange into a 12-unit apartment complex was completed. The apartment complex did not solve all John's problems, nor was it the final goal. But it did move his equity to Ft. Lauderdale and the apartments were fairly priced. The best part was that the income from the apartments was a positive cash flow to John, who had gotten rid of the Lido Beach home. Had John stopped right there, he would have accomplished something most investors would find ideal. But he wanted to move up into something bigger.

How 'bout an ocean-front hotel? Exactly, and before the year was out John had exchanged the apartments as a down payment on a beautiful resort hotel right on the beach.

Each of these transactions required a balance of the equities. In a simple one-on-one transaction, the balance is accomplished using the following balance board.

Two-Party Balance Board

	First Party	Second Party
Value of property given	$	$
Less existing mortgage		
	_____	_____
Equity		
Balance mortgage		
	_____	_____
Second equity		
Pays cash		
Gives paper		
Gives boot		
Gives other		
	_____	_____
Balance		
Gets cash		
Gets paper		
Gets boot		
Gets other		
	_____	_____
Balance		
Sweetener	_____	_____

Balance Board Terms

First party. One of the parties of the transaction. Can be referred to by the property owner's name, or by the property itself, e.g., Lido Beach. Each party is a giver, in respect to the property given up, and a taker, in respect to the property received.

Second party. Another party to the transaction. In multileg transactions there can be many parties shown on the balance board. Third-party transactions are very common and frequently become deferred or delayed exchanges, as described in Chapter 2.

Value. Values established by the originating party. As a transaction progresses these can change.

Less mortgage. The total of all existing debt and mortgages that will be assumed by the party taking this property. It is possible that during the negotiations, new information will indicate that the original mortgage data was incorrect and adjustments must be made. Paper or purchase money mortgages held by the giver are not calculated on this line.

Equity. The original equity based on the offering value less the existing debt. This is the point from which the balance of equities must begin.

Balance mortgage. This is a purchase money mortgage only. Purchase money mortgages are deferred payments to the giver and are calculated separately from the existing debt (which is generally inflexible) and third-party paper or notes that are not secured by this specific property (and that are treated as a form of boot). If there is no existing debt, the balance mortgage may be a first mortgage, unless the contract indicates that the taker (the person who ends up with the property) plans to obtain a new first mortgage. Any mortgages behind existing or "to be placed" mortgages will be in a secondary position.

Second equity. This shows the net equity to which the property will be held by the taker of the original property, item, or service. It is possible that the equities balance, at this point, because the actual balance was accomplished with the paper held by one or more parties. When the equities do not balance, one or more parties must add something else, in the form of cash or boot, to balance the equities. In the end, it is possible that a sweetener must also be added to close the transaction.

Pays cash. The simple way to balance anything is to write out a check. At times cash is essential to bring about a close. Cash in the deal does not necessarily mean that the giving party has had to reach into his own pocket for it; refinancing the property taken can often be the way the needed cash is created. The amount of cash paid always shows up in the column of the person who pays the cash. More than one party may end up with that cash in a multiparty transaction, where the total cash may be divided according to the contract.

Gives paper. Notes, mortgages, due bills, script, and other items, which are not tied to the property being given, will be treated as a future item to be received. Keep in mind that third-party-related items are treated by the IRS as cash. In final tax accounting, however, you can discount the value to bring it to a fair market value. For example, if you took an unsecured note, at a less-than-current interest rate, at the face amount owed of $10,000, you could discount the note in your tax computations to a lesser amount. One way to determine the market value would be to have a mortgage broker give you an assessment of the market value of that paper.

Gives boot. Anything else that comes into the transaction, with the exception of the sweetener (which from the IRS's point of view is also considered boot), is shown here.

Gives other. Other like-kind property given that would not be calculated as boot is shown here.

Balance. The final equity where all properties are in balance. The equities balance at this point only because the offering party is adjusting the values to his benefit. During the negotiations, which can include several offers and counteroffers, these values may vary.

Gets cash. The cash that has been put on the board. The total amount paid out must equal the total given. Show these amounts in brackets as a deduction from the balance.

Gets boot. The party or parties who actually get other boot as has been shown on the board. As with cash, boot may be more than one item and may also be divided between two or more parties. Show these amounts in brackets as a deduction from the balance.

Gets other. This shows the second equity in the other property that is going to the taking party. For example, if the first party is giving up a Lido Beach home and taking the apartments in exchange, the apartments equity will show as the equity that the party gets. Show these amounts in brackets as a deduction from the balance.

Balance. A properly balanced board will show zero at this point under each column.

Sweetener. The sweetener should not show on the balance board until absolutely neces-

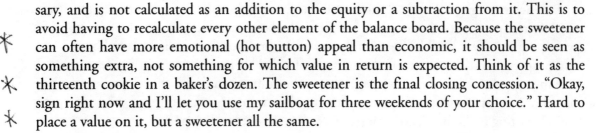

sary, and is not calculated as an addition to the equity or a subtraction from it. This is to avoid having to recalculate every other element of the balance board. Because the sweetener can often have more emotional (hot button) appeal than economic, it should be seen as something extra, not something for which value in return is expected. Think of it as the thirteenth cookie in a baker's dozen. The sweetener is the final closing concession. "Okay, sign right now and I'll let you use my sailboat for three weekends of your choice." Hard to place a value on it, but a sweetener all the same.

Using the Balance Board

Keep in mind that the balance board's primary function is to allow you to keep track of your offer. Both players in the game may keep their own boards, showing different values as they would relate to them. A broker may have a third viewpoint, and may use the balance board as a selling tool to explain the situation as it develops from offer to counteroffer. Once the transaction is completed you should put down the total deal as it has resulted, using the real values as they reflect your end result. It is likely that the original values (prices of all the properties and services offered) are inflated slightly. This does not mean that the values are not justifiable, only that each party takes into consideration some room for negotiation. Do not lose sight of that as you go along.

To use the balance board that follows, review the information below:

John's Lido Beach home value:	$375,000
Existing debt:	$125,000
12-unit apartment complex value:	$412,000
Existing debt on apartment complex:	$215,000

Two-Party Balance Board

	First Party: John	Second Party: Apartments
Value of property given	$375,000	$412,000
Less existing mortgage	125,000	215,000
Equity	$250,000	$197,000
Balance mortgage		
Second equity	$250,000	$197,000
Pays cash		53,000
Gives paper		
Gives boot		
Gives other		
Balance	$250,000	$250,000

Gets cash	(53,000)	
Gets paper		
Gets boot		
Gets other	(197,000)	250,000
	———————	———————
Balance	0	0
Sweetener	———————	———————

In this balance of equities, the second party adds $53,000 cash to the amount of his equity ($197,000) to match John's equity of $250,000. However, the apartment complex owner could have balanced the equity in many other ways. For example, instead of adding cash, the apartment complex owner could ask John to hold a second mortgage for the same amount ($53,000). Because this would increase the total debt on John's Lido Beach home, the balance calculations match the equity in the home to that of the apartment complex.

Two-Party Balance Board

	First Party: John	Second Party: Apartments
Value of property given	$375,000	$412,000
Less existing mortgage	125,000	215,000
	———————	———————
Equity	$250,000	$197,000
Balance mortgage	(53,000)	
	———————	———————
Second equity	$197,000	$197,000
Pays cash		
Gives paper		
Gives boot		
Gives other		
	———————	———————
Balance	$197,000	$197,000
Gets cash		
Gets paper		
Gets boot		
Gets other	(197,000)	197,000
	———————	———————
Balance	0	0
Sweetener	———————	———————

In the following example, the apartment complex owner gives John a vacant lot next to the apartment complex. However, as the lot is only valued at $30,000, there is still an imbalance to be made up. John agrees to hold a small second mortgage for $15,000, but wants the apartment owner to add $8,000 cash to the deal.

Two-Party Balance Board

	First Party: John	Second Party: Apartments
Value of property given	$375,000	$412,000
Less existing mortgage	125,000	215,000
Equity	$250,000	$197,000
Balance mortgage	(15,000)	
Second equity	$235,000	$197,000
Pays cash		8,000
Gives paper		
Gives boot		
Gives other		30,000(lot)
Balance	$235,000	$235,000
Gets cash	(8,000)	
Gets paper		
Gets boot		
Gets other	(197,000)(apts.)	(235,000)(Lido)
	(30,000)(lot)	
Balance	0	0
Sweetener		

So far, so good. Each offer and counteroffer is matching equity in one way or another. The apartment complex owner makes a counter to the original offer and agrees to accept the deal, provided that John will pay him for six months' management worth $5,000, give the owner free rent in one unit for a year, worth $7,200, and hold a second mortgage for $48,000.

In this counter the apartment owner is not accepting the original values as stated. The point is not whether he feels his property is worth more than the $197,000 or that the Lido

Beach home is worth less. What is important is he feels that he needs to receive those benefits. Because each party has a point of view with respect to the values of the property to be given up or received, each person should keep track of how the equities are being balanced, so that they can ascertain in their own mind exactly what they have invested in the property they will end up with. In the counteroffer shown below, the numbers are balanced against the equity of the apartment complex. If John believed the apartment complex to be worth less than the $197,000 equity indicated, then that will reduce the equity (and correspondingly the value) of his Lido Beach home. The counteroffer and reevaluation of the properties is common in making offers and getting them accepted. Each party views the end results on the basis not so much of the original value but of the value each party anticipated he would ultimately get.

Keep Your Original Goals Clearly in Sight

The ultimate balance is usually accomplished more quickly if the parties look to the end results desired. Having clear goals is very important, because it allows you to maintain your priority of benefits, the ones you want to get and those you are willing to give up to satisfy the majority of your needs. It is good to keep track of your transaction with the following adage:

"I'll pay your price if you accept my terms."

By using creative means you can greatly mitigate a price. Often, by exchanging a like-kind property that is not providing you with any benefits or benefits that substantiate its value, you can take advantage of the upgrade of benefits and the tax advantages of the 1031 exchange to overtrade (in your own mind) for a property that suits your needs and moves you closer to your goal.

Apartments Owner's Two-Party Balance Board

	First Party: John	**Second Party: Apartments**
Value of property given	$375,800	$412,000
Discounted to	357,000	
Less existing mortgage	125,000	215,000
Equity	$232,800	$197,000
Balance mortgage	(48,000)	
Second equity	$184,800	$197,000
Pays cash		
Gives paper		
Gives boot	12,200(R&M)*	

Gives other

Balance	$197,000	$197,000
Gets cash		
Gets paper		
Gets boot		(12,200)(R&M)*
Gets other	(197,000)	184,800
Balance	0	0
Sweetener		

*Rent and management value

The end result of any exchange will depend on the exchange of benefits. Many property owners are not aware of what their net benefits are. Good exchange brokers or salesmen who are acquainted with the exchange process can be helpful to "close the deal"—by showing each party how to solve their problems and move in the direction of their goals.

In the Lido Beach transaction, the lack of benefits through the continued ownership of the home in Lido Beach were strong closing elements that motivated John to accept the idea of taking the apartments. It is certain that John never would have purchased the apartment complex had he sold the Lido Beach home for cash. But that comparison was not available to him. There was no buyer in sight for the house, so he had to weigh the possible exchange transaction against the reality of keeping the Lido Beach home until a buyer was found.

Creative Balances Make Deals Fly Straight

In any kind of transaction, there is a moment when the salesman homes in for the kill. The salesperson who is watching every move being made in the transaction knows that all purchases or acquisitions are best closed on a small point. People do not like to make major decisions, so they will avoid making them altogether. Because of this, many deals fall apart—because the parties cannot come to a decision, or one side becomes frustrated at the indecision of the other.

Creative closing is a part of using the balance form. You will find that the more ways you have to put the deal together, the more combinations you will have to successfully conclude your contracts. There are a thousand and more ways which John and the apartment complex owner could balance their exchange, but what is important is to find **the way that will be mutually acceptable**.

Mutual acceptance of a contract is essential, because until there is an accepted contract there will be no closing. Each party will attempt to get the best deal they can, and as long as both keep sight of their goals and understand the benefits they will gain and problems they will give up, prolonged negotiations are not the usual rule. The major question should always be: Does this exchange move me closer to my goals?

Remember! Some exchanges are made when the only motivation is to get rid of a problem. One person's problem can be another's gold mine.

Sometimes it is the motivation that makes the deal work. John had a beautiful home, and were it not for the slow market and tight financing at the local level, it might have sold outright. Because it did not, it was a negative for John, and his motivation to sell or exchange grew each day he had to worry about the Lido Beach property.

To bring the Lido Beach deal to a close, John made the following counteroffer, which was accepted. He agreed to hold a second mortgage, but in the amount of $50,000; and he would not hire the owner as manager, but would allow him and his wife three months' free rent to wrap up their Ft. Lauderdale affairs prior to moving into the beautiful Lido Beach home.

On the following balance board I have left only the essential information. You will notice that what is missing is "values." These have become unimportant except for accounting or the IRS's benefit. In most exchange agreements the actual value or price is not shown. In the following exchange the only elements that are important are what you gave and get, and how much mortgage you had to pay.

Balance Board of John's Counteroffer

	First Party: John	**Second Party: Apartments**
Mortgage	$125,000	$215,000
Balance paper	50,000	
Total debt	$175,000	$215,000
Final result		
Gives boot	1,800*	
Gets boot		(1,800)*
Gets other	Apartments	Lido Beach house
Assumes debt	$215,000	$175,000

*Prepaid rent

Close with a Sweetener

The nice thing about exchanges is the ability to move some property that is next to impossible to sell on the open market. Some properties just don't sell if the market conditions are against them or if financing dries up. There is no doubt in my mind that if the apartment owner had had some minor item or personal property he wanted to include in the deal, he could have done so. For example, had he owned a diamond ring with a valid appraisal showing it worth $6,000, the deal would have closed with that ring as a part of the deal. John would have agreed to reduce the mortgage to $44,000 and take the ring. Or it might have been that the apartment complex owner needed to sweeten the deal just a bit to wrap it all up and "throw" the ring into the pot at the last minute.

Even if John had no interest in the ring he might turn to his broker and suggest that if the broker would take the ring as part of his commission, John would accept the deal right then and there. Many a ring has ended up on a broker's wife's finger in much this way.

Balance Board Form for Multiparty Transactions

	First Party	Second Party	Third Party
Value			
Less mortgage			
Equity			
Balance mortgage			
Second equity			
Pays cash			
Gives paper			
Gives boot			
Gives other			
Third equity			
Gets cash			
Gets paper			
Gets boot			
Gets other			
Balance			

Three-Leg Deals

An Emerald + a Lot + a Condo

Let me set the stage for a three-leg transaction. Tom owned a two-bedroom condominium in a South Florida town. It was worth $45,000 and had a $35,000 mortgage on it. His equity was $10,000. Gunner owned a vacant lot in North Carolina, free and clear and worth $10,000. Jim owned a nice emerald that was appraised at $11,500. Here is how this looked in the first balance.

Balance of Equity

Item	First Party Condo	Second Party Lot	Third Party Emerald
Value	$45,000	$10,000	$11,500

Less mortgage	35,000	0	0
Equity	$10,000	$10,000	$11,500

This transaction was easy because the third party, Jim, decided to let the emerald go for a flat $10,000 and there was no further balance needed to add or subtract from the equities.

A More Complex Three-Party Balance

In a more complicated transaction with three different parties, Al has a six-unit apartment building worth $180,000 with a $55,000 mortgage. Tom has a ranch in Ocala worth $260,000 with a $110,000 mortgage. Bill has a stamp collection appraised conservatively at $150,000 and will use any or all of it as necessary if he can end up with the apartment building. Al wants Tom's ranch in Ocala and Tom wants out with a minimum of $50,000 cash in his pocket.

Balance of Equity

Item	Al Apartments	Bill Stamps	Tom Ocala
Value	$180,000	$?	$260,000
Less mortgage	55,000	0	110,000
Equity	$125,000	$?	$150,000

At this point there has been no consideration given for the equity of stamps as we do not know exactly how many it might take to make a deal. Because Bill, the owner of the stamps, is flexible he becomes the pivotal point of this exchange and everything will be adjusted first through him, then later with the normal balance of equities until each party is satisfied with the end results.

To simplify the end results of the negotiations, Tom indicates that as long as he gets a minimum of $50,000 cash he will accept up to $52,000 worth of the stamps (subject to his satisfying himself as to their value). The rest due to him, $48,000, can be in the form of a second mortgage against the ranch. Bill agrees to come up with $50,000 cash if necessary. So far the exchange looks like this:

Balance Board

Item	Al Apartments	Bill Stamps	Tom Ocala
Value	$180,000	$ 52,000	$260,000
Less mortgage	55,000	0	110,000
Equity	$125,000	52,000	150,000
Balance mortgage			(48,000)(2nd mtg.)
Second equity		$ 52,000	$102,000
Pays cash		50,000	
Gives paper			
Gives boot			
Gives other			
Third equity		$102,000	$102,000
Gets cash			(50,000)
Gets paper			
Gets boot			(52,000)(stamps)
Gets other		(102,000)(Ocala)	
Balance			0

Bill is the pivot of this exchange; since he is coming in with the least equity it is logical that he will pay the $50,000 cash required. That sum plus the $52,000 worth of stamps makes Bill's total contribution or equity $102,000.

The Ocala ranch has an existing debt of $110,000 plus the additional $48,000 second mortgage Tom is going to hold. Tom gets $50,000 cash and is out of this deal with what he wanted. At this point Bill has control of the Ocala ranch and could stop the exchange right now if he became a taker for the ranch under the circumstances shown above.

To balance the board to bring the apartments into the picture (which was the original purpose of the transaction) all we have to do is bring Al's equity down to the same $102,000 to balance across the board. In the following example this is done with a balance mortgage whereby Al agrees to hold a second mortgage for $23,000 against his apartments.

Balance of Equity

	Apartments	Stamps	Ocala
Value	$180,000	$ 52,000	$260,000
Less mortgage	55,000	0	110,000
Equity	$125,000	$ 52,000	$150,000
Balance mortgage	(23,000)(2nd mtg.)		(48,000)(2nd mtg.)
Second equity	$102,000	$ 52,000	$102,000
Pays cash		50,000	
Gives paper			
Gives boot			
Gives other			
Third equity	$102,000	$102,000	$102,000
Gets cash			(50,000)(cash)
Gets paper			
Gets boot			(52,000)(stamps)
Gets other	(102,000)(ranch)	(102,000)(apts.)	
Balance	0	0	0

At this point, if it is acceptable to Tom, he would get $50,000 in cash and $52,000 in stamps and would hold a second mortgage against the Ocala ranch in the amount of $48,000.

Bill has a clear role. He is into this deal with $50,000 cash and $52,000 worth of stamps. The cash may not be out of his own pocket, however, as he might be able to raise it from a private or other lender against the apartments in the form of a third mortgage.

Considering that Bill now controls Tom's property, the balance of the negotiations can continue. Only slight modification needs to occur with Tom, as long as Al falls into place, as is shown in the previous balance board. On the other hand, should Bill have some problems he always has the a sweetener of adding more stamps, increasing the paper Al will hold, or in the last resort, add more cash.

On the following board, Al countered that he will accept the ranch with the $48,000 second mortgage and the $110,000 first mortgage, but because he does not believe the ranch is worth the full $260,000 he wants a sweetener of $20,000 worth of stamps. Tom reviews the deal and accepts if Bill adds half of the stamps required to go to Al. Because Bill cannot close without all the parties being satisfied, he agrees.

Balance of Equity

	Apartments	Stamps	Ocala
Value	$180,000	$ 52,000	$260,000
Less mortgage	55,000	0	110,000
Equity	$125,000	$ 52,000	$150,000
Balance paper	23,000		48,000
Second equity	$102,000	$ 52,000	$102,000
Pays cash		50,000	
Gives boot			
Third equity	$102,000	$102,000	$102,000
Gets cash			(50,000)
Gets boot			(52,000)(stamps)
Gets other	(102,000)	(102,000)	
Pays bonus		$ 10,000(stamps)	$ 10,000(stamps)
Gets bonus	$ 20,000(stamps)		
Balance	0	0	0

Keeping Good Records of Closed Transactions

When it is all over get the equity straight. No matter how well you document your balance board, when you are finished and have closed the transaction be sure you use the following **closed-transaction equity record** form for your files. This form will be helpful when you do your year-end income tax and if you include this property in a future exchange or sale. Attach copies of mortgages and documents relating to other details.

Closed-Transaction Equity Record

Date closed: _____   Closing agent: _____

Property acquired: _____

Legal description: _____

Address: _____

Justified value of property taken $_____

Less

Mortgages assumed at closing $_____

Secondary financing obtained $_____

Market equity at closing $_____

How you obtained this property

Exchange of equity (your cost)   + $_____

Add cash paid   + $_____

Add boot paid   + $_____

Add bonus paid (your cost)   + $_____

Add other exchange given (your cost)   + $_____

Less total debt assumed   - $_____

Less other value you got   - $_____

Your real investment equity $_____

Other important information

Mortgage on your exchanged property $ _____

List any other item, boot, or service you got in this exchange and show real value.

_____

_____

_____

When you fill in the closed transactions equity record you should be as accurate as you can. Most critical is the information on how you got the property. When you fill in the information on what you paid or gave in the exchange you should use your actual cost. This will allow you to maintain a proper perspective on your investment portfolio. You should have a growing difference between your real investment equity and the real market equity.

You should make an additional list of the reasons why you made the exchange in the first place. Indicate the benefits you expected to obtain from the new property and what problems you wanted to escape with property you gave up. Be honest, as the only person you kid will be you.

Why Everything Comes Back to the Benefits Gained

While location, location, location governs the ultimate value of any vacant property and improvements built on that land, from the investor's point of view, value is only a measure and not a final benefit. You may own the most valuable property in town and not have any benefits flowing your way. Possibly the cost to own it is such a drain on your other assets that the property has a negative benefit to you.

Train yourself to look for the benefits available in any potential investment. Review the following list of benefits that might attract you. You will think of others to add to your own list.

The 20 Benefits from Ownership of Real Estate

Income	Perks
Financial Security	"Free Living"
Pride of Ownership	Family Jobs
Equity Buildup	Great Way of Life
Image	Retirement
Pays for Staff	"Free Travel"
Shelters Other Income	Security
Gives You Something to Do	Appreciation of Value
Makes You Your Own Boss	Being Responsible
Gives You Roots	Self-Confidence

All of these benefits can be found in the same property, while only some may be present in others. Unless you get some of these or other benefits, you may need to think again about acquiring the property.

International Deals

Before you get settled down, thinking that exchanges are for the locals only, take a look at what is going on around the world. Recently Mexico made a deal to swap oil for a long shopping list of products and commodities. Russia is a master at bartering everything from diamonds to caviar for what they need. Barter and exchange transactions occur between all countries and when the economy gets tight and money is in short supply, the only economy that exists is the barter and exchange going on.

Caravans cross the Sahara, long paths up mountains are made by the natives of Tibet or Afghanistan or countless other out-of-the-way places where the trek to move goods from one area to another is a daily way of life. Each item has its value in relation to another item or service. Those values are the measure of the benefits to the person who will end up with the item or service. The price or value you set on the property you want to sell or exchange makes no difference if the **value of the benefits of owning that property** are not clearly visible. When you see property that is grossly overpriced it is generally because the "benefits" that the owner sees are **not visible to anyone else.**

Balance your exchanges by keeping this in mind; when you have a problem getting your counteroffers accepted it is likely that the real reason for rejection is that the other party does not see the benefits you see. A reselling of those real but not-yet-visible benefits is the next step to be done. It is not as hard as it might seem at first, and it's the only way to get the deal back on the right track.

If you cannot demonstrate value through benefits, your deal will never get back on the track unless **you** are willing to accept that the benefits you thought you saw are not really there at all (which might be the case).

Getting Started in Real Estate Exchanges — Turn Your Comfort Zone into a Gold Mine

Questions abound: "What kind of real estate should I start with? Where and how do I find it? How do I know it is a good deal? When should I buy or sell it?" Have any of these run through your mind? Have you avoided real estate because you had no idea where to turn for the answers? Read on; all the answers you need to know are about to be given.

Your Comfort Zone

All success in real estate investing begins with your comfort zone. The comfort zone is actually an area that is bounded by three different parameters. They are:
- The outer boundaries of the geographical area
- The type of real estate which you will acquire in this geographical area
- Your own abilities and goals

Each of these three zones will grow by a natural force that is hard to explain—but happens just the same. Take a look at an example of a comfort zone in action.

Rachel's Comfort Zone

Rachel discovered that it was taking more and more of her hard-earned salary as an airline stewardess to pay her rent. She looked back over the past five years and realized that each year the rent went up, and her utilities cost more. And at the end of each year there was nothing to look forward to except a rent increase, or worse, the need to find another apartment because the building had been sold and the new owners wanted that apartment for themselves or more rent from Rachel. Rachel knew the day would come when she would look back and see all her past landlords driving fancy foreign cars while she was puttering about in a 10-year-old Ford.

The first step was to get out of the rental apartment and into an ownership position. Rachel did some soul searching about her goals. Did she see herself working for airlines all her life? Was marriage in the wings? Or did she know what kind of lifestyle she wanted in the future? Did she have aspirations to change her job and do something else? Was she happy with her work? Did she feel something else would make her happier? Did she feel that she could meet her goals in South Florida, or would a move to another geographical area be necessary? Where in South Florida would she want to live, and in what style?

Plenty of other questions sprang up just getting to these decisions, but as real estate is geographically situated the first step in becoming a real estate investor is to establish the broad boundary as to **where** you want to start investing. It is neither reasonable nor practical to want to live in South Florida, but invest in California. Later on, when you can, you may expand your comfort zone to include California, but in the beginning you first decide where your backyard is going to be, then invest there.

Rachel was determined to stay in South Florida and saw her job with the airlines as a solid, exciting, and worthy profession for the moment. What she wanted to do was to use her other skills to augment her income and build a base of wealth that would allow her to become independent of outside employment as soon as possible. Her skills included interior decorating, the ability to fix up old furniture, refinish interiors, and with little money turn a blah-looking room or apartment into a vibrant and fresh place to live. Because she had some control over her working hours by bidding for blocks of flying time, she knew that she could devote ample time to her own "sweat equity" in fixing up properties to sell or rent.

Step 1: Stop Renting

Rachel's idea of what it would take to become a real estate investor was distorted by the things she had been told by others. She had gone to several "investor seminars," which were interesting and motivated her to invest and own. At the same time they were intimidating: if real estate investing was as easy as these seminars made it appear, then she would have to "fight it out" with all those other seminar graduates who were smarter, richer, and had more time to put into this venture than she. However, one thing was clear: she knew she had to stop renting. The $650 each month she was paying for her apartment was simply going into someone else's bank account. She had saved up about $5,000, her car was paid off, and, most important of all, she was determined to succeed. With these assets she spent a week driving around the community, trying to decide which part of town she liked the most and which was likely to give her opportunities to acquire properties she could fix up. At the end of the first week she was more confused than ever. What she had found was depressing. Each area that was better than where she had been renting seemed to be beyond her capabilities. She saw run-down properties here and there, but all they looked like were run-down properties, not opportunities. What was holding her back was the fear she would make a mistake. She had become her own brick wall.

To save time, she decided to pick an area of town with a good cross-section of property values but where almost everything was nice. She felt that she could live in any part of the area with the idea that it offered a chance to upgrade along the way.

She met with several real estate salespeople who specialized in that part of town and began looking at different properties for sale. She followed up owners' signs, looked at dozens of rental properties, and started to get a sound mental picture of what was going on in the area, economically as well as politically. Within a few weeks she began to see the trends of her chosen geographical area and could see which part of it was improving, and which was slipping behind.

Step 2: Become an Owner

She found a three-bedroom home that had a detached garage and a second-floor apartment over it. The owner had died and the property was in an estate. It was a bit run-down, the house was not occupied, and the apartment over the garage rented month-to-month below the current market price for the area. The zoning permitted up to seven multifamily units on the lot. The broker for the estate said the asking price was $65,000.

One thing led to the other and after several offers and counterproposals, Rachel obtained a two-year lease for the entire property, with the right to purchase it for $62,000 anytime within the two-year term. The estate even agreed to hold a second mortgage of $15,000 at the time of sale, provided that she paid off the balance by obtaining new financing not to exceed 70 percent of the value of the property. The contract called for Rachel to pay $700 per month rent, plus taxes and other maintenance. Rachel had the right to make improvements in the building provided that she did so with her own money.

As a bonus the estate gave her 60 days' free rent if she put up a security deposit of $1,400. She took that amount from her savings account, moved into the house, and started to work.

By the end of six months Rachel had converted the garage into two apartments and divided part of the house to convert it into two nice apartments. She went along bit by bit, adding units, getting them rented, taking the extra income from those additional tenants and plowing it back into the property to fix up, improve, and decorate. She gave notice to the tenants over the garage that they would have to move out because she was going to divide that apartment to convert it to a smaller apartment for herself, plus a nice studio to rent out. By year's end she had a total of six apartments, five of them paying her rent. She had changed the value of the property by increasing its income potential, putting herself in a good position to refinance the deal and exercise her option to buy.

The total income from the five apartments rented out was $26,000 per year. Her expenses consisted of $2,500 for real estate tax, $500 for insurance, and $3,800 for her utility bill. Adding a continuing fix-up budget of $4,000 per year and miscellaneous expenses of another $3,000 per year, she was left with $15,200 a year, out of which she had to pay the $700 per month rent to the estate, which still owned the property.

By the end of the first year a local savings and loan agreed to lend her $85,000 for a monthly payment that included principal and interest (P.I.) of $1,200 per month. She closed on the option to buy, paying cash that she got from the savings and loan. She paid $62,000 to the estate, $1,600 to the bank for the closing costs of the mortgage, and was left with $21,400 in her bank to launch herself into another property.

Her benefits were fantastic, as you can see. Living free, making money, building equity, and creating a foundation on which to build. She had become an owner.

But better, she had found her comfort zone. Her abilities had paid off, so now she knew exactly what kind of property worked best for her, and she could begin looking for similar properties. Armed with this information, she was able to establish geographic boundaries within which she could become the expert on everything available for rent or sale.

She quickly became more knowledgeable about what was going on within her chosen area and was able, little by little, to expand that geographic area to include more kinds of property.

It was hard work all the way. Not easy, as the seminars had said. And she made some mistakes, too. But she persisted and continually added to her skills and abilities. She bought books on how to fix the plumbing, learned more about gardening, and discovered that any-one could have a green thumb in the tropics with plenty of cow manure and water to back them up. She was well on her way.

The 7 Key Steps to Building Your Comfort Zone

1. Be honest with yourself about your abilities.
2. Decide to be an owner.
3. Convert your past rent into future ownership.
4. Find a property you can convert to improve the income potential.
5. Add to your skills to fix up or manage real estate.
6. Build equities from which you can generate cash or values to leverage or exchange into new investments.
7. Reevaluate your goals, adjusting your comfort zone as you do.

Your First Basic Need: Shelter

Every first investment should solve the need for shelter. This is so basic that I am constantly amazed at investors who overlook the need to solve their housing needs first. Of course, I acknowledge that there are sound reasons to rent when the circumstances require or even warrant it. Rachel, as an example, used the rent with option to buy as a tool to take over a property and fix it up. In an earlier example, Chapter 1, a "sweat equity" exchange helped one family move up into a better rental apartment. Rent, when it is a temporary or eco-nomic tool to move up, or when you can rent for less than you could own, is okay. All other rent puts you in the position of being OPM (other people's money) for the owner of that apartment.

The irony in the rent-vs.-own struggle is that in high-rent areas, such as New York City or Los Angeles, the would-be investor frequently becomes discouraged at the inability to find attractive "buys," and feels forced into the rental market.

In reality, it is the high rents that provide the opportunity to leverage up in any invest-ment that can be converted into a greater economic potential. Each investor will find that to maximize the cash spent on building a portfolio of investments, finding other people willing to spend more money to rent what you have is a key to success.

How to Set Up Your Comfort Zone

List Your Assets
Make an honest list of all your assets. Do not short-change yourself, nor should you overevaluate the items or property you own. No one will see this list unless you want them to, so be honest with yourself.

Describe Your Abilities
Take stock of yourself and your other investment team members. If your spouse is extra handy at something, then make note of it—even if you see no direct or even remote connec-tion with investing in real estate.

Decide Where You Want to Live

This is the most important decision you will make, because it will fix the geographic area of your comfort zone.

Budget Your Time

Time is critical because you may not have a lot of it to spend. Set aside as large a block of time as possible once a week for actual "in-the-field-looking," then budget research and "thinking" time to go over what you are looking at. Fortunately, the real estate industry generally swings into high gear on the weekends because that is when more people have free time to look at property for sale or for rent. You will find that if you make your time profitable you will look forward to your "Sunday in the field." The time you spend looking at property within your geographic zone should be your learning foundation where you become the expert of that zone.

Have a Plan

Your plan should be a road map that you can follow to these goals:

Initial Comfort-Zone Goals

- To learn your zone like the back of your hand
- To discover what is going on within the zone
- To determine values and trends within the zone
- To determine which property you would like to own

The goal that most people include or even try to have as their sole goal is "to buy a property." That is an ultimate step that will not enter the picture until you have first reached the four goals shown above. Remember that you want to accomplish the "insider trick" of reducing your risk and seeing opportunities that others miss. You will do that by first reaching the above goals.

The plan you devise will be tailor-made to your own experiences and abilities. The geographic area you first select may change as you look around, and such adjustments are common and should not be frustrating. Do not be led to greener pastures just because you do not see the diamond in the rough that may be in your own backyard. Give your "time in the field" time to sink in.

Develop Your Team

Your investment team will include your spouse, and other financial partners if there are any. Advisers will include a good tax accountant or tax lawyer, several different real estate brokers or salesmen, and other contacts that you develop and include in your circle of reference as you familiarize yourself with your comfort zone.

Establish Yourself

There is nothing more rewarding than to have a continually widening circle of influential friends and business acquaintances. Have a personal card printed that sets these activities apart from other work you do. "Bob Jones—International Investor," or "Phil Zimmer—Zimmer Investments" is all that is necessary. Include as a part of your "in the field" time a step-by-step building of contacts with these influential people. Make an effort to meet people who may be helpful to your future.

People Whom You Should Meet and Who Should Know You

Mayor	Deputy mayor
County officials	State representatives
Congressional representative	Governor
Police chief	Sheriff
Heads of building and zoning departments	Traffic planner
City planner	Bank presidents
Bank president's secretary	Local builders
Savings and loan presidents	Local insiders
Real estate brokers	

Granted, you may never meet all these people, and even if you do there may be no immediate benefit. But little by little, by getting to know the influential people in town and making sure that they know you, you will be becoming one of the town's influential people.

It is so much better to have the door open to you when you need help than to have to break it down. Start out from a position of working to meet your original objectives by building a strong foundation before trying to build the walls.

Keep Good Records

Everything you are doing that relates to the comfort zone should be well documented and filed away in a way that will make the information available to you when you need it. Review the following outline of records that are basic for any comfort zone. Add to this outline specific information that relates to your comfort zone and investment interests.

Comfort-Zone Records

    A. Goals

          1. Written and dated goals

          2. List of things to do to reach them

    B. Geographic zone

          1. City maps and plans

          2. Aerial map or photograph of comfort zone

          3. Bus and other public transport routes

          4. Schools and school zones

          5. Hospitals

          6. Parks shown

          7. Shopping centers marked

          8. Other specific areas of public benefit

          9. Bad sectors shown

               a. City dump

        b. Heavy industrial
        c. Other areas to avoid
C. Property information
    1. Property inspected—date, comments
    2. Rentals—location, price, comments
    3. Offered for sale—location, price, comments
    4. Sold—date, price, comments
D. Contacts—name, date contacted, telephone number and address
    1. Governmental
    2. City planning
    3. Town associations
    4. Banks and S & L's
    5. Lawyers
    6. Accountants
E. Offers made—Counteroffers, balance boards, etc.
F. Correspondence—file by name or service
G. List of assets—keep up to date
H. List of expenses—daily record

You do not have to start with all the records indicated, but as you add to your comfort zone you will want to upgrade the level of your data keeping. Of all your records make sure you keep detailed information on the property you have inspected. A good record of what you have looked at, with detailed comments on the property itself will enable you to make a valid comparison with another property in the future. In this way you will be able to make offers that take advantage of the opportunities you now recognize.

Make Offers

Every acquisition begins with an offer. As you begin to take control of your own destiny you should be willing to make offers. In fact, make a lot of offers.

In later chapters I will cover many creative techniques that allow you to build your real estate investments quickly and to reach your goals in the minimum time.

How Exchanges Fit into Your Comfort Zone

Of all the real estate investment techniques, exchanging is the only one that gives you a measure of control over both buying and selling. Exchanges give you a two-pronged attack in the real estate investment game. You can use real estate exchanges to leverage your investments by having a **cashless** vehicle to acquire properties as well as the opportunity to move up from one investment to another without paying a tax on gains along the way. There are only three basic methods of acquiring real estate. Cash. Paper. Exchange. Of these three the first two make up the conventional real estate market. By putting the total power of exchanging into your "bag of tricks" you become a rounded investor able to flex with the market. You will succeed because you are in control.

5

Documenting Your Exchange Portfolio —
A Pretty Picture Is Worth a Million Words

Profit is the measure of how well you play the real estate investment game. Successful players know that once in a while they will score by accident, but to win game after game requires hard work and careful preparation. You need to **discover the importance of good property presentation.** The winning part of making the facts and photos work for you is that it shows you to be a professional who takes care in how you offer your property for sale or exchange. A presentation with clear and precise detail is worth its weight in gold.

Find the Sizzle, Then Sell It

Rarely does a property sell itself for the highest return to its former owner. Benefits are what are bought and sold, and most of your transactions will be a result acquiring a property that can provide the right benefits for the buyer willing to pay the most money. However, you will have to "sell" the property and the total benefits picture if you expect the highest return. Elmer Letterman, the master salesman of all times, hit the nail on the head when he looked for that single element—the sizzle. The best sales effort, and resulting profit, begins before you actually acquire the subject property. A sound investment plan is one where you constantly look to improve the worth of the property you acquire, the end result being a profitable sale or exchange. The ultimate event, successful profit on the investment, depends on more than your "dream of wealth"; you should constructively plan for the eventual presentation of the property to prospective buyers, or "takers." The actual presentation you or your broker makes to prospective buyers should become an extension of your own experience with the property. Everything you know about the property should become a part of your portfolio of that investment. This portfolio will help you unlock the buyer's purse strings.

For Your Eyes Only

Begin with your personal private file on each property or service you have to offer. I have broken the data into the following three informational sections.

    1. Confidential information

2. Your property's potential benefits
3. General data, and income and expense information

The first is information that may never be shown to another party but that could be critical to your assessment of the property you are giving up or to a comparison with another property you may take. Some of this confidential information may be shared with your lawyer or accountant or both.

1. Confidential Information

-   A copy of the deed you received
-   All closing documents when you acquired the property
-   Your net cost when you acquired the property
-   A list of the benefits you expected when property acquired
-   A real assessment of the benefits and problems you received
-   Detailed income and expenses
-   Your goal with respect to this property (current date)
-   Your tax base in this property (current)
-   Lawyer's and accountant's opinions relating to this property
-   Depreciation schedules
-   Additions and improvement costs

The above information should actually form the basis of any property file when you acquire the property. Additions to the file will contain information or documents relating to your ownership of the property. Because you need to maintain an accurate account of your ownership for your own information, do not alter the data as you go along because you think a would-be owner would want to see something better than reality. This file and all the material in it is for you first, another owner second.

The first three items on the confidential information list will concern your closing on the investment when you acquired it. You should make copies of each of the items: the deed, all the closing documents, and your investment cost. Then store the originals in a bank safety box and keep copies in your files. The closing documents encompass many different items, depending on the property and how you acquired it. Copies of mortgages, notes, inventory, insurance policies, warranties from the previous owner, and so on are all very important and should be kept in a safe place.

2. Your Property's Potential Benefits

Every property has a potential use or uses that will provide benefits. Remember that not all of these benefits may actually be worthwhile to you at the time you acquire the property. Some of them may never be utilized by you, but they do provide value and latent profit centers for other buyers.

It will be helpful for you to maintain a list of all potential benefits as you become aware of them. Your goals may change, giving you a reason to take another look at a benefit you have not capitalized on. When it is time to sell or exchange, the person who ends up with the property is likely to have goals completely different from yours. In that situation, the benefits needed to meet those goals could require a different approach to the use of the same property.

Here once again are the 20 benefits to ownership listed in Chapter 3.

Income	Perks
Financial Security	"Free Living"
Pride of Ownership	Family Jobs
Equity Buildup	Great Way of Life
Image	Retirement
Pays for Staff	"Free Travel"
Shelters Other Income	Security
Gives You Something to Do	Appreciation of Value
Makes You Your Own Boss	Being Responsible
Gives You Roots	Self-Confidence

List the Benefits That Fit the Investor

Any property should provide one or more of these benefits directly to you. It is equally possible that your circumstances do not allow you to take advantage of one or more of these benefits. For example, if the property is a 50-unit motel, virtually every one of the above benefits could flow through it to the owner. If you are a bachelor-orphan (to carry this to an extreme for a moment), your goals and needs would not be directed to family jobs, yet many motels are family-run properties. The larger the family, the more jobs that can be taken over by family members. Certain groups of real estate investors seek out investments that can provide income to more family members. It is not uncommon to find whole family units of new immigrants owning and working the same property. Their needs dictate the kind of property they acquire.

To properly market your property for the highest price on the best terms suitable to your goals, you should constantly look for the total picture of benefits possible and not just those that satisfy your present needs. By opening your own eyes to the potential of a property you may discover that you have overlooked something that can also provide added benefit to you.

A good example of this would be a vacant property. Investing in vacant land can be one of the most lucrative forms of real estate investing—if you do your homework and/or luck out. Fortunately, most investors buying vacant land ensure their profit by the amount of homework they do. However, vacant land is a passive investment and unless you develop it or find a use for it, you will be spending money each year just to pay the taxes and insurance.

How to Find "Creative Benefits" You Overlooked

If the property value is going up at the rate of 20 percent per year or more, it might be worthwhile to hold on to it, depending on what else you could invest in. Vacant land can give you pride of ownership, image, can shelter other income, give you something to do, give you roots, as well as appreciate in value. But what about the potential of income, financial security, equity buildup, and "free travel," just to mention a few other benefits? How would you get them? Read on.

Sign companies will rent space for billboards. If your vacant land is in a good location and the zoning permits billboards, then the amount of rent you collect might pay your annual tax bill.

Warning! Read any billboard lease very carefully. In very fine print you may discover that what starts out looking like a 12-month lease automatically renews itself for a much longer time (like forever). Other leases might require you to notify the sign company a year in advance of when you want to terminate the lease, and may even require you to pay them back for rent they paid to you. Make sure you have provisions that clearly limit the term of the lease and allow you to terminate it (after a certain time) on thirty days' notice—for any reason.

Some farmers will lease their land to grow crops on. If the location has good traffic flow and a substantial population nearby, a you-pick-it type of farmer might come along and pay extra for the location. Better yet, you might discover that you can plant strawberries or other you-pick-it crops yourself and give some family members a job while you are generating income at the same time.

Radio and other communications companies often will lease a site for a tower antenna. The amount of land needed for this may not be more than a small fraction of the total tract, so you can get other uses and additional cash from the land and still have the antenna on the site.

Car lots, sales lots for boats, recreational vehicles, trucks, farm equipment, flea markets, produce sales, landscape nursery sales and growing fields, campgrounds, Christmas tree sales lots, fireworks sales stands, parking lots, are just a few of the many uses vacant land can be put to that do not require a large capital expense and do not distract from the natural appreciation of the land.

As you begin to discover potential benefits you will begin to expand on the uses. For example, I mentioned a parking lot. A parking lot could be for a nearby restaurant, bar, or other commercial venture that constantly finds itself with more business potential than existing parking will support. The parking lot could also be for a car dealer several miles away to store inventory, or for storage of equipment for a development company or a transport or moving company. Local circumstances will determine what uses are feasible for your land, and you will discover that the more you look, the greater the number of potentials you find.

Each potential benefit and corresponding use will create the need for questions to be asked and answers to be found. What will the current zoning allow? What are the necessary steps to change the zoning? What will other zoning allow? Each time you get to a new level of knowledge about a property you own you begin to see greater potential to satisfy other needs, both your own and those of a prospective buyer.

Economic Conversions—The Insider's Secret Tool

If there is one key to profit making in real estate it is the concept of "economic conversions." The idea is to take something and change it into something worth more. The cost, time, and effort it takes affect the end result and these three factors are significant in the selection of what you might economically convert.

An example of this would be the 50-unit motel the bachelor-orphan owns. All his needs and goals could be met by this property and yet a greater economic return might be available by the conversion of the motel into doctors' suites, or a medical clinic, or a health spa, or some other completely different use.

The owner of the motel may not have any interest in turning his motel into some other use, but a prospective buyer may need a change of use to meet his own goals. The seller, recognizing this potential, would find that the value he could receive in the sale or exchange of the property could be much greater by dealing with this buyer rather than a conventional motel buyer.

Most properties can be changed into something else. In some cities and zoning areas, even a single-family home can be used for professional offices—say, a doctor's or insurance office. When you can take a property that has a lower economic return (rent you can collect), for example, a single-family home, and convert it to a doctor's office, the bottom line for success will depend on the cost, time, and effort it took. If the total of those three elements cost less than the increased value in the subject property then you are bound for success.

You will begin to recognize the potential of economic conversions once you start to examine all the potential benefits that the property can throw off.

Why and How to Keep Track of Your Problems

Acknowledging your problems and keeping a record of the solutions you find will be a learning process. All real estate is capable of generating problems. If you are alert to potential problems, either by studying examples in this or other books, or through your experiences, you will cut off most problems before they bloom into major catastrophes.

The key is to see through the symptom to the actual problem. For example, the problem of late rents may really be the result of (1) not being selective enough in tenants, (2) not enforcing late-rent penalties, or (3) your reluctance to evict.

Whatever the problem is, it will have more than one solution. Some solutions may seem more costly at first but save you money in the long run by solving the root of the problem and not what turns out to be just the symptom.

3. General Data, and Income and Expense Information

There is an old story about the property owner who keeps two sets of financial books. One, for himself, shows the actual income and expenses as they relate to the property; one, for the IRS, shows a distorted view of the income, to lessen its tax liability and to augment the expenses to provide greater deductions and even less tax at the final accounting. After my many years as a Realtor I can sadly tell you that not only is this often true, there can also be a third set of financial records—what the prospective buyer sees, which are designed to play up the economic bonanza a buyer will gain when he buys the property. Remember:

To Thine Own Self Be True

All income and expense records should be as accurate and as up to date as you can possibly make them. You will want to take advantage of all legal applications of the tax code to your own situation, and above all, not kid yourself as to what is actually going on with this property. You do not have to be a CPA to keep detailed records of your expenses, and to record all the income from the property in a timely manner. If you use an accountant to deal with the IRS and take care of other financial matters, ask the accountant to set up records for you to keep. The more you do "hands on," the better you will learn what is going on with your investments and your money. Never be too busy to bother with the details of the income and expenses. Even if you have staff working on the rent collections and dealing with the daily expenses of management and property operations, you should review the property, the income and expenses, and the benefits you are getting on a frequent basis.

I am never surprised to find that many property owners have no idea of what is really happening. They have turned over the management to staff or a company professional and have grown distant from the events. The best property manager and the most loyal staff can never place themselves fully in your shoes. Property owners who have become distant from the actual events of their property can unwittingly mislead a prospect buyer or listing broker.

Build Your Reputation on Ethics

Worse than a careless property owner is one who deliberately "invents" a statement or pro forma of income and expenses to give to the prospective buyer instead of a real account of the income and expenses that the property can produce.

It is possible that no one will ever know if you sell a property to a buyer who trusts in the material you give and you deliberately lie to or cheat him. Indeed, even if someone finds out or strongly suspects that you defrauded the buyer there may be nothing to be done legally. But that does not make it right. Your success as a real estate investor, or in any other venture, will be assured if you follow a strict code of ethics. It is best to remember to "do unto others as you would have them do unto you." Honesty is the single factor that will help you keep out of trouble.

Keep Your Goals Clearly in Sight

Get a five- by seven-inch card and write down your goals as they relate to this property. Put a date on the card and every time you open the property file take a look at this card. If your goals have changed or your current plans have altered slightly then review the property in its totality to see if it is still giving you what you need or expect.

Keep Reliable Records

Know your tax base. This is the "book value" of property and is a very important bit of information for your ultimate calculation of any gain or for all tax-free exchange computations. Your tax basis is the value established initially when you acquire a property. This amount changes over the years because it will be decreased by depreciation or demolition of assets or by selling off parts of the property. The tax basis will be increased by improvements or by capitalization of expenses that you might otherwise have deducted as expenses.

It is a good idea to maintain a **log of your tax basis.** It would have a beginning value obtained from the closing statement or closing accounting when you acquired the property. Each year, as you either improve the property, add to your base through capitalization of expenses, or deduct from the value through depreciation, you will have a current **tax basis value.**

Tax-related or legal opinions. Anything your accountant or lawyer has recommended to you about this property should be kept.

Depreciation schedules. This is an accounting procedure and if you use a CPA or other accountant to keep your records make sure that you have copies of all the depreciation schedules the accountant has set up for this property. This information is used in calculating your tax basis as well as determining the "paper" expense for that investment. Keep this with your files as a reminder to add all new depreciable items to the list.

Costs of additions and improvements. This information will serve to maintain the tax basis as well as provide a clear record of not only the dates of improvements and additions to the property but the exact cost as well. A detailed record of this sort can be a good selling tool to document the improvements made to the property and it will show a prospective buyer or "taker" your professionalism as a real estate investor.

Keeping detailed records need not be a chore, if you have a definite place to put the data as you accumulate it. Once it is filed it will be out of your way, so you can clear your desk and mind for other matters. Keep business ethics a high priority. You will have a higher regard for yourself in the process.

When to Get Rid of an Investment

I don't know why so many people struggle with this question, for the answer is so easy to arrive at. You will sell, exchange, or otherwise dispose of your investments the moment they no longer are moving you toward your goals as would some other investment or benefit. That said, you can see that while the answer is simple, the recognition that you are at that stage is not so easy. Many investors hold on to property that no longer serves their interests or goals because they do not know how to find another investment that would.

Other investors get rid of a property because it begins to interrupt their normal or desired flow of "things." The problem with this reaction is that the problems may signal that more attention must be given to that property. An owner may end up disposing of a property that would help him meet his needs and move him toward his goals if the problem were isolated and solved. People generally tend to hold on to the comfortable properties and sell off the problem ones. Because comfortable properties may not be moving you in the right direction (out of sight, out of mind), you should pay close attention to all your properties and especially those that seem to be running smoothly.

The 8 Steps to Knowing What and When to Sell

1. Review your goals.
2. Assess the property's benefits.
3. What is your property's economic value?
4. Find the real market value of each property.
5. Should you sell or exchange?
6. What are the market trends?
7. Is there a time problem?
8. Are you ready to act now?

Let's take a look at each step in detail.

1. Review Your Goals

Goals are everything when it comes to plans. Your investment goals will form the basis for all your plans and only a frequent review of these goals will allow you to make needed changes in your investment strategy. By "frequent" I would suggest that you sit down and take a look at your progress toward your established goals once a month. By the way, your established goals must be written down so that you will have no misunderstanding about what they are. Do not hesitate to make changes in these goals as events change.

When you see that your goals have evolved to something new, or that you have reached a goal and now must focus your thinking on some higher goal, carefully reflect on what this new goal should be. Write it down and let it marinate in your mind for a day or two. Look at it several times a day after that and if you are comfortable with the new goal, set it down as the target for all activities. This means you should examine the investments you have and determine their worth as a pathway to the adjusted or changed goals. Clearly, if your total purpose was to arrive at financial independence and you just struck it rich with a $20 million lottery ticket, your investment strategy would most likely need to change. If your wife becomes pregnant and the doctor informs you that it will be triplets, I can assure you that your plans for the future will need a drastic overhaul.

2. Assess the Property's Benefits

Before you jump to the conclusion that the property you own will not effectively and economically move you in the direction of your goals, take another look at the benefits possible. Remember, you have been looking at things in a certain frame of mind, and now you have to anticipate a different future or a change of priorities. Whatever the event or circumstance, you gain a total view of your property only if you are open-minded about the totality of benefits possible. You will adapt best to sudden or gradual changes in your goals if you have taken a frequent look at the potential benefits your properties offer. If you discover that the property does not serve your new goals, it becomes a candidate for disposition.

3. What Is Your Property's Economic Value?

This has very little to do with the actual value, although the values can be equal. Your economic value is a relative review of how much it might cost you to replace the totality of the benefits you get from this property. For example, you own an office building that is rented to one tenant on a triple net lease (the tenant pays all costs to maintain the building as well as the real estate tax), and this tenant is stable, has never missed a month's rent in 12 years, and their business looks strong. If the net rent you get is $20,000 per year and the market would support a price for the building of $200,000 above your debt, your economic value would depend not on the $200,000 but on what this investment is worth to you from the total benefits you get. The important part of this exercise is for you to examine the total possible benefits available from this investment. If you are taking advantage of them all (a most unlikely event) then you need to remind yourself that income is only one benefit. You might be able to replace the income for $200,000 above your equity, but will you be able to replace all the other benefits you have—or could have?

4. Find the Market Value of Each Property

Some properties are not salable at the true economic value because the vast majority of buyers cannot or do not recognize the benefits they can obtain, or do not have a need for the totality of benefits available. A good example of this would be the labor "family jobs" form of investment, say a 50-unit motel, where the owner has enjoyed a nice income from the motel and at the same time supported other family members. For this family to dispose of this investment they should first decide what they will replace the total benefits with. The net operating income, while important, is not the most critical criterion for making the decision to keep the property or not.

Why Time Is Everything to Value

Market value is a function of the market and the time you allocate to the market. Time becomes the key to obtaining the best price. If you want to sell your property tomorrow at 12 noon on the dot, and are able to notify every investor within a thousand miles who might be interested in buying the property, you would likely not be satisfied with the price offered you.

5. Should You Sell or Exchange?

Real estate is not an instant commodity such as gold or potatoes. To be sold or exchanged the property must first meet the needs of and provide the path to the goals of the buyer. Except for very unusual market conditions and even more unique property, all prospective sellers must anticipate that to get the best price will take time. If price is less critical than the amount of time, the seller can lower the price to fit the market conditions.

6. What Are the Market Trends?

A more practical approach is to look at the market and ascertain what is moving and how long it is taking to sell. If the market is hot and sellers of similar properties are selling within 15 to 30 days, you are in a seller's market for that kind of property. You can get help from your real estate broker to establish a table of similar properties and the prices at which they have sold. From this homework you can come pretty close to what you might expect in the marketplace, and approximately how much time it might take to sell.

To be conservative in any such market study, it is my practice to deduct 10 percent from the "expected value" and add 50 percent to the "anticipated time" it might take to go to closing.

The time a satisfactory transaction is likely to take is usually more critical than the value, although there will be a correlation between them. However, certain market conditions create lulls in the sale of certain properties, and even a substantial drop in price may not produce a buyer. You will have an edge in these situations if you have the added opportunity to be an aggressive seller through the techniques of exchange, but a flat market will elongate every plan.

Most Realtors have access to computer programs that show the status of the local Multiple Listing Service, which is a databank of listings and sales information shared by members of the local Board of Realtors. While not all properties sold in your community will have been listed through an MLS member, the information you get from your broker will be helpful when you acquire property as well as when you are determining when to sell.

Some communities—Hilton Head, South Carolina, is a good example—publish all deed transfers in the local newspaper. This information can easily be obtained in any community through the courthouse records of property transfers and generally includes the names of the buyer and seller as well as the address or other description of the property and the price recorded in the contract. Make a habit of keeping track of what is going on in your comfort zone, even though you may not be thinking of buying or selling right now. It is a good idea to keep detailed records of all transfers in the immediate area where you own property so that you are on top of any trends.

Sometimes just being aware of local events puts you way ahead of people who live in the same area but are not aware of what is happening.

By following trends and being on top of local events and proposed development, you may have lead time to put a property on the market that may be headed for a flat market in the near future. For example, new road construction planned to start in two years may be a big boost to your property value 10 years from now, but for two years during the construction could flatten out any prospects for a sale. If your plan was to sell next year you may want to move that plan up a year. On the other hand, your original plan to hold for two to three years might be extended to five or six years, to take advantage of the appreciation you may gain through the new road and other development sure to follow.

Warning! New road plans have a way of not coming through on schedule. A proposed road that has not gotten funding from the federal, state, or local government agencies may linger as a proposal for years.

7. Is There a Time Problem?

Everything keeps coming back to time and goals. You should keep these two elements close to heart and constantly think of your goals in a time frame. Plans should be time-oriented so that you can judge how you are doing and where you are in your total picture. When you invest in real estate time will play the major role in the appreciation of value.

The whole idea is to anticipate the time/goal situation before there is a problem. If you have acquired property with the idea that you would sell or exchange it, and you have an interest-only mortgage that balloons in five years, you must allow yourself time to find a "taker" well in advance of the balloon payment on the mortgage.

However, even the best of plans can falter, so when you find yourself with a critical time problem you will need to use all your creative ability to salvage the deal. By following the steps in this chapter you will have more lead time than most investors, who don't seem to understand how desperate things can get until they actually get the foreclosure notice. Don't let that happen to you.

8. Are You Ready to Act Now?

Making decisions can be tough, and even tougher when they involve money. Assume for a moment that you are following the first seven steps properly, you are up on the market, know your goals, and have a good feel for where you are going. Suddenly you see a trend in the market that points toward a possible change for the worse. But time is still on your side if you act now. Are you ready to act now?

Moving with the flow of events is always the best way to go. You do not have to pioneer in real estate and you can learn from the mistakes of others. Going with the flow can, in some circumstances, carry you over the waterfall. Knowing when to come ashore is important.

The same can be said for standing on shore about to be devoured by a hungry lion: knowing when it is time to jump back into the stream of things and go with the flow can be equally important.

Your ability to make good decisions quickly is crucial. Overkill in study and comparison of properties can give another investor the added time to make the decision to acquire that property ahead of you. Holding on too long to the wrong property (for you) can put you into a time problem where the end result is a greatly reduced value or worse—a foreclosure.

As you gain confidence in your comfort zone and build knowledge of creative deal making you will find that decision making will not be as difficult as you think. Opportunities will open up and you can jump in and take advantage of them, both as buyer and seller. As a seller or exchanger you will need to develop property presentations that will knock their socks off.

How to Make a Property Presentation

A property presentation is what you give to a prospective taker for your property. The presentation itself can take several different forms, depending on the benefits you are attempting to highlight. For example, a vacant tract of land that has a dozen different uses could be presented in different formats. One presentation, directed at fast-food operators, would have all the necessary information showing competition, traffic counts, locations of schools and parks, and other public attractions. A presentation on this property directed to new-car dealers would contain information of interest to that business.

By careful examination of all the benefits and uses of a property, you will be able to ascertain a variety of potential markets or different takers. To make sure you have the information necessary to sell the property, review the Property Presentation Checklist.

Property Presentation Checklist

1. **Your name and address.** Make sure you double-check all address and phone numbers. Printers make mistakes. If there is any reason not to provide your own name and address then use a broker or other intermediary.
2. **Your phone and fax numbers.** Do not forget the area code.
3. **Property location.** The obvious information is the street address, city, and zip code. Not so obvious but important are directions on how to get to the property. A sketch or photograph is helpful if that information is a selling tool by showing proximity to important landmarks.
4. **Description.** A clear description of the property is always a good selling tool. "A modern, five-story, blue-glass-covered medical building, one block from Memorial Hospital, consisting of 55,000 square feet of rented offices. . . . " Descriptions should not oversell the property but be enough to pique the imagination.
5. **Value.** Unless the property is very expensive, or some other kind of property where the price would be misleading in view of the other information (such as an apartment house priced at $200,000 per apartment with monthly rents of only $1,000 per apartment), you should always include the price. By putting the price in a presentation you qualify the prospects.

The price you establish should be supported by the other information. Overpriced property just sits on the market until someone comes along and makes you an offer you will take. If you are in no hurry and have all the time in the world, you can, as conditions suggest, increase the price (value) of the property.

6. **Debt and debt service.** How much is the mortgage and who holds it? If there are several mortgages on the property, list them all, for example: "As of July 31, 1991, the first mortgage of $250,000, payable at $2,500 per month at 12 percent interest only for a remaining 10 years is held by United First Federal Savings and Loan." It is not necessary to go into great detail.

   If there is a balloon payment, be specific as to the actual date of the balloon. If there is a balloon payment of $100,000 due in three years with continuing interest-only payments until the last payment at the end of the 10th year, you would say "As of July 31, 1991, there is a first mortgage, held by United First Federal Savings and Loan, of $250,000 payable interest only at 12 percent per annum, monthly payments of $2,500 until July 31, 1994, at which time $100,000 of principal balloons. Payments are then $1,500 per month (interest-only at 12 percent) with the final principal due in full on July 31, 2001."

   Mention other details only if they are a sales tool, for example a mortgage that could be subordinated to additional financing without being paid off.

7. **Benefits.** You may list all the benefits as you see them, or be more specific as to the potential taker you are making the presentation to. You would approach a fast-food chain with different benefits than you would a car dealer, even though many of the attributes of the property would appeal to both.

8. **Your motivation.** In essence, why are you disposing of this property? The obvious answer is that the property is not doing for you what you want it to accomplish. This suggests something negative about the property; you need to be positive in your motivation. "Owner wants to acquire larger apartment complex" or whatever goal you want to obtain is best. By giving the specific directions you want to go, you open the door to other real estate investors who may have what you want and who are willing to take what you have to meet their own goals.

9. **Preference to buy/exchange.** This is an extension of your motivation. If you have a clear need then state it. "Owner wants to open new fast-food restaurants in South Florida and will take one or more commercial locations in exchange."

10. **State that you are the owner.** If you are making the presentation yourself rather than using a broker, be sure you make clear that you are the owner. "For sale/exchange by owner" generally does the trick nicely.

11. **What you can add.** If you have other property or items, including cash, that you can add to acquire a larger property, list them. For example, "To exchange up, owner can add other Florida and California real estate, value to $550,000, plus up to $50,000 cash." The word "cash" always attracts attention.

A simple property presentation can look like the two-page brochure that follows.

★ ★

★ FAMOUS COCONUT GROVE RESTAURANT ★
ON COMMODORE PLAZA
"The Essence of the Grove"

★ ★

CAFE EUROPA

3157 Commodore Plaza, Coconut Grove, Florida

FOR SALE

LOCATION:	Located on the northeastern side of Commodore Plaza in the heart of the bustling Grove.
DESCRIPTION:	This well-known Continental restaurant is located in a free standing, 2 story building with a popular, covered, open-air dining terrace. The indoor dining area includes a full bar and the kitchen is fully equipped. The second floor has offices and storage areas.

BUILDING SIZE:

First Floor:

    Dining area, bar, kitchen: 3,104 sq. ft.

    Outdoor dining area: 1,608 sq. ft.

Second floor office, etc.:   <u>2,350 sq. ft.</u>

Total, as per survey: 7,062 sq. ft.

YEAR BUILT: 1925

ZONING: SPI-2 (City of Miami - Special Public Interest District).

TAXES: 1989: $17,124.

LIQUOR LICENSE: 4 COP/SRX

SALES PRICE:

Business only: $900,000

Business and property: $2,400,000.

TERMS: Seller is willing to hold PMM or Wrap. To be negotiated.

COMMENTS: The business may be purchased separately or with the property. All leasehold improvements, fixtures, equipment, supplies and good-will are included.

FOR SHOWING & DETAILS: Contact **DAVID CASSEL**, or **JEROLD I. HORWITZ**, Realtor-Associates at **(305) 667-8871**.

Esslinger • Wooten • Maxwell Realtors

1360 South Dixie Highway • Coral Gables, Florida 33146 • (305) **667-8871**

NOTE: This offering subject to errors, omissions, prior sale or withdrawal without notice.   NML 97805-L 8 90

LOCATION MAP

ƎШM

Esslinger • Wooten • Maxwell Realtors

1360 South Dixie Highway • Coral Gables, Florida 33146 • (305) **667-8871**

Almost any quality copyshop has the ability to produce a brochure like this. A modern copier can turn out beautiful work in a very short time, and if you like it professionally typeset they can do that, too, usually inexpensively.

If you are listing your property with a broker, make sure that the listing agreement requires the broker to make up a detailed property presentation that contains the information in the checklist. Some real estate offices consider this a natural aspect of their professionalism, while others will attempt to get by with copies of MLS brochures, which are nothing more than reprints of the broker's Multiple Listing Service data. It is intended to be used by professionals and not by prospective buyers. MLS listings contain condensed information that is often in code or uses abbreviations that even many brokers don't understand. Do not believe for one minute that a prospective buyer or "taker" will be sold by this kind of listing presentation and insist on quality brochure presentations.

Build to Win

Think of yourself as an army of ants capable of being everywhere at once, doing a thousand things at the same time, building your nest, collecting food for life and thought, defending your position, attacking and being aggressive to gain more territory. Sound impossible? Not so, all it takes is a little time each day to build, store, and learn. Everything will fall into place the moment you have begun to assess your comfort zone. Risk and fear will be replaced by security and confidence. Just remember that everything looks easier when it is done by someone who knows what he is doing. In the early stages you will be learning more than doing. Once you begin to do, the world will be yours.

6

Get Ready to Make Offers

Set Up Your Property Records Correctly

In the beginning, you will not have a serious filing problem because you won't have much to file. But unless you tackle the potential organizational problem right away you will soon be overwhelmed with the amount of material you will have to contend with.

The most important files you keep will be those on the properties you own. The material on those specific properties I mentioned earlier will be filed in separate folders for each property.

The second most important files will be the records you maintain on properties you consider purchasing or exchanging into. Let me suggest an easy way to keep track of your offers and property records.

The 3 Steps to Good Record Keeping

1. Maintain one combined ledger of purchases, sales, exchanges, and inspections.
2. Put a descriptive heading on every offer.
3. File by property title.

Take a look at each of these steps in detail.

1. Maintain a Ledger: Calendar / Purchases / Sales / Exchanges / Inspections

You should have a three-ring binder in which you make five sections.
1. Calendar
2. Purchases
3. Sales
4. Exchanges
5. Property Inspections

Calendar. The calendar is a **chronological** account of all your offers, sales, and exchanges. Place in this section a dozen pages that have been ruled so that you have place for a date and a description of events. A sample of such a page with several entries follows.

96

Sample Binder Page from "Calendar"

Date	Transaction	Description of Event
6/21/91	Offer to buy	Offered to buy the Johnson tract of land in Palm Beach County. See Palm Beach 400 Acres.
6/23/91	Sale	Contracted with Bigallo to sell him Tract R in Eagle's Nest, NC.
6/25/91	Counteroffer	Johnson counteroffer
6/29/91	Offer to exchange	Brickhouse deal/mortgage for townhouse
6/30/91	Purchase	Signed deal with Johnson PB 400

This is a log of events and does not have to contain a lot of information other than provide a chronological record. Over the years, when you need to reconstruct a tax base in a property that has gone through several exchanges or just to maintain details on what you have done, this log will be worth its weight in gold.

Purchases. The second section of the binder, labeled "Purchases," will have a separate sheet of paper for each purchase. Do not put other deals on the same sheet. Over time you may add to the paper or move it to other files. In this and the following sections of the binder the property will be listed by its **property title.** The following entry in the "Purchases" section concerns a property called Palm Beach 400.

Sample Binder Page from "Purchases"

```
Palm Beach 400
```

A tract of land consisting of 400 acres of land located between Lake Forest Road and Hypoluxo Road with the Florida turnpike as the westerly boundary of the property. The property is located in Palm Beach County. See legal description in the contract and survey on file. Original asking price was $70,000 per acre. Contract price agreed to was $62,400 per acre.

1. Contract signed and executed June 30, 1991, with Bill and Wilma Johnson.

2. Contract closing date set for August 15, 1991.

Sales. Five years from now you might decide to sell this property or exchange it, and the sheet or sheets of information can be transferred to the next section of the binder, or if sold or exchanged you can retire it to a separate file kept elsewhere labeled "No Longer Own."

Take a look at the Palm Beach 400 several years from now in the "Sales" section of the binder.

Sample Binder Page from "Sales"

Palm Beach 400

A tract of land consisting of 400 acres of land located between Lake Forest Road and Hypoluxo Road with the Florida turnpike as the westerly boundary of the property. The property is located in Palm Beach County. See legal description in the contract and survey on file. Original asking price was $70,000 per acre. Contract price agreed to was $62,400 per acre.

1. Contract signed and executed June 30, 1991, with Bill and Wilma Johnson.

2. Contract closing date set for August 15, 1991.

3. Closed late due to title problems, October 1, 1991.

4. Submitted rezoning petition to county, November 15, 1991.

5. Property rezoned and platted for industrial park, July 1, 1992.

6. Offer from IBM to purchase, September 1, 1992.

7. Deal accepted with IBM, September 15, 1992.

8. Closing set for October 1, 1992.

9. Deal closed by Wm. Beggs, Esq. Contract price of $162,400 per acre.

Exchanges. The next section of the binder will be labeled "Exchanges." This form is a record of the specific property you are exchanging. The first entry will be the lead through which you first acquired the property. It could be that instead of selling the Palm Beach 400 to IBM you enter into an exchange; in fact, considering the profit you would have made from the above-described IBM deal ($40,000,000), an exchange could have saved you a lot of money. Keep in mind, however, that you still could affect the exchange by using a delayed exchange provision. In another transaction, you are exchanging a condo apartment you took in an exchange several years ago. You will end up with equity in a small apartment complex.

Sample Binder Page from "Exchanges"

El Mar Condo

A two-bedroom apartment, Unit 603, located at 110 Ocean Drive, acquired in an exchange with Tom McAndrews, on March 1, 1987. I exchanged into this unit giving McAndrews two residential lots in Jupiter, Florida (see the Jupiter Lots 8 and 9 Tract R file in the closed records). Value quoted in the exchange of the apartment was $55,000 with a first mortgage held by Amerifirst Federal of $30,000. There were no other fees paid or earned.

1. Exchange closed by Beggs March 1, 1987.

2. Condo rented to Alex Penrod (see "Leases" file) for $475 per month on March 15, 1987.

3. New lease with Madelain Monfort, April 1, 1990, at $525 per month.

4. Offer to Bob Montgomery subject to my mortgage balance of $27,000 to take his 11 units at 1313 S.E. 3rd Street, Ft. Lauderdale. His mortgage is $120,000. August 1, 1992.

5. Beggs closes the deal, September 1, 1992 (see "Rio Vista 3rd St. Apartments")

Property Inspections. This is a very important part of your ledger because personal inspections of property are essential to your becoming comfortable with the real estate in your comfort zone and its real value to you.

Chapter 7 describes the property inspection in great detail.

2. Use a Descriptive Heading on Every Offer

Successful real estate investors make offers, and they make a lot of offers. Insiders know that unless you make an offer no one will ever know you want to buy or exchange the property in question. Because most sellers don't know exactly what they will do until an offer actually comes in, it pays for you to be aggressive and make offers that suite your needs and interests. Keep in mind that your offers will therefore be designed to the price and terms that you **know** will make that investment a good investment. Sometimes your initial offer is just something that starts the ball rolling, and sometimes the door gets shut in your face forever. Usually persistence will win out if the property is a good one and you are able to put your deal together before another buyer comes along or the seller tires of the transaction and falls back in love with the property.

Because many of the offers you make will be on standard forms, they will all start to look alike after a while. Sure, all you need to do is read some of the details to distinguish the offers, but there is a simple way to keep everything clear. Use a descriptive heading on every offer.

Have a standard two-line heading typed across the top of every page of the offer. A sample heading would look like this:

```
June 15, 1992                        Cummings/Leadership Homes

Exch: Vero Land/West Commercial Blvd. land   Date Closed:_____
```

You can design your heading any way you like, but be sure you have the date the offer was first made (to distinguish from any counteroffers or your subsequent offers). List your name first and then the other party's. On the second line is a short description of the deal. In the above case it is an exchange of the Vero land for the West Commercial Blvd. land. When the deal closes fill in the closing date. Thus, any offer heading without a closing date clearly has not yet closed.

If you are making 10 offers a week, you will quickly find the right offer out of a pile of 20 or more without having to look at more than the first two lines.

So far I am only talking about keeping track of what you are doing. As you begin to acquire property you will need to set up complete files on each property. These files should contain everything important regarding the subject properties.

3. File by Property Title

As you set up files on your properties you should give them titles. You will remember your properties better this way and never be at a loss as to where they are filed. There are two key factors to having titles: never begin a title with a number and always keep the titles short. Some examples have already been shown: Palm Beach 400, El Mar Condo. Should you break up a property, for example, sell or exchange part of the Palm Beach 400, as you still have part you would change the name to reflect the remainder of the property: Palm Beach 150, if you had disposed of 250 acres.

The title should also describe the property. If it is the name of a building or a subdivision or plat name then you are constantly jogging your memory about this property as you examine the file or review the information.

Get Ready to Make Offers—Some Sample Contracts

Most offers to acquire real estate can be made on a standard purchase form used by the local Board of Realtors. Generally there will be several different kinds of "standard" forms for different categories of property. For example, in Florida the local Realtors' associations use the following types of forms, which are self-explanatory. There are slight differences owing to state laws and customary closing practices. Condominium and co-op sales have specific requirements, frequently that the new owner be approved by an association board. Here are some standard purchase contracts in use in Florida.

COOPERATIVE APARTMENT
Deposit Receipt and Contract for Sale and Purchase

8/87

_____ his wife, of _____

(PH _____) hereinafter called the Seller, and _____
_____ his wife, of _____
_____ (PH _____) hereinafter called the Buyer, hereby agree that the Seller shall sell and the Buyer shall buy the following described property UPON THE TERMS AND CONDITIONS HEREINAFTER SET FORTH.

I. DESCRIPTION OF INTERESTS TO BE SOLD AND PURCHASED: (NOTE: THIS IS NOT A FEE SIMPLE INTEREST IN REAL PROPERTY, BUT MERELY THE USE OF AND EQUITY IN AN APARTMENT GRANTED BY THE COOPERATIVE ASSOCIATION AS OWNER OF ALL THE COOPERATIVE PROPERTY.)

(a) The Proprietary Lease or other occupancy agreement (hereinafter called the "Proprietary Lease") relating to Apartment No. _____ of _____ (hereinafter called the "Apartment"),

(Name of Building)

owned by _____ , a corporation not for profit

(Name of Cooperative Association)

(hereinafter called the "Corporation"), between the Corporation, as Lessor, and the Seller, as Lessee, covering the Apartment with any necessary executed assignments or consents; Tax Folio No. _____ ;

(b) _____ shares of the capital stock of the Corporation or other similar membership rights, which shares or rights carry the privilege of receiving the Proprietary Lease described in (a) above; and

(c) The Seller's right, subject to the provisions of the Proprietary Lease, in and to all the fixtures, machinery and equipment now contained in the Apartment, plus the personal property described as follows: _____
_____
_____

PURCHASE PRICE .... (In U.S. Funds) $_____
METHOD OF PAYMENT:
Deposit herewith .... $_____
Additional deposit to be paid on or before _____ , 19___, after acceptance of $_____
contract by both parties. $_____
Time is of the essence as to additional deposit.
All deposits to be held in trust by _____
Principal balance of first mortgage, or other financing arrangements, which buyer shall assume ( ) or
obtain ( ) (CHECK ONE). $_____
Existing Lender _____ Loan _____
At Int. _____%, with Mtg. Pmt. $ _____ , incl. PI ( ) T ( ) I ( )
Fixed Rate ( ), Variable ( ), Balloon ( ) CHECK WHERE APPLICABLE
Other: _____ $_____
PM Financing to Seller: Terms: _____ $_____
_____ Due on Sale ( ) or Assumable ( ) CHECK ONE.
Principal balance of Seller's percentage share of blanket mortgage, or other financing arrangements, of
the Corporation which the Buyer shall assume is calculated in the purchase price $_____
OR Principal balance of Seller's percentage share of blanket mortgage, or other financing
arrangements, of the Corporation which the Buyer shall assume ($ _____) is not
calculated in the purchase price.
Balance of funds due at closing (subject to adjustments herein) in U.S. Currency, certified or cashier's
check. Said funds may be held in escrow pursuant to provisions of Paragraph N in this Contract. $_____
TOTAL PURCHASE PRICE .... $_____

3. SPECIAL CLAUSES: (See page 4 or Addendum attached, if any.)

(a) This Contract is contingent upon the sale being approved and the Buyer being approved for occupancy by the Corporation. The Buyer shall apply for such approval within _____ days from the date of this Contract being signed by both parties or be in default. The Buyer shall diligently submit such references and appear before any board or committee as may be reasonably required by the Corporation. The Transfer Fee or Application Fee (if any) charged by the Corporation shall be paid by the Buyer.

(b) The Seller represents that: (i) the current assessment for maintenance, operation, taxes, Mortgage if any and Lease if any, insurance, etc. is in the amount of $_____ per _____ ; and (ii) the Corporation has a freehold interest in the land upon which the Apartment is situated, or a leasehold interest having an unexpired term of _____ years. (If blank not filled in, it is presumed to be a freehold interest.) The Seller further states that the assessments will be current as of the Closing and may be subject to further change as determined by the Corporation.

(c) The Seller represents that he is not aware of any pending special assessments by the Corporation, except those disclosed to the Buyer for the following purpose(s). _____ .
_____

Any such pending special assessments shall be the obligation of the Buyer and any special assessments assessed on or before the date of this Contract shall be the obligation of the Seller.

(d) Seller represents that the Proprietary Lease, or other corporate documents, rules or regulations DO restrict the following: Pets _____, Children _____, Leases _____, Form of Ownership _____. CHECK WHERE APPLICABLE.

(e) There will be no proration of the assets or liabilities, including the reserve accounts, if any, held by the Corporation.

4. PARKING SPACE(S): (CHECK WHERE APPLICABLE)

a) _____ the right to use the parking space # _____ is included in the sale of this apartment.

b) _____ no parking space is included in this sale.

c) (Other): _____ .

BE ADVISED: When this agreement has been completely executed, it becomes a legally binding instrument. The form of this "Cooperative Apartment Deposit Receipt and Contract for Sale and Purchase" has been approved by the Broward County Bar Association and the Fort Lauderdale Area Board of REALTORS, Inc.

5. ACCEPTANCE DATE: This offer shall be null and void unless accepted, in writing, and a signed copy received by _____ _____ on or before ___ day of _____ 19___, by _____ AM/PM.
6. CLOSING DATE: This Contract shall be closed and the item described in Section 1 above and possession shall be delivered on or before the ___ day of _____ 19___, unless extended by other provisions of this Contract or separate agreement.

STANDARDS FOR REAL ESTATE TRANSACTIONS

A. WARRANTIES OF SELLER: The Seller covenants, represents and warrants that he is the sole owner of the shares in the Corporation (or other membership rights), the Proprietary Lease (or other occupancy agreement), and the fixtures, machinery, equipment and personal property heretofore described; that the same are free and clear of all liens, encumbrances, restrictions on transferability and adverse interests, subject, however, to any liens or mortgages on the real property of which this Apartment forms a part and the rights of the Corporation. The Seller further covenants, represents and warrants that the shares in the Corporation are duly paid for and are non-assessable and that all assessments of the Corporation are current, except as herein provided. Also, there exists no default under the Proprietary Lease or other occupancy agreement.

B. SELLER'S DOCUMENTS: (1) Within ten (10) days of the execution of the Contract by all parties, the Seller shall deliver to the Buyer where applicable, copies of the Articles of Incorporation, By-Laws and any amendments thereto of the Corporation and any house rules, and a copy of the proposed Proprietary Lease.

    (2)   At or before closing, the Seller shall deliver the following:

        (a)   Certificate or certificates for the number of shares described in Section 1(b) (or other evidence of member rights), and if the Seller is a fiduciary, there shall also be delivered all documents necessary or required by the Corporation for the purpose of transferring such shares or other membership rights, including, but not limited to, certificates of authority to act.

        (b)   Stock powers or endorsements on such stock certificate or certificates, together with all necessary documentary stamps duly affixed thereto to cover the transfer thereof into the name of the Buyer.

        (c)   Original Proprietary Lease or other occupancy agreement of the Seller described in Section 1(a) above, together with any such assignments or consents as may have been necessary to transfer the interest of the Lessee named therein to the Seller.

        (d)   Assignment of the Proprietary Lease and its appurtenances, duly executed for the purpose of conveying to the Buyer all the Seller's right, title and interest as Lessee in the Proprietary Lease.

        (e)   Consent of the Corporation to the Transfer of such shares and the Proprietary Lease to the Buyer, or in the alternative, a certificate by an officer of the Corporation that a consent to such transfer is on file with the Corporation.

        (f)   Bill of Sale conveying personal property to the Buyer.

C. BUYER'S DOCUMENTS: At or before the Closing, the Buyer, in addition to the payment of the balance of the purchase price and adjustments, shall deliver the following:

    (1)   Agreement signed and acknowledged by the Buyer in form approved by the Corporation, accepting the assignment of the Proprietary Lease and assuming and agreeing to perform and comply with all the terms, covenants and conditions of the Proprietary Lease, including observance of house rules and any special provisions with respect to such shares, on and after the effective date of the assignment; one of such executed agreements to be delivered to the Seller and the other to the Corporation.

    (2)   If the Corporation so requests, the Buyer shall surrender the assigned Proprietary Lease and in place thereof shall enter into and execute a new Proprietary Lease with the Corporation in substantially the same form and covering the same apartment as the Proprietary Lease so assigned and surrendered.

    (3)   If the Buyer is assuming the Seller's percentage share of the blanket mortgage of the Corporation, an assumption agreement, if required by the Corporation or the mortgagee.

D. POSSESSION: The Seller agrees that as of the closing, the Apartment will be vacated and possession and keys delivered to the Buyer.

E. EXISTING FINANCING: The Seller shall obtain and furnish a statement from the Corporation, or from a holder thereof, as to blanket mortgages, if any, setting forth the principal balance, method of payment, interest rate, and whether the financing is in good standing. The Seller shall obtain and furnish a statement from the lender, under any other financial arrangement, setting forth the principal balance, method of payment, interest rate, and whether the Seller's percentage share of other financing is in good standing. If there is a charge for the change of ownership records by the mortgagee or Corporation, it shall be borne equally by the parties to the transaction. Any variance in the amount of a mortgage to be assumed from the amount stated in the Contract, shall be added to or deducted from the cash payment or the purchase money mortgage, as the Buyer may elect. In the event such mortgage balance, or any other financing is more than three percent (3%) less than the amount indicated in the Contract, Seller shall have the option to adjust the purchase price to where differential is no more than the 3% allowed, or the Seller shall be deemed to be in default under the Contract.

F. NEW FINANCING: Any Purchase Money financing arrangement to Seller shall follow the forms generally accepted and used in the county where the property is located. A Purchase Money financing arrangement shall provide for annual proof of payment of taxes and insurance, if not provided by Cooperative Association, against loss by fire with extended coverage in an amount not less than the full insurable value of the improvements. In a first Lien, the Note and Lien shall provide for acceleration, at the option of the holder, after thirty (30) days default and in a junior Lien, after ten (10) days default. Junior Liens shall require the owner of the property encumbered by said Mortgage to keep all prior Liens and encumbrances in good standing and forbid the owner of the property from accepting modifications, or future advances, under a prior Lien. Any prepayment on Lien shall apply against principal amounts last maturing. In the event Buyer executes a financing arrangement to one other than the Seller, all costs and charges incidental thereto shall be paid by the Buyer. If this Contract provides for Buyer to obtain a new financing arrangement, then Buyer's performance under this Contract shall be contingent upon Buyer's obtaining said financing arrangement upon terms stated, or if none are stated, then upon the terms generally prevailing at such time in the county where the property is located. Buyer agrees diligently to pursue said financing arrangement, but if a commitment for said financing is not obtained within _____ banking days (15 banking days if this blank is not filled in) from date of this Contract, and the Buyer does not waive this contingency, then either Buyer or Seller may terminate this Contract, in which event, all deposits made by Buyer pursuant hereto shall be returned to him, and all Parties relieved of all obligations hereunder. (NEW FINANCING ARRANGEMENTS MAY REQUIRE ASSOCIATION APPROVAL.)

G. CONTRACT ASSIGNMENT: This Contract is not assignable.

H. INSPECTION: 1. The Buyer shall have the right to make the following inspections of the individual unit at Buyer's expense subject to the provisions of Paragraph 4 below. All inspections described in Paragraphs 1 (a) and (b) below shall be completed on or before five days prior to closing.

    a)   Termite: The Buyer shall have the right to have the individual unit inspected by a licensed exterminating company to determine whether there is any active termite or wood-destroying organism present in said unit. If there is any such infestation or damage, or any prior damage from wood-destroying organism, the Seller shall pay all costs of treatment and repairing and/or replacing all portions of said unit which are infested or have been damaged.

    b)   General: The Buyer shall have the right to have a roof, air conditioning, electric and plumbing inspection of the individual unit made by persons or companies qualified and licensed to perform such services. If such inspection reveals functional defects (as differentiated from aesthetic defects), Seller shall pay all costs of repairing said defects.

c) Personal Property: The Seller represents and warrants that all appliances and machinery included in the sale shall be in working order as of the date of closing. Buyer may, at his sole expense and on reasonable notice, inspect or cause an inspection to be made of the appliances and equipment involved prior to closing. Any necessary repairs shall be made at the cost of the Seller and, unless otherwise agreed in writing by the Parties, the Buyer shall, by closing, be deemed to have accepted the property as is.

2. Escrow for Repairs: If treatment, replacement or repairs called for in subparagraph a, b, and c hereof are not completed prior to closing, sufficient funds shall be escrowed at time of closing to effect same.

3. Reinspection: In the event the Seller disagrees with Buyer's inspection reports, Seller shall have the right to have inspections made at his cost. In the event Buyer's and Seller's inspection reports do not agree, the Parties shall agree on a third inspector, whose report shall be binding upon the Parties. The cost of the third inspector shall be borne equally between the Buyer and Seller.

4. Limitation and Option Clause: Seller shall be responsible for all costs of the above treatment, replacement or repairs up to $ _____ (or 2% of the purchase price if this blank is not filled in). In the event the total cost of items to be accomplished under subparagraphs a, b, and c exceed this amount, then either Party shall have the option of paying any amount in excess, and this Contract shall then remain in full force and effect. However, if neither Party agrees to pay the additional amount above the dollar amount or applicable percentage of the purchase price, then, at the Seller's or Buyer's option, this Contract may be cancelled by delivery of written notice to the other Party or his agent, and the deposit shall be returned to Buyer.

I. SUBLEASE: There shall be no Sublease or Right of Occupancy encumbering this property unless indicated under Special Clauses (U). The Seller shall, within 10 days of acceptance of this Contract, furnish to Buyer copies of written Sublease, if any, and 10 days prior to closing, an estoppel letter from such tenant specifying the nature and duration of said tenant's occupancy, rental rate, advance rents and security deposits paid by such tenant. In the event Seller is unable to obtain said estoppel letter from tenant, the same information may be furnished by Seller to Buyer in the form of a Seller's Affidavit.

J. PLACE OF CLOSING: Closing shall be held at the office of the Buyer's attorney or closing agent, if located within Broward County; if not then at the office of the Seller's attorney, if located in Broward County.

K. EXPENSES: Documentary stamps required to be affixed to the stock certificates and documentary stamps required to record the Proprietary Lease or other occupancy agreement shall be paid by the Seller. The cost of recording the Proprietary Lease or other occupancy agreement or documentary stamps on a Purchase Money Promissory Note and the cost of recording Purchase Money Security Agreement shall be paid by the Buyer. Florida State Sales Tax shall be paid as applicable.

L. PRORATIONS: Service contracts assumed by the Buyer, interest, assessments (other than special assessments) and other expenses and revenue of the Apartment being assumed by the Buyer shall be prorated through the day prior to Closing.

M. RISK OF LOSS: If the Apartment and personalty being conveyed to the Buyer are damaged by fire or other casualty before delivery of the Seller's Documents and can be restored to substantially the same condition as now existing within a period of sixty (60) days thereafter, Seller may restore the damaged items and the closing date and date of delivery of possession heretofore provided shall be extended accordingly. If Seller fails to do so, the Buyer shall have the option of (1) taking the property as is, together with insurance proceeds, if any, or (2) cancelling the Contract and all deposits will be forthwith returned to the Buyer and the parties released of any further liability hereunder.

N. MAINTENANCE: Between the date of the Contract and the date of closing, the Apartment and personalty, if any, being conveyed to the Buyer, if any, shall be maintained by Seller in the condition as it existed as of the date of the Contract, ordinary wear and tear excepted.

O. ESCROW: · The party receiving the deposit agrees by the acceptance thereof to hold same in escrow and to disburse it in accordance with the terms and conditions of this Contract. Provided, however, that in the event that a dispute shall arise between any of the parties to this Contract as to the proper disbursement of the deposit, the party holding the deposit may, at his option: (1) take no action and hold all funds (and documents, if any) until agreement is reached between the disputing parties, or until a judgment has been entered by a court of competent jurisdiction and the appeal period has expired thereon, or if appealed, then until the matter has been finally concluded, and then to act in accordance with such final judgment; or (2) institute an action for declaratory judgment, interpleader or otherwise joining all affected parties and thereafter complying with the ultimate judgment of the court with regard to the disbursement of the deposit and disposition of document, if any. In the event of any suit between Buyer and Seller wherein the escrow agent is made a party by virtue of acting as such escrow agent hereunder, or in the event of any suit wherein escrow agent interpleads the subject matter of this escrow, the escrow agent shall be entitled to recover a reasonable attorney's fee and costs incurred, including costs and attorney's fees for appellate proceedings, if any, said fees and costs to be charged and assessed as court costs in favor of the prevailing party.

P. ATTORNEY FEES AND COSTS: In connection with any litigation arising out of this Contract, the prevailing party, whether Buyer, Seller or Broker, shall be entitled to recover all costs incurred, including reasonable attorney's fees, for services rendered in connection with such litigation, including appellate, bankruptcy and postjudgment proceedings.

Q. DEFAULT: In the event of default of either party, the rights of the nondefaulting party and the Broker shall be as provided in this contract and such rights shall be deemed to be the sole and exclusive rights in such event: (a) If Buyer fails to perform any of the covenants of this Contract, all money paid or deposited pursuant to this Contract by the Buyer shall be retained by or for the account of the Seller as consideration for the execution of this Contract as agreed and liquidated damages and in full settlement of any claims for damages by the Seller against the Buyer; (b) If seller fails to perform any of the covenants of this Contract, all money paid or deposited pursuant to this Contract by the buyer shall be returned to the Buyer upon demand, or the Buyer shall have the right to specific performance. In addition, Seller shall pay forthwith to Broker the full professional service fee as provided for in this Contract.

R. PERSONS BOUND: The benefits and obligations of the covenants herein shall inure to and bind the respective heirs, personal representatives, successors and assigns (where assignment is permitted) of the parties hereto. Whenever used, the singular number shall include the plural, the plural the singular, and the use of any gender shall include all genders.

S. SURVIVAL OF COVENANTS AND SPECIAL COVENANTS: Seller covenants and warrants that there is ingress and egress to subject property over public or private roads or easements, which covenants shall survive delivery of Seller's Documents. No other provision, covenant or warranty of this Contract shall survive the delivery of the Seller's Documents, except as expressly provided herein.

T. FINAL AGREEMENT: This Contract represents the final agreement of the parties and no agreements or representations, unless Incorporated into this Contract, shall be binding on any of the parties. Typewritten provisions shall supersede printed provisions and handwritten provisions shall supersede typewritten and/or printed provisions. Such handwritten or typewritten provisions as are appropriate may be inserted on the face of this form or attached hereto as an addendum. The date of this Contract shall be the day upon which it becomes fully executed by all parties.

U. SPECIAL CLAUSES:

ALL PARTIES ARE ADVISED THAT THE I.R.S. CODE REQUIRES THE BUYER TO WITHHOLD TEN PERCENT (10%) OF THE SALES PRICE FOR TAX ON SALES BY CERTAIN FOREIGNERS. THE TAX WILL BE WITHHELD UNLESS AFFIDAVITS OF COMPLIANCE WITH THE I.R.S. CODE OR AN I.R.S. QUALIFYING STATEMENT ARE PROVIDED TO BUYER AT CLOSING.

WITNESS: Executed by Buyer on _____ 19 ___ Time: _____

_____   BUYER _____ (SEAL)

_____   BUYER _____ (SEAL)

ACCEPTANCE OF THIS CONTRACT & PROFESSIONAL SERVICE FEE: The Seller hereby approves and accepts the offer contained herein and recognizes _____ as Broker(s) in this transaction, and agrees to pay, as a fee _____% of the purchase price, or the sum of _____ _____ Dollars ($_____) or one-half of the deposit in case same is forfeited by the Buyer through failure to perform, as a compensation for service rendered, provided same does not exceed the full amount of the agreed fee.

WITNESS: Executed by Seller on _____ 19 ___ Time: _____

_____   _____ (SEAL)
                                                             SELLER
_____   _____
                                                             I.D. TAX NUMBER OR SOCIAL SECURITY NUMBER

                                                             _____ (SEAL)
                                                             SELLER
                                                             _____
                                                             I.D. TAX NUMBER OR SOCIAL SECURITY NUMBER

Deposit received on _____ 19 ___ to be held subject to this Contract; if check subject to clearance.

By: _____   By: _____
            Broker or Attorney

BE ADVISED: When this agreement has been completely executed, it becomes a legally binding instrument. The form of this "Cooperative Apartment Deposit Receipt and Contract for Sale and Purchase" has been approved by the Broward County Bar Association and the Fort Lauderdale Area Board of REALTORS, Inc.

JANUARY 15, 1992   Cummings / Sher   Vero Ocean Land

FLORIDA REALTOR®

F.A.R. Exchangor Form No. 3, Rev. 1975

OFFER TO EXCHANGE PROPERTY WITH ACCEPTANCE

The undersigned, first party, at the time and place stated below, hereby offers to exchange the real estate and/or personal property described herein for the real estate and/or personal property of the second party described herein upon the terms and conditions set forth herein.

Wherever the singular is used herein, the same shall apply to the plural if the context so requires. The word "Grantor", when used herein, shall designate the owner of or the person conveying title to any property herein described; and the word "Grantee", when used herein, shall designate that party to this agreement who will receive title to said property according to the terms of this agreement.

The handwritten or typewritten portions hereof shall prevail over the printed portions hereof where they are in conflict.

AS TO ALL PARCELS OF REAL PROPERTY AFFECTED BY THIS AGREEMENT, THE FOLLOWING TERMS SHALL APPLY:

1. All the items mentioned in this paragraph as may now be on the property shall be deemed to be part of the real property and shall be delivered free and clear of encumbrances: all garden bulbs, plants, shrubs and trees; screen doors and windows; storm doors and windows; electric lighting fixtures; window shades; curtain rods and venetian blinds; bathroom accessory fixtures; heating and air conditioning units and attached fixtures; water heaters; linoleum cemented to floors; carpeting attached to floors and stairs; awnings; exterior antennas.

2. Ad valorem taxes levied in the year of closing shall be prorated at the time of the closing, at the option of Grantee, on the basis of the ad valorem taxes for the preceding year, or the actual ad valorem taxes for year of closing, if determinable at time of closing, or the amount resulting from multiplying the assessed value of the property times the latest available tax rate.

3. Interest, prepaid rents, fuel oil and water charges shall be prorated as of the date of closing. Accrued income and expenses, including taxes for the day of closing, shall accrue to the Grantor. At the time of closing, tenant's security deposits shall be delivered to the Grantee. Existing leases shall be assigned to the Grantee. The Grantee acknowledges he has examined each of the leases referred to in schedule "A" annexed hereto and made part hereof and has initialed said leases for identification.

4. Legal possession of the premises shall be delivered to Grantee on the date of closing. Physical occupancy of premises shall be delivered to Grantee on the date of closing subject to tenants' rights if any.

5. Special assessments and all deferred charges of any kind, for work actually commenced prior to the date of the acceptance of this offer, chargeable to the property involved shall be paid by the Grantor, otherwise to be paid by the Grantee.

6. Grantor represents that he has no notice or knowledge of any planned public improvements which may result in special assessments and that he has not been served any notice requiring repairs, alterations or corrections of any existing condition unless specifically mentioned herein and that there are no existing orders against the property.

7. Grantor shall convey the property by Statutory Warranty Deed or by other conveyance provided herein, free and clear of all liens and encumbrances, excepting governmental zoning and/or regulations, recorded easements for public utilities and recorded building restrictions. Grantor, however, warrants that the property does not violate governmental zoning and/or regulations or recorded building restrictions.

8. The Grantor shall furnish and deliver, whether this agreement calls for a deed or a land contract, or any other type of conveyance, to the Grantee for examination at least fifteen (15) days prior to the date set for closing, the Grantor's choice of either:

A. A complete abstract of title made by an abstract company extended to within twenty (20) days of the closing, said abstract to show Grantor's title to be marketable and in the condition called for by this agreement. The Grantee shall notify the Grantor, in writing, of any valid objection to the title within twenty (20) days after the receipt of said abstract and the Grantor shall have a reasonable time, but not exceeding sixty (60) days within which to rectify the title (or furnish a title policy as hereinafter provided) and in such case, the time of closing shall be accordingly extended; or

B. A commitment by a responsible title insurance company licensed by the State of Florida to issue, upon compliance with the requirements of the commitment and upon recording of the proper documents as agreed herein, an owners policy of title insurance in the amount of the full insurable value of the real estate, naming the Grantee as the insured. The policy to be issued shall insure the Grantee's title to be in the condition called for by this agreement, subject only to the terms and stipulations set forth in the policy and/or as are imposed upon the insuror by the laws of the State of Florida.

9. Should the Grantor be unable to carry out this agreement by reason of a valid legal defect in the title which the Grantee is unwilling to waive, all money or other considerations shall be returned and this entire agreement shall be void.

10. In the event any parcel shall be damaged by fire or elements prior to the time of closing, in an amount of not more than ten per cent (10%) of the fair market value, the Grantor shall be obliged to repair same. In the event such damage shall exceed such percentage, this contract may be cancelled at the option of the Grantee. Should the Grantee elect to carry out this agreement in spite of such damage, such Grantee shall be entitled to all the credit for the insurance proceeds resulting from such damage, not exceeding, however, the exchange value.

AS TO ALL ITEMS OF PERSONAL PROPERTY AFFECTED BY THIS AGREEMENT, THE FOLLOWING TERMS SHALL APPLY UNLESS SPECIFICALLY PROVIDED TO THE CONTRARY HEREIN:

1. Personal property tax shall be prorated at the time of closing; sales tax shall be paid as prescribed by law.

2. Grantor shall deliver possession of the property on date of closing and shall convey the property by good and sufficient bill of sale, or by other conveyance as provided herein, free and clear of all liens and encumbrances, subject to tenants' rights, if any.

PARTIES HERETO AGREE TO THE FOLLOWING GENERAL PROVISIONS:

1. Grantee agrees that, unless otherwise specified, he will pay all costs of securing any financing to the extent permitted by law, and to perform all acts necessary to expedite said financing.

2. Where this contract requires that Grantee accept property subject to a mortgage, it is understood that Grantee will assume and agree to pay said mortgage unless specifically stated to the contrary. This agreement is subject to Grantee being permitted to assume said mortgage without acceleration by holder. Grantee shall pay any assumption charge and shall purchase escrow accounts from Grantor at time of closing.

3. Should the amount of any mortgage which is to remain a lien on any of the properties mentioned herein after conveyance not be set forth herein this contract shall be voidable at option of the Grantee; should said amount, however, as stated be more or less than the true balance of said mortgage then cash adjustments shall be made at the time of closing, it being understood that this transaction is to be closed on the basis of the mortgage being in the amount as represented. However, in lieu of cash adjustments, Grantor shall, at his option, increase or decrease said mortgage balance to the amount represented herein.

4. The parties hereto warrant and represent, unless otherwise specified, that they have full authority and right to bind to the terms of this contract all of the persons who hold title to the properties herein described and that they are acting within the scope of their authority and agency.

5. Grantor agrees to convey the property described herein to the Grantee, his nominee, or assigns named in writing.

6. Grantee, at his expense, may obtain a survey of Grantor's property. If the survey shows any encroachment except as otherwise provided herein, Grantee shall notify Grantor in writing within 45 days from date hereof but, in no event, less than 10 days prior to the closing date specifying the encroachments. Grantor shall have the same duty and time to remove such encroachments as is provided for the correction of defects in title.

7. Grantor shall pay for documentary stamps and surtax on the deed for the property he is conveying. Grantee shall pay for recording the deed. Mortgagor shall pay for the documentary stamps, intangible tax, and recording costs on the purchase money note and mortgage.

8. Within ⁸ days from full execution of this agreement, Grantor shall furnish to Grantee or his attorney any approvals or waivers required by any condominium documents in connection with a resale of the property. Grantee agrees to cooperate with Grantor to the extent necessary to secure approval or waiver. If Grantor is unable to secure any approval or waiver required by the condominium documents within the specified time, Grantee shall be entitled to the return of all money or other considerations and this entire agreement shall be void.

9. If this offer is accepted, it shall not become binding upon the first party until a copy of the accepted offer is deposited, postage prepaid, in the United States mails, addressed to the first party at his residence or by personal delivery thereof or by delivery to

Jack Cummings, 2669 E. Commercial Blvd. Ft. Lauderdale, Florida 33308

10. This offer shall be deemed revoked unless accepted in writing within   15 working   days after date hereof.

11. This transaction is to be closed at the office of   Bill Beggs Lawyer - Ft. Lauderdale   on or before

90 days from the acceptance date of this contract, or at such other time and place as may be designated in writing by the parties hereto.

12. Should either party default in the performance of this contract, the defaulting party shall pay as liquidated damages at the option of the other

party, the sum of   Five thousand dollars ($5,000)   Dollars.

13. This agreement shall be binding upon the heirs, personal representatives, administrators, executors, successors, and assigns of the parties hereto.

14. The warranties and representations made herein survive the closing of this transaction.

First Party   Land given is zoned for 5 units per acre

Exchanges the following property   103 Acres of land in Saint Lucie County, Florida,
Known as the Vero South Land Trust, Plat book 65 - page 12,

(List mortgages, amounts & terms) $1,200,000 payable interest only in annual payments at 9% for 7 years with full balloon at the end of the term with no penalty for prepayment in all or part.

Broker for the First Party is   Steve Engels - Cummings Realty

Second Party   VAL SHER

Exchanges the following property   80 acres of land located in Collier County, Florida
Known as the SHER TRACT # 66.

(List mortgages, amounts & terms)   FREE AND CLEAR

Broker for the Second Party is   Rainbow Realty of Chicago, Ill.

THIS AGREEMENT IS SUBJECT TO AND-OR CONTINGENT UPON THE FOLLOWING TERMS AND CONDITIONS

Each party has a period of 10 days to inspect the property offered to them and unless either party rejects the property offered this contract shall e set for closing within 90 days of this date

IF THERE IS NO ACCEPTANCE OR REJECTION IN WRITING BY JANUARY 30, 1992, then this agreement shall be considered null and void and each party released from any further obligation to the other

Brokerage fees are by separate agreement. However, all parties to this contract agree that Broker for any party may cooperate with other Brokers and divide commissions in any manner satisfactory to them. The Broker (Brokers) is (are) authorized to act as Brokers for all parties hereto and may accept commissions therefrom.

The undersigned, first party, has read and fully understands and hereby makes the foregoing offer at   the offices of

CUMMINGS REALTY   on this   15   day

of   January   , 19 92   , and acknowledges receipt of a copy of said offer.

Witness   First Party

Witness   First Party

The undersigned, second party, has read and fully understands and hereby accepts the foregoing offer at

on this   day

of   , 19   , upon the terms and conditions stated and acknowledges receipt of a copy of this agreement.

Witness   Second Party

Witness   Second Party

MARCH 5, 1992   CUMMINGS / ENGELS   CONDO

DEPOSIT RECEIPT AND CONTRACT FOR SALE AND PURCHASE
(IF FHA, VA OR CONDOMINIUM CONTRACT, RIDER REQUIRED.)

BUYER __JACK CUMMINGS AND OR HIS ASSIGNS__

of __Ft. Lauderdale, Florida__ (Tel: (_305_) _771-6300_) and

SELLER __STEVEN ENGELS__

of __Of Fort Lauderdale, Florida__ (Tel: (___) __NO PHONE__

hereby agree that the Seller shall sell and the Buyer shall buy the following described property together with existing improvements thereon, UPON THE TERMS AND CONDITIONS HEREINAFTER SET FORTH.

1. LEGAL DESCRIPTION of real estate located in __BROWARD__ County, Florida.   Tax Folio # _972-33-49-001_

Apartment 1106 of the Condos by the Sea, located at 977 North Atlantic Road, Ft. Lauderdale, Florida, 33308

COMPLETE PROPERTY ADDRESS: __See Above__
(Address)   (City)   (Zip)

PERSONAL PROPERTY INCLUDED: All fixed equipment, all window screens, treatments and hardware, all attached floor coverings and attached lighting fixtures as now installed on said property. Also included are the checked major appliances: range ____, refrigerator ____, dishwasher ____, disposal ____, microwave oven ____, trash compactor ____, washer ____, dryer ____, owned pool equipment ____, ceiling fans ____.   ALL OF THE ABOVE

ADDITIONAL PERSONAL PROPERTY INCLUDED: _____ None - See attached list to be removed.

PERSONAL PROPERTY NOT INCLUDED: ~~See attached list of items Seller will remove~~

LEASED EQUIPMENT: ____none____

Seller represents that the property can be used for the following purposes: __Single Family Home__

2. PURCHASE PRICE IS: (In U.S. funds) . . . . $_550,000._

   METHOD OF PAYMENT:
   (a) Deposit herewith . . . .(paid by check). . . . . $ _50,000._
   (b) Additional deposit due within __20__ United States
       banking days after date of acceptance. Time is of
       the essence as to additional deposit . . . . $ _100,000._
       ALL DEPOSITS TO BE HELD BY: __CUMMINGS REALTY INC.__
   (c) Amount of new note and mortgage to be executed by the Buyer . . . $_____
       to any lender other than the Seller.
       TYPE OF MORTGAGE:
       (CHECK ONE) Conventional (X), FHA ( ), VA ( )
       (CHECK ONE) Fixed Rate ( ), Variable ( )
       Interest Rate _11_%, with initial Monthly Payment of $ __As approved by Buyer__
       Other terms: _____
   (d) Existing mortgage balance encumbering the property $250,000
       to be ASSUMED by the Buyer approximately . . . . $_____
       Name of the mortgagee _____
       Loan No. _____
       At an interest rate which may be changeable to the rate of
       interest at time of closing not to exceed the rate of _____%
       per annum. (CHECK ONE) Fixed rate ( ) or Adjustable rate ( )
       with a maximum ceiling of _____%.
       Buyer is assuming a balloon mortgage. YES ____ NO ____.
       Balloon due date _____.
       Other terms _____ . . . . $ _150,000_
   (e) Purchase money note and mortgage, first ( ) second (X), to Seller
       bearing interest at the rate of _9_% per annum and payable
       $XXXXXXXXXXXXXXXXXXXXXXXXXX interest per _ONLY_ based upon
       an amortization period of _10_ years. If balloon mortgage, final
       maturity date (balloon payment) shall be _10_ years from closing. . . $_____
   (f) OTHER CONSIDERATION: _____
   (g) Balance of funds due from Buyer in the form of U.S. currency, cashier's check or
       equivalent drawn on a Broward County financial institution, on closing and delivery of deed
       (or such greater or lesser amount as may be necessary to complete payment of purchase
       price after credits, adjustments and prorations). Said funds may be held in escrow pursuant
       to provisions of Paragraph U of this contract. . . . . $ _0_

   TOTAL PURCHASE PRICE . . . . $ _550,000_

3. FHA, VA or Condominium Contracts: See required rider attached hereto and made a part hereof which shall control.

4. SPECIAL CLAUSES: See Page __na__ or Addendum, if any.

5. ACCEPTANCE DATE: This offer shall be null and void unless accepted, in writing, and a signed copy received by __JACK Cummings__ on or before __15__ day of __MARCH__, 19_92_ by _12:NOON_ AM/PM.

6. CLOSING DATE: This Contract shall be closed and the deed and possession shall be delivered on or before the __1__ day of __APRIL__, 19_92_, unless extended by other provisions of this Contract or separate agreement.

Form FS-001 (Rev. 8/89)   PAGE 1 OF 4

STANDARDS FOR REAL ESTATE TRANSACTIONS

A. EVIDENCE OF TITLE: The Seller shall, within _____ banking days (ten (10) banking days if this blank is not filled in), order for Buyer a complete abstract of title prepared by a reputable abstract firm purporting to be an accurate synopsis of the instruments affecting the title to real property recorded in the Public Records of that county to the date of this Contract or alternate title information acceptable to Buyer's closing agent, in his sole discretion, showing in Seller a marketable title in accordance with title standards adopted from time to time by the Florida Bar subject only to liens, encumbrances, exceptions or qualification set forth in this Contract, and those which shall be discharged by Seller at or before closing. The abstract shall be delivered at least fifteen (15) days prior to closing. Buyer shall have fifteen (15) days from the date of receiving said abstract of title to examine same. If title is found to be defective, Buyer shall, within said period, notify the Seller in writing, specifying the defects. If the said defects render the title unmarketable, the Seller shall have ninety (90) days from receipt of such notice to cure the defects, and if after said period, Seller shall not have cured the defects, Buyer shall have the option of (1) accepting title as it then is, or (2) demanding a refund of all monies paid hereunder which shall forthwith be returned to the Buyer, and thereupon, the Buyer and Seller shall be released of all further obligations to each other under this Contract.

B. CONVEYANCE: Seller shall convey title to the subject property to Buyer by statutory warranty deed or fiduciary special warranty deed, if applicable, subject to: (1) zoning and/or restrictions and prohibitions imposed by governmental authority; (2) restrictions, easements and other matters appearing on the plat and/or common to the subdivision; (3) taxes for the year of closing; and (4) other matter specified in this Contract, if any.

C. EXISTING MORTGAGES: The Seller shall obtain and furnish a statement from the mortgagee setting forth the principal balance, method of payment, interest rate, and whether the mortgage is in good standing. If there is a charge for the change of ownership, including charges for an assumption fee, and any other costs, exclusive of documentary stamps and recording charges, it shall be borne by the Buyer unless the total charges exceed one percent (1%) of the unpaid balance of the mortgage. In the event the total cost of the above-referred to items exceed one percent (1%) of the unpaid balance of the mortgage to be assumed, then either party shall have the option of paying any amount in excess so that the entire cost is paid, and this Contract shall remain in full force and effect. However, if neither party agrees to pay the additional amount, then, at the Buyer's or Seller's option, this Contract may be cancelled by delivery of written notice to the other party or his agent, the deposit shall be returned to the Buyer and all parties shall be released from all further obligations hereunder.

Buyer shall make application for assumption of the existing mortgage within _____ banking days (five (5) banking days if this blank is not filled in) from the date of this Contract. Buyer agrees to make a good faith, diligent effort to assume the existing mortgage and agrees to execute all documents required by the mortgagee for the assumption of said mortgage. In the event the mortgagee does not give written consent to permit the Buyer to assume the existing mortgage at the rate and terms of payment previously specified, within _____ banking says (twenty (20) banking days from the date of this Contract if this blank is not filled in) then, either party may terminate this Contract by delivery of written notice to the other party or his agent, the deposit shall be returned to the Buyer and all parties shall be released from all further obligations hereunder. This right of termination shall cease upon the Buyer obtaining written approval for assumption of the mortgage prior to the delivery of the notice of termination.

Any variance in the amount of a mortgage to be assumed and the amount stated in the Contract shall be added or deducted from the cash payment. In the event the mortgage balance is more than three percent (3%) less than the amount indicated in the Contract, Seller shall have the option of adjusting the purchase price to an amount where the differential is no more than the three percent (3%) allowed, and if he declines to do so, then either party may terminate this Contract by delivery of written notice to the other party or his agent, the deposit shall be returned to the Buyer and all parties shall be released from all further obligations hereunder. The notice must be given no less than five five (5) days prior to the closing.

D. NEW MORTGAGES: Except as specifically hereinafter provided, any purchase money note and mortgage to Seller shall follow a form with terms generally accepted and used by institutional lenders doing business in the county where the property is located. A purchase money mortgage shall provide for an annual proof of payment of taxes and insurance against loss by fire with extended coverage in an amount not less than the full insurable value of the improvements. A first mortgage and note shall provide for acceleration, at the option of the holder, after thirty (30) days default, and a junior mortgage shall have a ten (10) day default clause. The note shall provide for a late charge of five percent (5%) of the payment due if payment is received by the mortgagee more than ten (10) days after the due date and mortgagee has not elected to accelerate. Junior mortgages shall require the owner of the property encumbered to keep all prior liens and encumbrances in good standing and shall forbid the owner from accepting modifications or future advances under any prior mortgages. Any prepayment shall apply against principal amounts last maturing. In the event Buyer executes a mortgage to one other than the Seller, all costs and charges incidental thereto shall be paid by the Buyer. If this Contract provides for Buyer to obtain a new mortgage, then Buyer's performance under this Contract shall be contingent upon Buyer's obtaining said mortgage financing upon the terms stated, or if none are stated, then upon the terms generally prevailing at such time in the county where the property is located. The Buyer agrees to apply within _____ banking days (five (5) banking days if this blank is not filled in) and to make a good faith, diligent effort to obtain the mortgage financing. In the event a commitment for said financing is not obtained within _____ banking days (thirty (30) banking days if this blank is not filled in) from the date of this Contract, then either party may terminate this Contract by delivery of written notice to the other party or his agent, the deposit shall be returned to the Buyer and all parties shall be released from all further obligations hereunder. This right of termination shall cease upon the Buyer obtaining a written commitment letter for mortgage financing at the rate and terms of payment previously specified herein prior to the delivery of the notice of termination.

E. ASSIGNMENT: This Contract is not assignable without the specific written consent of the Seller if new mortgage financing or an assumption of an existing mortgage is a contingency.

F. SURVEY: The Buyer, within the time allowed for delivery of evidence of title and examination thereof, may have the property surveyed at his expense. If the survey shows any encroachment on said property or shows the improvements located on the subject property in fact encroach on adjoining property, or violate any of the covenants herein, the same shall be treated as a title defect.

G. INSPECTIONS: The Buyer shall have the right to have the following inspections at Buyer's expense, subject to the provisions of paragraphs 1-5 below. Seller agrees to provide access and utilities for inspection upon reasonable notice. Seller's agent has the right to be present at inspection and should be given reasonable notice of the date and time of inspections. All inspections shall be completed and written reports submitted to Seller upon completion but not later than _____ days prior to the closing (ten (10) days if blank not filled in). However, the Buyer is entitled to a walk through inspection immediately prior to closing to check the items below to ensure no major functional defects have occurred subsequent to the professional inspections and compliance with subparagraphs below.

   1. Termite: The Buyer shall have the right to have the property inspected by a licensed exterminating company to determine whether there is any active termite or wood-destroying organism present in any improvements on said property or any damage from prior termite or wood-destroying organism to said improvements. If there is any such infestation or damage, the Seller shall pay all costs of treatment and repairing and/or replacing all portions of said improvements which are infested or have been damaged subject to paragraph 5 below.

   2. General: The Buyer shall have the right to have a roof, seawall, pool, electric, plumbing, appliance, machinery, structural and environmental inspection made by persons or companies qualified and licensed to perform such services. If such inspection reveals functional defects (as differentiated from aesthetic defects), Seller shall pay all costs of repairing said defects subject to paragraph 5 below.

   3. Escrow for Repairs: If treatment, replacement or repair called for in subparagraphs 1 and 2 hereof are not completed prior to closing, sufficient funds shall be escrowed at time of closing to effect same.

   4. Reinspection: In the event the Seller disagrees with Buyer's inspection reports, Seller shall have the right to have inspections made at his cost. In the event Buyer's and Seller's inspection reports do not agree, as submitted to all parties, the parties shall agree on a third inspector, whose report shall be binding upon the parties. The cost of the third inspector shall be borne equally between the Buyer and Seller.

   5. Limitation and Option Clause: Seller shall be responsible for all costs of the above treatment, replacement or repairs up to $_____ (or 2% of the purchase price if this blank is not filled in). In the event the total costs of items to be accomplished under subparagraphs 1, 2 and 3 exceed this amount, then either party shall have the option of paying any amount in excess and this Contract shall then remain in full force and effect. However, if neither party agrees to pay the additional amount above the dollar or applicable percentage of the purchase price, then, at the Seller's or Buyer's option, this Contract shall be cancelled by delivery of written notice to the other party or his agent, and the deposit shall be returned to Buyer.

H. ENVIRONMENTAL CONDITION: Seller is not aware of any prior or existing environmental condition, situation or incident on, at, or concerning the subject property or any adjacent property that may give rise as against Seller or the subject property to an action or to liability under any law, rule, ordinance or common law theory. This representation shall survive the closing.

I. RADON GAS: Radon is a naturally occurring radioactive gas that, when it has accumulated in a building in sufficient quantities, may present health risks to persons who are exposed to it over time. Levels of radon that exceed federal and state guidelines have been found in buildings in Florida. Additional information regarding radon and radon testing may be obtained from your county public health unit.

J. INSURANCE: The premium on any hazard or flood insurance policy in force covering improvements on the subject property, shall be prorated between the parties, or the policy may be cancelled as the Buyer may elect. If insurance is to be prorated, the Seller shall, on or before the closing date, furnish to the Buyer all insurance policies or copies thereof. The Buyer has the option of accepting or rejecting any continuation of service contract if accepted, the charge thereof shall be prorated providing the service contract is assignable to Buyer. Any transfer fee shall be borne by the Buyer.

K. LEASES: The Seller shall, ten (10) days prior to closing, furnish to Buyer copies of all written leases and estoppel letters from each tenant specifying the nature and duration of said tenant's occupancy, rental rate, advance rents or security deposits paid by tenant. In the event Seller is unable to obtain estoppel letters from tenants, the same information may be furnished by Seller to Buyer in the form of a seller's affidavit. Unless indicated under special clauses, at closing there shall be no lease or right of occupancy encumbering the property.

L. SELLER'S AFFIDAVIT: Seller shall furnish to Buyer at time of closing an affidavit attesting to the absence of any claims of lien or potential lienors known to Seller. If the property has been improved within ninety (90) days prior to closing, Seller shall deliver to Buyer an affidavit setting forth names and addresses of all contractors, subcontractors, suppliers and materialmen and stating that all bills for work on subject property have been paid, and Buyer may require releases of all such potential liens. Furthermore, the affidavit shall state that there are no matters pending against the affiant that could give rise to a lien that would attach to the property between the disbursing of the closing funds and the recording of the instrument of conveyance, and that Seller has not, and will not, execute any instrument that could adversely affect the title to the property.

M. PLACE OF CLOSING: Closing shall be held at the office of the Buyer's closing agent, if located within the county where the property is located, and if not, then at the office of Seller's agent, if located within the county where the property is located, and if not, then at such place as mutually agreed upon.

N. DOCUMENTS FOR CLOSING: Seller shall prepare and provide deed, purchase money mortgage, mortgage note, bill of sale, Seller's affidavits regarding liens, FIRPTA affidavit, survey or affidavit regarding coastal construction control line, F.S. 161.57, if applicable, and any corrective instruments that may be required in connection with perfecting the title. Buyer's closing agent shall prepare closing statement.

O. EXPENSES: Abstracting prior to closing, state documentary stamps which are required to be affixed to the instrument of conveyance and the cost of recording any corrective instruments, shall be paid by the Seller. Intangible personal property taxes and documentary stamps to be affixed to the purchase money mortgage, if any, or required on any mortgage modification and the cost of recording the deed and purchase money mortgage shall be paid by the Buyer.

P. PRORATION OF TAXES (REAL AND PERSONAL): Taxes shall be prorated on the current year's tax, if known. If the closing occurs at a date when the current year's taxes are not fixed, and the current year's assessment is available, taxes will be prorated based upon such assessment and the prior year's millage. If the current year's assessment is not available, then taxes will be prorated on the prior year's tax; provided, however, if there are completed improvements on the subject premises by January 1st of the year of closing, which improvements were not in existence on January 1st of the prior year, then the taxes shall be prorated to the date of closing based upon the prior year's millage and at an equitable assessment to be agreed upon between the parties, failing which, requests will be made to the county tax assessor for an informal assessment taking into consideration homestead exemption, if any. However, any tax proration based on an estimate may, at the request of either party to the transaction, be subsequently readjusted upon receipt of tax bill, and this agreement shall survive the closing. All such prorations whether based on actual tax or estimated tax will make appropriate allowance for the maximum allowable discount and for homestead or other exemptions if allowed for the current year.

Q. PRORATIONS AND ESCROW BALANCE: Taxes, insurance, assumed interest, utilities, rents, and other expenses and revenue of said property shall be prorated through the day prior to closing. In the event that Buyer assumes mortgage, Seller shall receive as credit at closing an amount equal to the escrow funds held by the mortgagee, which funds shall thereupon be transferred to the Buyer.

R. SPECIAL ASSESSMENT LIENS: Certified, confirmed and ratified special assessment liens through the day prior to closing (and not as of the date of this Contract) are to be paid by the Seller. Pending liens as of the date of closing shall be assumed by the Buyer.

S. RISK OF LOSS: If the improvements are damaged by fire or other casualty before delivery of the deed and can be restored to substantially the same condition as now existing within a period of sixty (60) days thereafter, Seller may restore the improvments and the closing date and date of delivery of possession herein before provided shall be extended accordingly. If Seller fails to do so, the Buyer shall have the option of (1) taking the property as is together with insurance proceeds, if any, or (2) cancelling the Contract and all deposits will be forthwith returned to the Buyer and the parties released of any further liability hereunder.

T. MAINTENANCE: Between the date of the Contract and the date of closing, the property, including lawn, shrubbery and pool, if any, shall be maintained by the Seller in the condition as it existed as of the date of the Contract, ordinary wear and tear excepted.

U. ESCROW OF PROCEEDS OF SALE AND CLOSING PROCEDURE: The deed shall be recorded and evidence of the title continued at Buyer's expense, to show title in Buyer, without any encumbrances or changes which would render Seller's title unmarketable, from the date of the last evidence and the cash proceeds of sale may be held in escrow by Seller's attorney or by such other escrow agent as may be mutually agreed upon for a period of not longer than ten (10) days. If Seller's title is rendered unmarketable, Buyer's closing agent shall, within said ten (10) day period, notify Seller or Seller's attorney in writing of the defect, and Seller shall have thirty (30) days from date of receipt of such notice to cure said defect and shall use best efforts to do so. In the event Seller fails to timely cure said defect, all monies paid hereunder by Buyer shall, upon written demand therefor, and within five (5) days thereafter, be returned to Buyer and, simultaneously with such repayment, Buyer shall vacate the premises and reconvey the property in question to the Seller by special warranty deed. In the event Buyer fails to make timely demand for refund, he shall take title as is, waiving all rights against Seller as to such intervening defect except such rights as may be available to Buyer by virtue of warranties contained in deed. Possession and occupancy will be delivered to Buyer at time of closing. The broker's professional service fee shall be disbursed simultaneously with disbursement of Seller's closing proceeds. Payment shall be made in the form of U.S. currency, local cashier's check, local certified check, unless in the event a portion of the purchase price is to be derived from institutional financing or refinancing, the requirements of the lending institution as to place, time and procedures for closing and for disbursement of mortgage proceeds shall control, anything in this Contract to the contrary notwithstanding.

The foregoing notwithstanding, if title insurance is available, at standard rates insuring Buyer as to any title defects arising between the effective date of title binder and recording of Buyer's deed, proceeds of sales shall be disbursed to the Seller at closing.

V. ESCROW: The party receiving the deposit agrees by the acceptance thereof to hold same in escrow and to disburse it in accordance with the terms and conditions of this Contract. Provided, however, that in the event a dispute shall arise between any of the parties to this Contract as to the proper disbursement of the deposit, the party holding the deposit may, at his option: (1) take no action and hold all funds (and documents, if any) until agreement is reached between the disputing parties, or until a judgment has been entered by a court of competent jurisdiction and the appeal period has expired thereon, or if appealed then until the matter has been finally concluded, and then to act in accordance with such final judgment; or (2) institute an action for declaratory judgment, interpleader or otherwise joining all affected parties and thereafter complying with the ultimate judgment of the court with regard to the disbursement of the deposit and disposition of documents, if any. In the event of any suit between Buyer and Seller wherein the escrow agent is made a party by virtue of acting as such escrow agent hereunder, or in the event of any suit wherein escrow agent interpleads the subject matter of this escrow, the escrow agent shall be entitled to recover all attorney's fees and costs incurred, including costs and attorney's fees for appellate proceeding, if any, said fees and costs to be charged and assessed as court costs in favor of the prevailing party.

W. ATTORNEY FEES AND COSTS: In connection with any arbitration or litigation arising out of this Contract, the prevailing party, whether Buyer, Seller or brokers, shall be entitled to recover all costs incurred including attorney's fees and legal assistant fees for services rendered in connection therewith, including appellate proceedings and postjudgment proceedings.

X. DEFAULT: In the event of default of either party, the rights of the non-defaulting party and the broker shall be as provided herein and such rights shall be deemed to be the sole and exclusive rights in such event; (a) If Buyer fails to perform any of the covenants of this Contract, all money paid or deposited pursuant to this Contract by the Buyer shall be retained by or for the account of the Seller as consideration for the execution of this Contract as agreed and liquidated damages and in full settlement of any claims for damages and specific performance by the Seller against the Buyer. (b) If Seller fails to perform any of the covenants of this Contract, all money paid or deposited pursuant to this Contract by the Buyer shall be returned to the Buyer upon demand, or the Buyer shall have the right of specific performance. In addition, Seller shall pay forthwith to broker the full professional service fee provided for in this Contract.

Y. CONTRACT NOT RECORDABLE AND PERSONS BOUND: The benefits and obligations of the covenants herein shall inure to and bind the respective heirs, representatives, successors and assigns (when assignment permitted) of the parties hereto. Whenever used, the singular number shall include the plural, the plural the singular, and the use of any gender shall include all genders. Neither this contract nor any notice shall be recorded in any public records.

Z. SURVIVAL OF COVENANTS AND SPECIAL COVENANTS: Seller covenants and warrants that there is ingress and egress to subject property over public or private roads or easements, which covenants shall survive delivery of deed. No other provision, covenant or warranty of this Contract shall survive the delivery of the deed except as expressly provided herein.

FINAL AGREEMENT: This Contract represents the final agreement of the parties and no agreements or representations, unless incorporated into this Contract, shall be binding on any of the parties. Typewritten provisions shall supersede printed provisions and handwritten provisions shall supercede typewritten and/or printed provisions. Such handwritten or typewritten provisions as are appropriate may be inserted on this form or attached hereto as an addendum. The date of this Contract shall be the day upon which it becomes fully executed by all parties.

SPECIAL CLAUSES:

BUYER HAS A PERIOD OF 20 WORKING DAYS TO OBTAIN AND ACCEPT THE
TERMS OF THE NEW MORTGAGE OF $250,000 shown on the other page of
this contract. Unless approved then this agreement is null and
void and each party is herein after released from further obligations
to each other. Within the same time period the Buyer has the right
ro review and accept all the personal items which the Seller is to
remove from the property. Unless approved by the Buyer this agreement
will likewise be null and void.

All parties are advised that the I.R.S. code requires the Buyer to withhold ten percent (10%) of the sales price for tax on sales by certain foreigners. The tax will be withheld unless affidavits of compliance with the I.R.S. code or an I.R.S. qualifying statement are provided to Buyer at closing.

Executed by Buyer
on ___March 5,_____, 19_92_ Time: _1:00pm_

BUYER _____ (SEAL)

Social Security or Tax I.D. # _____

BUYER _____ (SEAL)

Social Security or Tax I.D. # _____

Deposit received on ____MARCH 5,_____, 19_92_ to be held subject to this Contract; if check, subject to clearance.

By: ___STEVEN WEIL_____ By: _____
           Escrow Agent   Steven Weil

ACCEPTANCE OF CONTRACT & PROFESSIONAL SERVICE FEE: The Seller hereby approves and accepts the offer contained herein

and recognizes _____CUMMINGS REALTY OF FORT LAUDERDALE_____
_____,

Address: 2669 East Commercial Blvd. Ft. Lauderdale, Fl 33308 Phone No. (305) 771-6300

AND _____

Address: _____ Phone No. _____

as Broker(s) in this transaction.

(CHECK and COMPLETE THE ONE APPLICABLE)

(   ) IF A WRITTEN LISTING AGREEMENT IS CURRENTLY IN EFFECT:
        Seller agrees to pay the Broker named above including cooperating sub-agents named, according to the terms of an existing, separate written agreement;

OR

(X) IF NO WRITTEN LISTING AGREEMENT IS CURRENTLY IN EFFECT:
        Seller shall pay the Broker(s) named above, at the time of closing, from the disbursements of the proceeds of the sale, compensation in the amount of (COMPLETE ONLY ONE) __7__ % of gross purchase price OR $_____, for Broker(s) services in effecting the sale by finding the Buyer ready willing and able to purchase pursuant to the foregoing Contract.

        If Buyer fails to perform and deposit(s) is retained, 50% thereof, but not exceeding the Broker's fee above provided, shall be paid Broker, as full consideration for Broker's services including costs expended by Broker, and the balance shall be paid to Seller.

Executed by Seller
on _____, 19____ Time: _____

SELLER _____ (SEAL)

Social Security or Tax I.D. # _____

SELLER _____ (SEAL)

Social Security or Tax I.D. # _____

BE ADVISED: When this agreement has been completely executed, it becomes a legally binding instrument.
The form of this "Deposit Receipt and Contract for Sale and Purchase" has been approved by the
Broward County Bar Association and the Fort Lauderdale Area Board of REALTORS® Inc.

REVISED 8/89

Each contract form has a section containing the standards that are common to that kind of property. In my exchange offers, I use these standards along with a simple exchange form. I have a blank form of the first part of the agreement in my computer, and I simply fill in the details of the offer, modifying specific paragraphs to suit the situation and the desired offer. (I recommend that you invest in a computer and a good word-processing program. Later on, as you get more sophisticated with property ownership you can add a database program, as well as real estate management software, to help you keep track of your property. More on computers later in this chapter.) When I have completed the initial portion of the offer I attach appropriate "standards" taken from the previously shown Board of Realtor contracts. A sample of my blank agreement follows:

Sample 4: Author's Simple Exchange Offer

```
JUNE 15, 1992                         CUMMINGS/

_____            DATE CLOSED:_____

            AGREEMENT TO EXCHANGE

FIRST PARTY The undersigned, JACK CUMMINGS
and or his assigns and hereinafter called FIRST PARTY, does
agree to exchange to the SECOND PARTY the following:
FIRST PROPERTY:

Subject to the following debt:

In addition the FIRST PARTY agrees to pay to the SECOND PARTY,
at closing of this exchange, the following:
_____


SECOND PARTY The undersigned, _____
and or his/their assigns and hereinafter called SECOND PARTY,
does agree to exchange to the FIRST PARTY the following:
SECOND PROPERTY:

Subject to the following debt:

In addition the SECOND PARTY agrees to pay to the FIRST PARTY,
at closing of this exchange, the following:
_____


            TERMS AND CONDITIONS

1. IRS 1031 EXCHANGE  It is the intention of the FIRST PARTY
that this agreement meet the requirements of the United States
Internal Revenue Section 1031 exchange and both parties agree to
cooperate with any documentation required at or prior to the
closing.

2. STANDARDS  Attached to this agreement are STANDARDS which are
common to real estate closings of this area. In that these stan-
dards refer to "buyer" and "seller" these terms shall apply in
that each party shall be treated as a "buyer" of that property
received and as a "seller" of that property given up. These
terms do not alter the provisions shown in paragraph 1 of these
terms and conditions.
```

3. INSPECTIONS OF THE PROPERTY TO BE RECEIVED The FIRST PARTY has a period of _____ days following the acceptance of this agreement by the SECOND PARTY to review the following: A recent survey of the subject SECOND PROPERTY, all leases, service and employment contracts and other documentation which may be listed herein, and to make inspections of the subject property as mentioned in the attached STANDARDS but not limited to those inspections. This agreement will become null and void unless the FIRST PARTY has accepted in writing the reviews and inspections called for in this paragraph by NOON OF THE _____ DAY following the date this agreement has been fully executed by both parties, and each party will therein after be released from any further obligation to each and the other and all deposits which are a part of this agreement will be returned. The SECOND PARTY may inspect the FIRST PROPERTY prior to execution of this agreement and the FIRST PARTY will cooperate to provide access to the property and any reasonable request for documentation on the subject property. Failure of the SECOND PARTY to execute the agreement before the date shown in paragraph 7 shall cause this agreement to be null and void.

4. CLOSING The closing of title for this exchange shall take place at a place to be determined by the FIRST PARTY, said location to be in the City of _____, State of Florida. The location will be selected no sooner than 30 days prior to the closing. The closing date shall be _____

5. BROKERS AND BROKER COMMISSIONS The FIRST PARTY is a registered real estate broker doing business with his own account and herein agrees that no fee is due to the First Party nor is any Fee to be paid by the FIRST PARTY to any other broker. The SECOND PARTY agrees to indemnify the FIRST PARTY against any legal action to collect a fee from the FIRST PARTY.

6. RECORDATION OF THIS AGREEMENT Both parties agree that this agreement shall not be recorded.

7. VALID CONTRACT Unless this agreement is fully executed by both parties on or before NOON the _____ day of _____ 199___ then the agreement is withdrawn and shall become null and void and all deposits shown returned.

8. OTHER TERMS AND CONDITIONS

WITNESS HERETO   DATE _____

_____   _____

                                                                       FIRST PARTY

WITNESS HERETO   DATE _____

_____   _____

                                                                       SECOND PARTY

To show you what a full exchange offer might look like, review the following offer which has been placed on my blank with the appropriate standards attached. My form has been modified slightly to take into account the special circumstances.

On January 15, 1992, Bill Gallagher offers to exchange a condominium apartment he owns in Miami, Florida, for a duplex in Atlanta, Georgia, owned by Harry Johns. The condominium has a first mortgage against it of $32,000, payable at $329.10 per month for approximately 20 years at 12 percent per annum. The duplex is free and clear, but to balance the equities Johns will hold a purchase money mortgage for $55,000, payable interest only for 12 years at 10 percent per annum, annual payments of $5,500.

The other details such as legal description and additional details are shown on the contract.

Sample 5: Author's Simple Exchange Agreement

```
JANUARY 15, 1992                              GALLAGHER/JOHNS

MIAMI CONDO/ATLANTA, GA. DUPLEX        Date Closed: _____
```

AGREEMENT TO EXCHANGE

FIRST PARTY The undersigned, BILL GALLAGHER and/or his/their assigns and hereinafter called FIRST PARTY, does agree to exchange to the SECOND PARTY the following:

FIRST PROPERTY: Apartment 205, Vista Atlantico, a 2 bedroom condominium apartment, with parking places 88 and 89, located at 355 Atlantic Road, Miami Beach, Florida. Unfurnished except for refrigerator, central air and heat, range, dishwasher, clothes washer and dryer, water heater and wall to wall carpets as in place.

Subject to the following debt: A first mortgage held by Miami Federal Savings and Loan in the amount of $32,000 payable at $329.10 per month for 20 years at 12 percent per annum. Assumable at a fee of $100.00 paid by Second Party.

In addition the FIRST PARTY agrees to pay to the SECOND PARTY, at closing of this exchange, the following:

```
_____   $ 100.000   _____
```

SECOND PARTY The undersigned, HARRY JOHNS, and or his/their assigns and hereinafter called SECOND PARTY, does agree to exchange to the FIRST PARTY the following:

SECOND PROPERTY: A duplex (2 bedroom 2 bath each side) located at 7789 Peachtree Lane, Atlanta, Ga. on Lot 17 Block H, Peachtree Subdivision # 9. Each side of the duplex is unfurnished except for central air and gas heat, water heater. This is a new building and is uninhabited, no leases in effect.

Subject to the following debt: SECOND PARTY to hold a Purchase money first mortgage of $55,000 payable in annual installments of interest only at 10 percent per annum, for 12 years. Principal may be paid in part or in full without penalty. Said mortgage to be common to the area with a 30 day grace period, with no sale or lease longer than 4 years allowed without the Mortgagee's approval.

TERMS AND CONDITIONS

1. IRS 1031 EXCHANGE It is the intention of the FIRST PARTY that this agreement meet the requirements of the United States Internal Revenue Section 1031 exchange and both parties agree to cooperate with any documentation required at or prior to the closing.

2. STANDARDS Attached to this agreement are STANDARDS which are common to real estate closings of this area. In that these standards refer to "buyer" and "seller" these terms shall apply in that each party shall be treated as a "buyer" of that property received and as a "seller" of that property given up. These terms do not alter the provisions shown in paragraph 1 of these terms and conditions.

3. INSPECTIONS OF THE PROPERTY TO BE RECEIVED The FIRST PARTY has a period of 30 days following the acceptance of this agreement by the SECOND PARTY to review the following: A recent survey of the subject SECOND PROPERTY, all leases, service and employment contracts and other documentation which may be listed herein, and to make inspections of the subject property as mentioned in the attached STANDARDS but not limited to those inspections. This agreement will become null and void unless the FIRST PARTY has accepted in writing the reviews and inspections called for in this paragraph by NOON OF THE 30th DAY following the date this agreement has been fully executed by both parties, and each party will therein after be released from any further obligation to each and the other and all deposits which are a part of this agreement will be returned. The SECOND PARTY may inspect the FIRST PROPERTY prior to execution of this agreement and the FIRST PARTY will cooperate to provide access to the property and any reasonable request for documentation on the subject property. Failure of the SECOND PARTY to execute the agreement before the date shown in paragraph 7 shall cause this agreement to be null and void.

4. CLOSING The closing of title for this exchange shall take place at a place to be determined by the FIRST PARTY, said location to be in the City of MIAMI, State of Florida. The location will be selected no sooner than 30 days prior to the closing. The closing date shall be ON OR BEFORE MARCH 31, 1992 as selected by the FIRST PARTY.

5. BROKERS AND BROKER COMMISSIONS The FIRST PARTY is a registered real estate broker doing business with his own account and herein agrees that no fee is due to the First Party nor is any

Fee to be paid by the FIRST PARTY to any other broker. The SEC-
OND PARTY agrees to indemnify the FIRST PARTY against any legal
action to collect a fee from the FIRST PARTY.

6. RECORDATION OF THIS AGREEMENT Both parties agree that this
agreement shall not be recorded.

7. VALID CONTRACT Unless this agreement is fully executed by
both parties on or before NOON the 30 day of JANUARY 1992 then
the agreement is withdrawn and shall become null and void and
all deposits shown returned.

8. OTHER TERMS AND CONDITIONS:

ONLY THOSE SHOWN ON THE ATTACHED STANDARDS - WHERE IN CONFLICT
THE PROVISIONS SHOWN HERE SHALL RULE. GENERAL STANDARDS contain
provisions for exchange of Duplex to Gallagher and CONDOMINIUM
STANDARDS contain provisions for exchange of Condominium to
Johns.

WITNESS HERETO   DATE: JANUARY 15, 1992

_____   _____
                                 BILL GALLAGHER - FIRST PARTY

WITNESS HERETO   DATE _____

_____   _____
                                 HARRY JOHNS - SECOND PARTY

Get Sound Legal Advice

Real estate contracts of any kind are serious business and can bind you to legal and financial obligations that you may not understand and that can become very expensive. You should know exactly what the contract says and where your obligations and liabilities are, and all the consequences, should you default on the agreement. Because of this I recommend that you establish your own offer format which will provide you with a "fill-in" form so you can crank out many offers. The best way to ensure that you are using the right kind of fill-in form is to do the following.

How to Develop a Good Fill-in Offer Form

1. Start with local Board of Realtor contracts. Get a Realtor, broker, or sales-
    man to show you the usual standard forms of contracts used in your area.
    Make sure that you understand every term used and how the different provi-
    sions contained in those contracts apply to each party. This is a learning
    stage for you so that later on, when you are talking to your lawyer, you will
    know what he or she is talking about.

2. Pick a good **real estate lawyer.** To find one ask around different real estate firms, explain that you are new to investing in this area and would like to meet several different real estate lawyers. After you have the names of several, set up appointments explaining that you are new to investing in real estate in this area (no need to explain you don't own any), and that you want to select a lawyer to represent you in future transactions. Generally a first appointment such as this would not cost you anything, but make sure that is understood before you go to the meeting.

At the meeting explain that you plan to make many offers that real estate and do not want to waste time by having the lawyer read and approve every offer prior to your making it. Present several of the local board offers which you have already become acquainted with and ask which ones would be most suitable and what would have to be added as **an escape clause** to allow you to make offers but not be bound until you are ready to commit to the property.

You should have three forms of offers that can be used as a template.

The 3 Template Offers to Develop

1. The letter of intent
2. The offer to purchase
3. The offer to exchange

In each of the above situations I urge you to make the offer appear as standard as possible. If the local Board of Realtors has a standard exchange form, use it as well as the standard offer to purchase.

The importance of the escape clause. The key to an escape clause is a provision that gives you the right to inspect any or all of the property following the commitment by the other party, during which allocated time you can still reject the deal. An escape clause gives you the opportunity to make offers without having to spend days or weeks or even months studying the property in question. Because your comfort zone will open up many opportunities that "look good" on the surface, you will be able to act on this first look without the fear of making a mistake. Once you tie up the property or get negotiations started you can spend more time looking into the details. Investors who look under every blade of grass prior to making offers generally end up watching other investors buy the property out from under them.

Because you can now make offers without the fear of commitment you will be inclined to offer on more and more properties. As your offers are designed to fit your needs and goals rather than those of the other party, you can expect that your initial offers often will be rejected or countered. Do not assume that your offers will be accepted right from the very first, but do be positive that if the property is good you will end up owning it.

Present your offer properly. You should not present your own offer. An intermediary such as a real estate broker or salesman can absorb the heat of the other party, who may lash out and say something that if said directly to you would put an end to any reasonable relationship between you. Many deals are ended with a simple statement like "This is a stupid offer." A positive attitude is helpful, not only for your self-confidence but to build up confidence in the intermediary who is presenting your offer.

Avoid potential negativity by not being around when the offer is presented. Do not assume from this that you can just mail your offer to the other party and get by that way. It is much better to have someone between you and the other party for best results. Even after 25 years of dealing for other people, I have someone present my offers. When it comes to presenting my offers I am just as quick to fly off the handle as you will be if that wrong slip of the lips finds a tender spot.

A Word About the Letter of Intent

A letter of intent is not really a contract, and will serve mostly as a starting point in some situations. The best circumstance to use the letter of intent would be if you were making an offer to a real estate professional for their own property. "Real estate professional" includes brokers and salesmen, mortgage brokers and bankers, developers and builders, and title insurance companies and members of the legal profession. Each of these "owners" is more apt to respond to you if they are interested in the kind of transaction you are proposing, even though you are not presenting them with a formal contract. Avoid using a letter of intent on other potential sellers or "takers." A letter of intent can be for a purchase or exchange. An example of a letter of intent that I might use follows.

Sample 6: Author's Letter of Intent

```
AUGUST 1, 1992                    CUMMINGS / AABA PROPERTIES

LYONS PARK / RIO VISTA 6     Date Formal Contract: _____
```

LETTER OF INTENT

This letter is to express the intent of JACK CUMMINGS, as FIRST PARTY, to acquire from AABA PROPERTIES INC. herein called SECOND PARTY, a six unit apartment recently constructed in Rio Vista Subdivision in Ft. Lauderdale, Fla., at 3339 Ponce de Leon Blvd.

If the terms and conditions of the proposal are acceptable and the SECOND PARTY indicates that acceptance below, then the FIRST PARTY will, within 15 working days, draft a formal contract (of sale / of exchange), to be presented to the SECOND PARTY for their approval.

It is understood that the formal contract will contain more provisions than shown in this letter of intent and that no binding contract will exist between the parties until the formal agreement to be presented is fully executed.

TERMS AND CONDITIONS

1. The First Party will deliver to the Second Party, at closing, a cashiers check in the amount of $120,000.

2. In addition to the above, the First Party will deed to the Second Party the following real estate:

Lot 12 of Block C, Lyons Industrial Park Sub., a commercial lot,

200' frontage on NW 57 Street, at a depth of 300' zoned B-2 Subject to a first mortgage of $45,000 payable at 9.5 percent for 12 years interest only annually installments.

3. The Second Party will deliver to the First Party the deed to the six unit apartments at 3339 Ponce de Leon Blvd. free and clear of all debt, and with central air and heat, full kitchen appliances and parquet floors in all rooms except garage which have finished concrete floors and bathrooms and kitchens which have Italian tile floors.

4. Unless committed by other agreement, there will be no broker- age fee due from or payable to either party to this transaction from the other.

Submitted: August 1, 1992

_____

JACK CUMMINGS

ACCEPTED BY SECOND PARTY: Subject to a review of and approval of the formal contract to be presented within 15 working days by the FIRST PARTY, or prior sale or withdrawal from the market, the Second Party will accept the above proposal.

Date: _____

_____

AABA PROPERTIES INC.

Computerize for Maximum Results

Why knock yourself out when it would be so easy to crank out the number of offers you should be making by setting up your offer templates on a computer. Sure, you can use forms and fill them in using a typewriter, but each offer will require certain details and terms that you will want to add.

You do not need an expensive computer, in fact, with the prices of excellent computers falling faster than snow in January in Buffalo, you will be able to fully equip yourself in style for less than $1,000. If you look around at some of the local computer shops in your area you might find a real bargain in a used machine that comes loaded with hundreds or even thousands of dollars of software too.

The idea is not to be intimidated by the equipment and the level of sophistication you actually need. To adequately computerize yourself you can do very nicely with the follow- ing items.

Start-up Computer Equipment

1. A basic computer that . . .
    a. is IBM-compatible
    b. has a minimum 20-megabyte hard disk
    c. has at least one floppy drive
    d. has an internal clock with calendar
    e. has parallel port (for printer)
    f. can be expanded to add other items such as a phone modem, color screen, fax card, etc.
    g. has good high-resolution monitor (go to color if you can afford it)
2. Recommended software
    a. WordPerfect (latest version)
    b. A utilities software package (ask dealer)
    c. Latest version of MS-DOS
3. A quality printer (laser-jet or 24-pin dot-matrix)

You will start to add soft- and hardware to your computer as you go along, such as a phone modem, which will allow you to communicate with other computers, or database programs such as REALTRON, or your county tax files. You can even add a fax card, which will turn your computer into a fax machine (with some limitations), a scanner to send anything via the fax, and so on. All these items add to the efficiency of the computer and can make your life much more interesting and trouble-free.

Your software should be kept to the absolute minimum until you master what you are using. Too many people load up with dozens of programs and games and then are burdened with learning how to use the darn things.

The best software programs require effort to learn, and even after months of using most programs you will still be finding additional applications that can smooth out your operations.

WordPerfect, like many other good word processing programs, has "mail merge," or simply "merge." This allows you to build a mailing and phone list, as an example, then write one letter that can become a personalized letter to each person you select from your mailing list.

To expand on this capability you can formulate standard offers or letters of intent that are sent to lists of property owners that you obtain, via your computer, from the local tax roll. Once you have your lists and property descriptions, the computer can print out separate offers or letters of intent to as many people as you tell it to.

Property Information via Computer

Most real estate brokers have one or more property-search databases available to them which they can access with their own computer. If you are going to be a valued client of this broker suggest that they do the searches for you, or, even better for them, that they allow you to access the database with your own computer. Some brokers may ask you to pay a fee for this, and as they are charged for the amount of time they spend in the database this would be understandable. If the data source has limitations on who can use it, you may have to be listed as an associate of that real estate firm. If you must get a real estate license, that is not a bad idea anyway because of the inside information you can gather as well as the commissions you can save.

Once you have a computer you will be able to keep track of every record you need. Every form and report mentioned in this book can be maintained with your computer and you will be thankful that you have made the investment.

Many people do not take the plunge into owning and using a computer because they are intimidated by it or computer salespeople. I admit that both can be intimidating, but you should persist. Insist that the firm that sells you the computer spend some time with you to show you how to use it. Some computer shops that sell software also have videotaped lessons on the software, and almost every software program has a built-in tutorial program, which will get you started in the basics. If you don't want to buy the videotape training program look at your local video rental shop; they may have the very tape you need for an inexpensive weekend rental.

Be a modern real estate investor: take the world by the horns and go for it.

7

The Who, Why, and How of Exchanges

To make the most out of real estate exchanges you should recognize that at any single moment, not everyone who owns property is ready, willing, and able to make an exchange—not with you, not with anyone. However, you should also realize that all property owners are susceptible, under the right circumstances, to making a deal that involves a real estate exchange . . . even an exchange for a property, service or item that they really do not want. In this chapter, I'll tell you who makes exchanges, why, and how you can make more of them.

Finding the Right Candidates for Exchanges

Real estate exchanges are made between two or more parties. Generally, each party can be categorized as one or more of the following seven types:

The Magnificent 7—Types of Parties to Exchange

1. Has not found a buyer.
2. Has a tax problem.
3. No investment connection.
4. Give me anything, I'm ready to make a deal.
5. Can be motivated to make a deal.
6. Is an aggressive investor who understands exchanges.
7. Has nowhere to turn and must save face.

Look at each of these seven categories of prospective deal makers and discover where you can find them and how to deal with them. Keep in mind that you can also be one or all of the above Magnificent Seven at one time or another.

1. Has Not Found a Buyer

The reality of real estate is that there are times when specific properties cannot be sold, even at a bargain price. You could be the most motivated seller in town but if there is no ready buyer for your property then it will not sell. Dropping the price below rock bottom may produce a buyer, but not always—and that is not an economic way to go if there is an alternative route.

Exchanges are a way for you to become a buyer rather than a "stuck-in-the-mud" seller. Yet many sellers do not know how to become buyers, nor do they have the luxury of being able to wait out a lull in the market. The longer their property remains on the market with no buyers in sight, the greater their motivation to sell. As the "sell now" motivation grows, there will be a greater acceptance level to take another property in exchange.

Who wants a white elephant? You may ask yourself the logical question, "If no one else wants to buy this property, why should I?" The answer to this question is the real "insider's secret" to real estate investing and profit making. Remember the **economic conversion?** Well, that is what it's all about. You need to look beyond the property as it is, and see the **benefits** that it can generate. You will always have the greatest success in real property when you buy something that would have greater value if used in some different or expanded way.

The potential for economic conversion does not always stand out like a ripe pumpkin in a field. Most of the time the potential is a simple change. Sometimes the change is not even a change of use, but an expansion of the current use. Add an extra apartment, fix up the property and raise the rents, that sort of thing. As you go through this book, you will begin to see how this investment strategy pays off, and how simple it will be for you once you have your comfort zone working for you.

Owners of unsold property stand out. The property owner with an unsold property is easy to spot. The FOR SALE sign has been in the yard for months, and often the property is vacant and starting to show signs of neglect . . . all signs that the owner is motivated and open to a solution to his problem.

☞ **Key Thought:** Solve Their Problems and You Solve Yours

One of the very best ways to find the anxious seller is to have your broker do a frequent computer search of properties in your comfort zone, to determine how long the unsold properties have been on the market. It is important for you to keep track of this information, because it can also point to a trend in your investment zone, and the data will come in handy when you are making offers. Keep in mind that the computer-generated information will give you only part of the total picture. A property that has been listed for only two months may have been on the market before with another broker. Check back to an earlier computer printout to see if it has been listed by another firm prior to the current listing. You may find a property that the owner has been unable to sell for a long time.

Why properties do not sell. Most properties remain unsold because of a problem with the property, the owner, or the circumstances of ownership. A structural problem that will be costly to fix can be considered a potential deduction from the price, if you can determine in advance the cost of repair. However, many construction problems cannot be so simply estimated and the property may not be salable as long as the problem exists. Personally, I do not recommend you acquire any property with a known structural problem unless you are very experienced in dealing with building construction, and can obtain or accurately estimate the cost to remedy the problem yourself.

A difficult owner or ownership circumstance might be a waste of time to confront. Some owners are just too nasty to deal with and have a completely unrealistic idea of the value of a property. But do not make hasty judgements. Sometimes the real problem is that the owner just does not have time or patience to deal with the property and its problems. People who have professions that consume their free time and occupy their every thought can be quick to want to get rid of a "problem property." Note that these property owners are prime owners with whom you can make deals.

When the property is burdened with a ton of debt or leases that cannot be broken and are half the current rental potential, you will have to weigh very carefully the difficulty or cash flow shortage you will have to deal with to turn the property around. Your experience in this area will grow very quickly.

Owners can be the reason a property doesn't sell. Often, an unsold property is not the fault of the property, the market, or the debt, but of the ownership itself. When the owners are going through personal problems, such as a death, marriage, divorce, birth, or job transfer, events can take place that generate strong motivation to do something, but at the same time remove absolute control of the decision-making process. Under the right circumstances an exchange can provide a way for the decision process to get back on track.

For sale for a year—look at it. When you find property that has been on the market for a long time, take a look at it. As a matter of fact, you should make it a habit to look at any property that has been on the market for 12 months or longer. In some areas with certain kinds of property this time might be six months.

Your real estate broker or salesman can help you find most of these properties. You will see some FOR SALE BY OWNER signs pop up from time to time in your comfort zone, and you should always be the first to show up to see the property. No matter what you think about the property or its price, keep track of its market history, because 12 months later you might become interested in that property at a price or on terms that suit you. The owner may also be motivated sufficiently to react in a positive mode to you then, even if neither of you was interested at first.

The inspection checklist. Whenever you inspect property you should bring an **inspection checklist** that follows. This checklist should be filled out while you are going through the property and filed by property address in your comfort zone files. Keep the inspection checklist in section 5 of your combined ledger of purchases/sales/exchanges described in the previous chapter. When you attempt to make a deal on this property, the inspection checklist will become a part of the property's active file. Even if you are 100 percent turned off by the property and can see no potential in it, be dutiful: fill out the form and keep it. Two years later things can change and something might come your way that makes that property ideal for your needs.

```
Inspection Checklist - Date: _____

  1. Property address:_____
     _____
  2. Owner's name:_____
  3. Owner's motivation:_____
     _____
  4. Legal description:_____
  5. Date listed:_____
  6. Salesman's name and phone:_____
  7. Price: $_____Mortgage amount: $_____
  8. Mortgage terms:_____
  9. Describe property:_____
```

_____

10. Present zoning and use:_____

_____

11. Potential uses:_____

_____

_____

12. Problems with this property:_____

_____

_____

13. Did you like it or not?_____

_____

Tips on Filling Out the Checklist

1. Do it while you are going through the property. This makes you concentrate more on what you are looking at. After you have this for a while you will start to ask the same questions, so that you can make better direct comparisons.

2. Write in pencil so you can make changes.

3. Put the date at the top and get the correct legal description—such as Lot 12 Block 21 of West Hills Subdivision so that you can keep the properties correctly filed and be ready to make offers.

4. Item 5, the date listed, is very important, as it tells you how long that broker has had the property on the market. Ask the salesman, "Was this property listed before?" Possibly the property has been on the market for years, with different brokers for several months each.

5. Item 9, the description of the property, is what you see: condition, repairs, special features, that sort of thing.

6. Ask questions about every item on the checklist that may be of special interest to you.

7. Most important of all: Item 13. Did you like the property? Make a note of why or why not.

2. Has a Tax Problem

More and more real estate owners are faced with large capital gains on which they will have to pay a large tax. This is where the "tax-free exchange" comes to the rescue, and boy-oh-boy, can it save a bundle of money.

Finding a property owner who is faced with this kind of problem is not that difficult. All you have to do is go back to your friendly real estate broker or salesman and look a bit harder at the property records they have access to via their computer. The longer a property owner has held a property the greater the potential increase of value. Most deed or tax records will show the date when the current owner acquired the subject property. A long tenure of ownership is a clue to a potential high gain in the event of a sale.

Take another look at the property records. Public records usually indicate the price, so you should be able to pinpoint the exact price the current owner paid. In some areas of the country the property records may not show the price, but may rather indicate the "transfer tax" paid. Once you know how the transfer tax is calculated you can back into the price. For example, if you see that Jones paid $220 in transfer tax and the tax is $1.10 per thousand, then the transfer was $200,000. (Take the amount of tax paid, $220, divide by 1.10 then multiply by 1,000.) The value of $200,000 may not be accurate because Jones might have increased the tax by overstating the value just to throw off investors like yourself. While this intentional misleading does happen, it is rare.

Some public records may show the original price paid (or the reported price) but not take into consideration additions and improvements made following the purchase. You should ask the broker or the owner if any improvements have been made after the original purchase.

Warning! Improvements should conform to local building codes and comply with required permits. Work done without proper building permits can be improper and against the code. Make sure that all improvements in a property you plan to acquire meet the code and that the work was done legally.

For example, Jones bought a property for $200,000 and spent $100,000 adding a second floor to the building. The work was properly done with a licensed general contractor and all the building permits were properly obtained and paid for. That $100,000 will add to his basis, moving it up $100,000. Deduct from that depreciation, say $160,000 over the next 15 years, and the result is a final basis of $140,000 ($200,000 plus $100,000 less $160,000 = $140,000). If Jones's property is now worth $1,000,000, he will have a gain of $860,000 ($1,000,000 less $140,000 = $860,000). Jones is a prime candidate for an exchange.

These bits of information may not allow you to calculate to the exact penny, since you may not be able to ascertain the improvements made or the depreciation taken, even so the facts will jump off the page: **This guy may have to pay a fortune in income tax if he sells.**

When reviewing properties listed by brokers, you can take advantage of the salesman's desire to make a deal and get a lot of information about the property and the owner. Do this for any property listed for lease or sale in your comfort zone. No matter if that property is of no interest to you, get the information when you can. Several years later you might become interested in that property. If the same owner has the property, you may have some very confidential information about that person's tax situation.

3. No Investment Connection

People end up owning property that they did not seek to buy. It might be they got it as a commission, or a "payment" in lieu of having to foreclose on a loan, or as a gift they could have done without, an inheritance, or under any of a dozen other circumstances. Remember, some "sellers" will take a property they don't want just to make a bigger deal. Look at Phil, who is desperate to get out from under a $200,000 mortgage on an empty warehouse he can't rent, so he takes a $30,000 lot in Shreveport he hasn't seen (and never will) as a part of the transaction. This vacant lot in Shreveport might be a real sleeper that someone can make a killing on, simply by giving Phil something else (that he may also not really want) that is closer to home.

Greater detachment leads to a greater "get rid of" motivation. Sounds logical doesn't it? Well, it is, and it works in exactly that proportion. I'll give you a prime example. Ever think of buying a time-share apartment? Despite what many people say or think about them, I honestly believe that everyone who loves to travel should own at least one. I personally own (as of this date) seven weeks' total. The problem with time-share properties is their price. Most buyers overpay for their weeks because they deal with the emotions of going through the "sales line" and buying direct from the developer. That is where all the markup is, and you can do much better if you read on.

Many time-share developers tend to pay their salesmen a combination of cash and time-share weeks. This procedure may not exist in every time-share project, but to test it out get hold of one or more salesmen from the time-share project you would like to own—if you can make **your** kind of deal. Tell the salesman that you would like to buy direct from an owner but that you will not pay more than half the listed price. You may suddenly find that the salesman is actually the owner of several good weeks and will discount them substantially. As the salesman has no real investment capital tied up in the weeks he owns, his motivation can be very high, and he will often deal for a combination of cash and exchange.

4. Give Me Anything, I'm Ready to Make a Deal

This is either a smart seller or a very anxious seller. Either way, the end result can be an attractive deal because it allows you to move off of something that is doing nothing to move you closer to your goals.

Consider two properties that can provide you with nearly identical benefits. Property A is for sale only, and while it is your first choice you have not been able to nail down the deal. Property B is good and will work for you, but is not even your third or fourth choice. Yet the seller of Property B, or his broker, suggests that the deal could be structured with you giving to the owner some property you have had for 10 years that is a zero benefit to you. To facilitate the deal, the seller agrees to take that property as the total down payment and will hold paper to balance the equities. You take a harder look at Property B, review the total benefits you get, and give up. You make the deal with Property B, even though you would not have done that transaction were it not for the exchange.

I am convinced that most sellers will take something in exchange if they are approached correctly. In later chapters I deal with the sticky subject of presenting the offer. Often the other party must be educated to the benefits of exchanges, and that process can take time. Patience wins out in the long run.

5. Can Be Motivated to Make a Deal

I love these guys. They might start out that morning looking themselves in the eye and saying out loud, "I will never take a trade," and before the day is over they end up owning 50 acres in the middle of Brazil. This person is much like most sellers who, when given the right circumstance, will take something in exchange. The difference is that the "to-be-motivated" seller may actually have a mental block about taking anything in exchange. This is one of the major hurdles you will have to overcome, and for these sellers the exchange often is the "sweetener" that you use just to close the transaction.

"Mr. Dorset, Mr. Cummings says this is his final offer. He will buy your apartment building for $400,000 if you agree to hold a first wrap-around mortgage on the property for $200,000 and will lease to him the land, which represents the other $200,000 of value, for $16,000 per year."

"Tell Mr. Cummings I will not do a deal where I get nothing down. Who does he think I am anyway?"

"Mr. Cummings has agreed to reduce your mortgage to $180,000 and will, at closing, give to you and Mrs. Dorset a $20,000 cruise around the world on the Royal Viking Sun."

If Mr. Dorset takes this deal it is still nothing down for me, because I can go to a barter company who deals in advertising and who has a credit with Royal Viking Line for future cruises. All I have to do is exchange them something for the $20,000 value that Mr. Dorset wanted to see invested.

Your key to motivating Mr. Dorset or any other seller will depend on how much information you have about that person. If the seller will open up to your broker as to what he would like to do after the "sale," it can provide some clues as to ways to motivate the person into a deal.

☞ **Key Word:** Sweetener

You can often close a deal with something the person would not have bought. The world cruise, a new car, jewelry, new carpet for his home, all become items that can put the final touch on the deal.

6. Is an Aggressive Investor Who Understands Exchanges

Knowledgeable investors who know the advantages of exchanges are far more accessible than the novice who is scared of his own shadow when it comes to deal making. You will find that the aggressive exchanger might also be very easy to find because he might seek you out before you find him.

Do not assume that all real estate investors know about exchanges. Most investors do not get involved in exchanges because they deal in the conventional real estate market. That is, they list their property with a real estate company to be sold. As most conventional real estate brokers and salesmen do not know how to put a real estate exchange together, this fantastic tool is lost to that investor. Nonetheless a knowledgeable investor will be more receptive to a creative concept such as exchanges, and will listen to the logic of the deal. Exchange clubs, which exist in many areas, are a good source of knowledgeable exchanges. In a later chapter I will give you the secrets to dealing with professional exchangers and exchange clubs, as well as how to start your own club.

7. Has Nowhere to Turn and Must Save Face

The ultimate rationalization to a real estate exchange may very well be that the deal offered provides a way out without failure. Let's face things as they are: we live in a tough society where no one wants to be labeled a failure. In real estate you "fail" by making a bad investment. It makes little difference if the events turned against you through no fault of your own; in short, there is no "bad luck" in real estate, only bad timing.

As many exchange offers do not involve "price," or even values, for that matter, who's to say that one side of the deal had to take a loss and was forced to bail out of the deal (i.e., fail as a real estate investor)?

To some degree, all investors have a bit of this "fear-of-being-labeled-a-failure" syndrome lurking in the back of their minds. When the market is tight and no one is ready to buy, given a choice between two offers—one where you clearly took a beating, and another where you seem to get out whole—the second will likely be accepted. Because exchanges do not **broadcast the price you or the other side had to take,** the value aspect of the transaction does not get in the way of acceptance.

Using this strategy is very touchy, as there can be no hint that the exchange will allow one party or the other to save face. Nonetheless, when you find a situation where the seller is concerned at what others may think about the deal, you can bet that this person is looking for a way out. The exchange can put you on your way in.

Looking for and Finding Owners Who Will Exchange

You will have to consider two factors: (1) the kind of property you want to own, and (2) the potential source of "insiders" who may have ownership of that kind of property. The first factor will be decided by your comfort zone and the goals you are attempting to achieve. The second factor will be your ability to access what I call the **prolific dozen**.

The Prolific Dozen—The Primary Source of Exchanges

1. Realtors	7. Doctors
2. Developers	8. Mortgage brokers
3. Lawyers	9. Heirs
4. CPA S	10. Known investors
5. Bankers	11. Exchange clubs
6. The newly divorced	12. Transferred to new job

The prolific dozen is the bank of property owners you will look at for motivated property sellers. At this point you are not looking for exchanges; you are looking for sellers ready, willing, and able to make a deal with you on terms that suit your abilities and needs and move you closer to your goals.

Because there will be many motivated sellers, you will do best if you learn quickly to avoid the unmotivated seller. Let your broker or salesman waste his or her time trying to knock on doors that go unanswered (most people don't know it is opportunity knocking).

How to Contact the Prolific Dozen

As you are working within a geographic area, it will be easy to isolate the prolific dozen you should contact. With few exceptions they will actually live in the area you have chosen as your comfort zone.

The 10-Step Program

To maximize your results in contacting property owners, and in particular members of the prolific dozen, follow the **10-Step Program** to establish yourself as a real estate investor, which will assume that you have already accomplished the basics of your investment strategy. Prior to beginning the 10-Step Program, review your status as a budding real estate investor.

Getting Ready for the 10-Step Program

1. Have you established your goals?
2. Have you selected your comfort zone?
3. Have you put together your investment team?
4. Have you determined what kind of real estate you want to acquire?
5. Have you begun to put your records in order?
6. Have you reviewed your goals daily?

If all is in order you are ready to move into the big time. The intermediate goal of the 10-Step Program is to expose you to opportunity and to create the potential that you represent opportunity for others. Investing in real estate does not have to be a lonely job; in fact, the greater your exposure to the market and the "insiders", the faster you will become an insider yourself.

The 10 Steps to Establish Yourself as a Real Estate Investor

1. Compile a mailing list.
2. Divide the mailing list into different categories.
3. Plan three mailings to each category.
4. Do phone follow-up.
5. Keep good progress records.
6. Set aside specific days for property inspections.
7. Be ready to make offers.
8. Advertise your successes.
9. Expand your comfort zone.
10. Acquire more property.

Take a look at each of the steps in detail by following a real estate investor who, like you, is using this program. To set the stage, Charlie Sopkins has decided to augment his income with real estate investments. He has reviewed his goals and knows that the best kind of property for him to own will be commercial properties like strip stores and small office buildings. He wants to keep an open mind about this, and expects to expand into other kinds of investments as he grows familiar with the property in his comfort zone.

Charlie has chosen a geographic area around where he lives, and has had a real estate broker become a member of his investment team. The broker has agreed to help Charlie in hopes of making a sale or two.

The geographic area itself consists of fewer than a thousand property owners. Because Charlie is looking for commercial properties, he has selected several "business" streets where the majority of properties fall into his desired property category.

Step 1. How to Compile a Mailing List

Using a deed search available through his real estate broker, Charlie obtains a property-by-property printout. Not only does this give him the name of the owner and the owner's address, but in most communities it also contains a wealth of additional information, including the owner's phone number, alternate business address and phone numbers, date purchased, price paid, tax assessment, breakdown between land and improvements, legal address, date improvements were made, previous owner, and other such information.

Charlie also goes through a cross-reference directory to add to this list members of the prolific dozen who may not actually own property in the area, but who work within the zone. The reason for this is to add to your list anyone from the prolific dozen's possible spheres of influence who may be of assistance to you. The cross-reference directory is a book that lists names the way a phone book does, but in addition provides a listing by street where you can get the names and phone numbers of people along any given street within the desired area—and by phone number. Most city libraries have these books, as do many real estate companies, check-cashing companies, and credit bureaus.

Let Your Computer Do the Hard Work

Using a word-processing program such as WordPerfect. Charlie can quickly create a computer file that contains the following information, which can be used to create mailing lists, information reports, and so on. Once the data is placed in a "field" you can access it as needed, for example, to print out a list of your entire file using only Fields 1, 2, and 3. This printout can be directed to mailing labels, or envelopes. In another form, you could print out only Fields 1, 5, and 6 to get a quick look at the property owners in your area and the kind of property they own. If you selected to code Item 6 to allow you to be specific with one word, say "strip-6" (meaning a strip store building less than 6,000 but more than 5,000 square feet), you could ask your computer to print out all information for properties with the description "strip-6".

Essential Data—Mailing Fields

1. Owner's name: First, Last
2. Owner's street address
3. Owner's State and Zip
4. Owner's phone, home and business
5. Property legal
6. Property description
7. Own other property?
8. Category of owner
9. Contact log

Not all of the above fields need to be filled in as you develop the list; in fact, it is likely that you will add to the list and your fields as you build a computer information file.

If Charlie is doing this by hand, the same information can be kept on 5" x 7" cards.

Step 2. Divide the Mailing List into Different Categories

Notice Item 8 in the computer fields above. You will want to break your mailing list into several different categories of property owners. The minimal breakdown should be: (1) members of the real estate, legal, accounting and mortgage professions; (2) doctors; (3) known investors; and (4) everyone else.

As you begin to fine-tune your list, you will change the category of some of the people as you discover where they best fit. Unless you know that a person would be in the Categories 1 through 3, list them in 4.

The reason for the categories is to allow you to send different signals to each type of target.

Step 3. Plan Three Mailings to Each Category

The initial mailing should be a simple introduction of yourself and your intent to acquire property. Charlie Sopkins is specific as to the kind of property he is interested in; to avoid wasting a lot of time explaining over the phone or via correspondence that he wanted Madrid, Georgia, and not San Francisco, he outlines where the property should be located.

Even though there are four different categories of letters to send out, they can be very similar. If you are using a mail-merge program, the letters can be printed out in a more personal way, using the owner's name in several places within the letter.

Sample Introductory Letter 1

```
Randy Osoff
Able Realty
2332 West Broad Street
Madrid, Georgia
                                    September 5, 1995


Dear Mr. Osoff,
    I am taking the opportunity to introduce myself to you and
your firm. After several months of study, I have decided to
acquire several commercial properties in the western area of
Madrid, and as your office is located on one of the major com-
mercial streets I hope that you can assist me in this quest.
    Attached to this letter you will see a list of the types of
property I would be interested in.  Should you own or have list-
ings of properties which would meet those criteria please send
me a presentation containing the salient facts, including price
and terms offered.
    I look forward to hearing from you at your first opportunity.

                            Sincerely yours,

                            Charles Sopkins
```

Sample Introductory Letter 2

```
Doctor Glynn Simons
2334 West Broad Street
Madrid, Georgia

                                    September 5, 1995

Dear Doctor Simons,
    I am taking the opportunity to introduce myself to you in the
hope that we may do business together in the near future.
    After several months of study I have decided to acquire sever-
al commercial properties in the western area of Madrid, and as
your office is located on one of the major commercial streets I
hope that you can assist me in this quest.
    Attached to this letter you will see a list of the types of
property I would be interested in. Should you own or know of any
such properties which are on the market I would appreciate hearing
from you with salient facts, including price and terms offered.
    I look forward to hearing from you at your first opportunity.

                                    Sincerely yours,


                                    Charles Sopkins
```

Both of the letters shown are to be sent to the professional people in your comfort zone and not the property owners. Your approach to a property owner will differ greatly, as you can see from the following example.

Sample of First Letter to a Property Owner

```
Mr. Frank Brunson
1995 West Eighth Avenue
Madrid, Georgia

                                    September 28, 1993

Dear Mr. Brunson,
    Following several months of research, I recently decided to
invest in real estate in the western Madrid area, and understand that
you own several properties along West Broad street. I would appreci-
ate learning if you would consider selling any of your properties.
    I can be reached at 943-7721 during business hours and if I am
out inspecting property please leave a message and I will get
back to you as soon as possible.
    If you are not interested in selling, perhaps you know of
property available in the western Madrid area. In any event, Mr.
Brunson, I look forward to meeting you in the near future.

                                    Sincerely yours,

                                    Charlie Sopkins
```

The difference is subtle and is designed to build a connection. Most property owners are used to getting letters from real estate brokers asking for a listing. Those letters often sound like this:

"Hi, I'm Bob Greatdeals, and as fellow neighbors [lives 45 miles away] you and I should meet. As **the** Realtor in town that loves our neighborhood, I would like to represent you in the sale of your property. I've taken the liberty to enclose some data I think you will find interesting. Let's have coffee soon. Sincerely, Bob" Makes you want to cry, doesn't it?

Along comes your letter, and how clean and refreshing it sounds. Remember, you are opening doors, planting your name in the field of dreams, putting up the "I'm open for **your** business" sign, and getting ready to cash in on your comfort zone.

Subsequent mailings to the same list need to come at regular intervals. Once every four months should be sufficient, and while you may include additional communications to people who begin to respond to you in a positive way, your mailings will become your major link to getting the first look at any property which might come on the market within your zone. You are **building** for the future. Your second and later mailings should be reinforcements to the first mailing and your follow-up phone calls. Cut out clippings from the local newspapers that are informative about what is going on in the community. Do not select articles that reflect up or down trends in real estate, because it is not your job to educate people to property trends and you want to remain distant in that respect. You are not trying to get a listing on their property, you want a shot at acquiring it.

Step 4. Do Phone Follow-up

Phone follow-up is important because it gives you candid feedback that you would not get otherwise. In the beginning you will pick names randomly for the phone follow-up, without any specific selection process. The idea is to practice this for a while and get a feel of what people expect to hear and how you are going to handle the phone conversations. There must be a method to your phone calls, however, or you will sound like a salesman trying to get an appointment to show some new kind of water-filter system.

Phone conversations can return their maximum benefit if you pay close attention to the **Phone Follow-up Checklist.** Until the phone follow-up becomes second nature to you, I would recommend that you print out a copy of the checklist and have it in front of you every time you start to make a follow-up call. For the items which require you to do advance homework, make sure you have answered all the questions "yes" before dialing.

First, read to yourself out loud:

> The goal of this follow-up call is to make sure the person I am calling knows
> I am a real estate investor who may someday be interested in acquiring their
> property. I must at all times remain calm, cool, and uncontroversial. I will use
> the word "fantastic" when I might think "bullshit," and my sole goal is to
> make a friend and a potential real estate deal. I am patient beyond all bounds,
> and nothing will cause me to have negative thoughts during this phone call. I
> have reviewed the items on the Phone Follow-up Checklist so that I will
> appear professional and in charge of my own future:

Phone Follow-up Checklist

1. Name and profession of the person I am calling.
2. The legal description and street address of the property they own.
3. I can mentally see what the property looks like.
4. I know of actual properties on the market in the same area.
5. I have a printout of every property sold in the general area in the past 12 months in front of me.
6. I know what information I would like to get.
7. I am ready to take notes.
8. I will succeed.

As you progress in the task of making phone follow-ups you will discover that things begin to build. As you start to meet people over the phone you will be establishing yourself within this community as a person; you will be invited to lunch, and will in turn invite people to lunch. Property that is not really on the market gets offered to you: "You know, Charlie, I've been thinking about selling, but you know how it is, I just never got around to facing the real estate guys. Why don't you come over and take a look at my building. Perhaps we can get together."

☞ **Key Words:** Opportunity Knocks . . . but if you have your door already open, you let opportunity in before anyone else can beat you to the draw.

By the time you send your second letter to your mailing list, you will begin to be more selective as to whom you call back. You will always want to include several random calls, just to keep yourself on top of the "hidden wealth within your zone," but because your time is limited, the majority of follow-up calls will be to the prolific dozen within your zone.

Step 5. Keep Good Progress Records

Memory is the first thing that fails in business dealings, so write information down and keep it where you can find it. There is no substitute for good record keeping. I've already suggested you invest in a computer and a good word-processing program to make your life easier. If you cannot afford that, use card files and binders to keep things together. Do not be like Cookie, a very sharp woman lawyer I know who has decided to make her niche in the real estate profession as a saleswoman. She does write things down, but can never remember where she put them.

You will shortly discover that **follow-up** is the sister of **persistence,** and that together those two attributes will help you gain the upper edge in everything you do. To follow up properly, you need to know exactly what has been going on, and where you are with respect to that property or that property owner.

Step 6. Set Aside Specific Days for Property Inspections

Inspecting property is essential. You already have your property inspection checklist ready, so plan on using it.

The best way to get into the habit of inspecting properties is to set aside one day a week when you will do all your property inspections. Later on add two or three days as the need arises. Keep in mind, too, that just because your usual inspection day is Friday, that does not mean that you should miss out on an appointment another day of the week if the situation warrants. Be flexible on this, but do set aside a day just for looking at real estate.

As you are going to be a busy person, you will want to fill that day with as many property inspections as possible. One interesting way is to check with the local Board of Realtors and find out if there is a specific day for your comfort zone in which it schedules **open houses** or **broker inspection tours.** If the Board won't help you, then ask your broker. Your broker will provide you with a list of such broker open houses, if you allow him or one of his salesmen to go with you (to register you).

Going to brokers' open houses with your own salesman is okay if you want to deal exclusively with that salesman. As a Realtor, I can give you a thousand good arguments why you would want to develop a relationship with one salesman who will look after your best interests and assist you all the way down the line. However, in the beginning you may not want to make that kind of commitment, or may not find the salesman you feel that comfortable with.

Trick of the trade: It's all in the name. So have a trade or corporate name that makes you sound important and like an insider already: "Realty Investments International" or "Atlanta Properties" or "Prime Investment, Inc."

Call a broker and properly identify yourself as the president of "Prime Investment, Inc.," and ask what day their open houses are for western Madrid, Georgia; then expect an answer.

Property inspections are a chore, but a necessary one. You are still and always learning about your comfort zone. Physical inspections are essential. When you travel through your comfort zone, you should make an effort to be alert to everything that is going on. Is there some new construction? Are local businesses doing well or are there a lot of vacant shops for rent? What about the cars parked in the residential areas? The kind of cars people drive is a key to the kind of people you will find living in the area, and is a key trend indicator to a change of living standard.

The minute you start to see abandoned cars in what was a nice middle-class area, you need to take a closer look at what is going on.

Step 7. Be Ready to Make Offers

Until you have your standard offer template ready you will be at the whim of your broker or lawyer. The broker will act quickly, but often thinking first of his client (the owner of the property you might be interested in). Your lawyer will act, but not so quickly, and in the heat of the moment many opportunities are surely lost because one member of the investor's team was not ready to give aid and assistance. Decide **now** that you will learn how to fill in a standard real estate purchase or exchange form, then stock up on a bundle of them and go to work. Do not forget to use a standard-looking **escape** or **out clause** that enables you to make offers, tie up property, and still have a way out if things go against you.

☞ **Key Words:** Out Clause or Escape Clause

This is the clause in a contract that makes the agreement unilateral and ties up the other side while you still have an out. Do not think for one moment that this is bad for the other

✳ side. The worst that will happen is they give you a "free look," to discover if you are truly as interested in the property as you first thought. And you will be interested and will end up closing on the transaction.

Step 8. Advertise Your Successes

Not in a flamboyant, Donald Trump style, please, but to show that **you are a *real* real estate investor.** In one of your usual mailings to your list you might mention, almost in passing, "Last Friday I closed on the First National Bank Building, adding to my commitment to invest in property in our neighborhood. Please keep me in mind should you or anyone you know be interested in selling."

Step 9. Expand Your Comfort Zone

Whatever the geographical area you originally selected, your first reaction, once you are working it, will be "It's too big." But as your self-confidence grows in what you are capable of doing, you will want to add to that area. Resist, for a while, the urge to begin to increase the size of your comfort zone, because it is likely that you still are not ready. But plan on eventually branching out to other kinds of property in other parts of town. That moment will have arrived after you have already acquired property in your comfort zone and need to look elsewhere for complementary properties, or when you realize you have chosen the wrong comfort zone and need to make a complete change in investment goals and strategy.

Step 10. Acquire More Property

Like the name of the game says, real estate investment means acquiring property. There is no need to sell for the moment; in fact, you should never acquire anything with the idea that you can make a quick turnover. Sure, there will be times when you are offered a nice profit the same day you go to contract on a property, but unless you must sell or take a fast profit or learn of some pending problem that might hint at an upcoming lull in the market, hang on to the property until you have a solid feel for it and its potential. If it turns out to do less than you thought with respect to your needs and your goals, do not hesitate to make an aggressive move to dispose of that property.

Finding Property Means You Spin Off Profits

Now that you have finished this chapter I'll let you in on a real insider's secret. Everything contained in this chapter follows one of the very best plans for a real estate salesman to follow to get listings. I started working on and perfecting a total package for real estate salesmen to follow that would be a surefire way to break into the business. The key to being successful as a real estate salesman is to get listings. **Listings** is the name of the brokerage game. Without them you fail, with them you succeed.

After over 25 years of working out bugs and perfecting the salesman's "comfort zone" program, I was also working on the investor's version of the program. The investor program has a distinct advantage over the salesman's program: sellers react more favorably to the buyer who contacts them directly than the salesman who, as we all know, is just trying to get a listing.

Despite this fact, both the investor and the salesman will find great success using a direct and clearly focused attack to reach their desired goals. The critical factor is knowing where to select your comfort zone, then maintaining it with complete follow-up. Don't worry about mistakes (if you don't make any, you don't make anything) or missed opportunities, because there will be more coming your way if you keep your eyes open.

The following chapter introduces an added element to the world of exchanges: **barter.** This is the ancient art of dealing in and with everything, from personal property to personal services. You can use barter as a tool or a sweetener, and it will open more doors than you ever thought possible.

8

Introducing Other Types of Barter to the Exchange

In the world of exchange, barter is a catchall term. It includes trades on everything from oil for farm tractors to an orthodontist's best efforts on buckteeth. Barter is a creative opportunity for you, once you understand how it works and where it can fit into your real estate transactions.

You Can Add Creativity to Exchanges with Barter

This chapter is designed to serve several needs: first, to expand your mental outlook on what exchanging is all about; second, to offer other avenues for you to follow in adding creative touches to any transaction you might entertain; and third, to show you that exchanges are available that do not include real estate.

Warning! Barter loonies lurk around the corner. There are fanatics who try to live a normal life, never spending money (which I presume they never have) by bartering for everything. "See this suit?" one of these guys might begin, a smile of pride on his face as he tugs sharply at the lapels of his polyester tweed. "Got it through barter."

Shock treatment, I presume; this fellow has been relying on barter for everything, too much of it, in fact. The whole idea of doing exchanges is not to try to live by exchanges alone, but to use the technique as an investment tool.

Even the most ardent Amway distributor cannot live (or won't) on Amway products alone. Exchanges are not to be the rule of your life, but the tool should be there when exchanges can work for you.

If you had never learned any swimming stroke other than backstroke, let me introduce you to the breaststroke of exchanges; it will keep you afloat in any investment pool.

How to Use Barter—The Deal Maker and Sweetener

Let's look first at barter as a form of exchange that does not include real estate. Every business, every service offered, every product made can be bartered. There is no exception at all. Own a restaurant, hotel, or apartment building. Then you have obvious services to "sell" by barter exchange for something else. Do you do window tinting, paint houses, tune pianos, give tennis, golf, or guitar lessons? Then you have something to barter. Are you a CPA, lawyer, do appraisals, sing at weddings, proofread on the side, type resumes, wax cars, bake donuts, or anything even close? If you do, then there is a potential barter deal waiting for you.

Perishables Are the First Line of Barter

If you deal in a product or service where the item of value is perishable, then you will be a prime candidate for barter. "Perishable" in barter means much more than a ripe banana; it means any item, product, or service that, unless used by a certain date, is lost forever.

An airline seat for a flight leaving New York City at 3:44 p.m. for Chicago on March 3, 1998, self-destructs once the aircraft has taken off. An empty seat on a flight, an unrented hotel room, the two or three extra students you could have added to the class you teach, all the uneaten garlic bread and veal marsala thrown out at the end of the night in your Italian restaurant, the extra work your employees could have done last week (because they were not busy), and the two hundred pounds of oranges from your garden all will be lost—unless you can sell them or barter their value before their time is past.

Airlines, hotel companies, restaurants, and all advertising media from radio to TV and newspapers to magazines, barter some of their product for other items—often among themselves. So why not you?

I know of doctors who'll barter away a surgical procedure, dentists who'll extract a dozen teeth (need it or not), and physical therapists who barter massages. You see what they give, now what do they get? Why, surgical procedures, meals in restaurants, airline tickets, hotel rooms, advertising time, and if they want, two hundred pounds of oranges or a massage. Get the idea? Or do you think barter is child's play?

International Barter Is Really Big Business

When Russia needs a million tons of wheat what do they do? Pay for it? No, they work out a barter deal. When an international airline needs to do something drastic, and they launch a major advertising campaign, do they pay for it with cash? Of course not, they pay for it with airline tickets. See how it works?

Okay, so you get the picture. How can this work for you? Where can you fit into this scenario to get some benefits, to move yourself closer to your goals?

Take Stock of Your Potential Barter Assets

The very first exchange example I put in this book was a barter transaction. It was a "sweat equity" deal where a prospective tenant worked out a deal with the owner of an apartment building to exchange work for rent—a simple deal that was, in effect, a barter transaction. Most barter transactions start with personal effort. You do roof repairs so you barter roof repairs. You are a cobbler so you barter shoe repairs. You are a cop (with a hobby of fixing air conditioners) so you barter air conditioner repairs. You are a secretary who teaches yoga, so you barter private yoga lessons. Somewhere you have the opportunity to do a direct barter transaction.

But even if you are a klutz, are the kind of person who is always taking lessons, not giving them, have no green thumb, can't get paint on a wall without putting twice as much on yourself, and in general have nothing worth bartering, **do not give up.** There is still hope for you.

Scrip

Skip the Obvious Barter Situations

Enter Scrip. Scrip is like money. You print it, you design what it looks like, and you control who gets it (initially) and how it can be spent. You are the bank. You are in control. You do not have to be Fort Knox.

Scrip is widely used as a form of barter. The Akbar restaurants in New York City contract with a "barter company" called Fun Time Guides for advertising. The Akbar, as well as other restaurants and companies who deal with Fun Time Guides, are paying for their advertising partly in United States greenbacks, and partly in Fun Time Guides scrip. A copy of the Fun Time scrip follows:

Aangan
Classic Indian Cuisine
330 W. 46th St.
581-1032

Abingdon Square
Gourmet Bistro
13 Eighth Ave.
727-7195

Athenian West
Mediterrean Cuisine
350 Hudson St.
691-9060

Cafe Americano
Classic Italian
105 Hudson Street
219-8802

Cafe Trio
Trendy Italian
90 3rd Ave.
353-2144

Cosmico
Greek-Israeli/Nt. Club
208 W. 70th St.
362-0007

Cronies
Wings-N-Things
1695 Second Ave. (88th St.)
860-1919

Donahue's
Hardy Irish Cuisine
770 2nd Ave.
883-1193

El Azteca
Authentic Mexican cuisine
783 9th Ave.
307-0616

Faros
Seafood Continental
3700 Riverdale Ave. - Bronx
549-7944

Ginger Man
Continental Cuisine
51 W. 64th St.
399-2358
(Catering also available)

J.P. Lofland's
Bar and Grill
29 W. 21st St.
924-3264

Landmark
Amer./Cont'l
626 11th Ave.
757-85ºº

Marbo
Chinese Cuisine
151 E. 60th St.
832-1210

Meson Sevilla
Authentic Spanish
344 W. 46th St.
262-5890

O'Neal Bros. Cafe
Continental Cuisine
60 W. 57th Street
399-2361

Pasta Pot
Pasta Galore
30 Mulberry St.
962-9249

Samraat
Authentic Indian
175 Madison Ave.
213-1377

Stubby's
Bar & Grill
1461 First Ave.
744-3800

Trattoria Alba
Italian Bistro
233 E. 34th St.
689-3200

Trattoria Tiziano
Italian Renaissance
165 Eighth Ave.
989-2330

In the initial contract with Fun Time Guides all the different restaurants or other services included agree to accept the Fun Time Guides scrip in payment for the meals or other services offered. They can control, to some degree, the time periods when they will honor the scrip, and can impose some restrictions on its use. They in turn can spend part of the scrip collected on advertising through the Fun Time Guides.

How and Why Scrip Works

When you have scrip to spend, you will go where it can be spent. Sound logical? Well, it is critical. Restaurants that start to deal in scrip find that with proper distribution of their scrip they will be generating business that may not have come to them in the usual course of business, and that spenders of scrip are apt to buy the high-priced (and highly profitable) items available. If the Akbar can buy advertising from Fun Time Guides that will work for them, and pay 75 percent of the advertising bill with the Fun Times scrip that they redeem, the actual cost of the advertising will be a function of (1) the cash added to the payment and (2) the out-of-pocket cost of the meals paid for by the scrip.

When you spend scrip you always must pay tax and tip in real money. Considering that a patron is apt to overspend, and therefore tip according to his bill, waiters love to see a scrip spender show up. Restaurant owners dealing with scrip know that they get added business, which makes the establishment look full and adds to the tips of the waiters. For the Akbar, a $1,000 advertising bill might actually cost only $500.

The Real Cost of the Akbar Advertising Bill

Invoiced bill from Fun Time Guides	$1,000
Paid as follows	
25% in US dollars	$ 250
75% in Scrip	$ 750
	———
Hard cost of $750 in meals	$ 250
Plus actual cash spent	$ 250
	———
Real cost to Akbar	$ 500

The above calculation is based on an actual cost to Akbar for the redemption of the $750 in scrip of only $250. General overhead of the restaurant is not calculated as this business is extra patronage not usual to the restaurant.

Remember what I said about perishables? Well, the scrip is not as perishable as yesterday's empty airline ticket or motel room. It may have a termination date three or four months away, and Fun Time Guides banks its scrip like money. They and hundreds of barter companies like them sell advertising or broker other transactions and create money that eventually sifts back to the very customers who come back to them to buy advertising or other services (with scrip and real money).

You can do exactly the same, on whatever scale you want.

Print Your Own Money—Two Keys to Printing Scrip

You can print your own scrip, spend it, and obtain the desired benefits you have been looking for now. There are two keys to this. It is simple, but you have to establish the product or service you plan to offer with your scrip.

1. Do you have a product or service? If you do, you can issue scrip as a payment for all or part of that product or service. Restaurant and hotel owners, for example, can print up $10 bills of scrip, which can be redeemed at their own establishments. If you have a service to offer, from car repairs to Swedish massage, you can do the same.

2. If you do not have a product or service, find one. This is not one of those sounds-easier-than-it-is plans. The idea is to cut your out-of-pocket expenditure whenever you can. If you can generate 10 percent of your down payment in the form of profit in a scrip you print, you are able to invest in more property without having to spend your hard-earned cash (or cash you don't have).

Finding a Product or Service You Don't Own

Think of some products or services you can "sell" that will pay you large commissions. A few such items are listed below:

The 12 High-Commission Items

1. Insurance	7. Advertising
2. Specialty travel programs	8. Jewelry
3. Select electronics	9. Designer apparel
4. Professional services	10. Country club memberships
5. Restaurant meals	11. Furniture
6. Hotel rooms	12. Nonproperty rentals

These 12 ideas are just the tip of the iceberg; it is hoped that you will tap your personal experience and expertise and find something that will work for you. To help your creative juices flow, take a quick look at each of the above.

Insurance

Some states require you to have a special specific license to sell insurance, but it may not be difficult to call an independent insurance company and find out. The kind of insurance you would want to know about are life and health insurance. The best is apt to be life, because in a major whole-life policy some life insurance companies have paid the "salesman" as much as 100 percent of the first-year premium. A continuing bonus can follow for each year the policy is maintained by the insured.

Assume you might want to add a sweetener or find something to close a deal you are getting close to. You offer to "pay" the first-year premium of a $1 million whole-life insurance policy. You actually make the payment for the other party, but get all or most of it back as your commission. This spells value to the "seller" of the property you want to acquire, at little or no cost to you. By the way, the first-year premium of a major whole-life policy for a person in his mid-fifties could easily be $15,000 to $20,000.

Specialty Travel Programs

Special tours, certain cruises, and other travel programs that airlines or tour operators offer can carry high commissions to the travel agent who sells them. You do not have to be an owner of a travel agency to become a "travel agent," and using travel as a bonus or as an exchange item can be a very simple way to make deals work and save some cash along the way.

The first step is to get to know one or more owners of travel agencies. Explain to them that you are a real estate investor and would like to use travel, from time to time, as a part of your "purchase price" when you acquire property. Show this chapter to them and let them draw their own conclusions as to how this arrangement will profit both them and yourself.

A word to the owners of travel agencies. I have been in the travel business as owner of my own firm for over 25 years. I got into the travel business because I represented builders in Spain and we were taking hundreds of people to Spain on a regular basis to buy property. Once in the travel business I found it interesting, and I looked for more ways to use the travel product I had available to me.

When a prospective real estate investor comes to you and says, "I want to buy travel programs and give them to people I buy property from," do not laugh or turn them away. They can become a new source of business for you.

All they want is to be treated as though they were an **outside travel consultant** and get the maximum commission you would pay to such an agent. If they also wish to partake of the perks of being a travel agent, consider that when the time comes and they have proved their worth to you in adding to your agency volume.

What you can expect with travel programs. In general the travel industry is a low-markup product. It works that way because the agency does not have to "buy" any product to sell (unlike a shop that must maintain a large volume of inventory). However, in off times of the year, or for some tours or cruises, tour operators and carriers offer the agents larger-than-normal commissions. About the largest I can think of was a 38 percent fee on a selected trans-Atlantic crossing of a major cruise line. Whatever it might be, if you could offer a "seller" a $25,000 cruise for two that departed New York City 18 months from now as a part of your purchase of their property, your ultimate cost (not now but prior to 18 months from now) would be the $25,000 less your commission. If the commission was 25 percent and you got 75 percent of that, your net cost for that cruise would be $20,312.50; and while you still are out of pocket, you have reduced that cash payment substantially and have pushed it to a future date.

Select Electronics

Computers, car phones, and other high-ticket items that may also require continuing payments often bring the salesman a nice commission in the form of all or most of the initial payment to acquire that product. Car phones, water systems, and that sort of thing are often "given away" by the selling company so that they develop a customer for their continuing service. Make a contact with one or more of these suppliers and, when the situation is ripe, offer the owner of the property you are trying to buy a package of 10 car phones as a sweetener to close now. Your actual cash outlay to connect him (and the nine other employees he may want hooked up) may turn out to be zero.

Professional Services

Just about any professional will pay you for a lead. You can offer their services if they agree to pay you a percentage of each contract, or a flat fee every time someone comes in and hires them.

If you are making an offer to buy a condominium apartment from a major builder and you offer him $5,000 worth of scrip that can be redeemed from a professional service he now has to pay real money for, he is apt to take the deal. If you make $10,000 back as your percentage of the total fee from the professional service actually rendered, not only have you saved $5,000, but you have also made an additional $5,000.

Professional fees that start out small and grow are just about anything dealing with real estate, from lawyer's fees to engineering.

Restaurant Meals

Pick a new restaurant; go to the owners and explain that you are a real estate investor and would like to help them develop customers by offering restaurant scrip, which you will print up at no cost to them, for patrons to spend at their establishment. Explain that tax and tip will not be included and that the restaurant can exclude heavy business days or evenings for redemption of the scrip.

You will print and distribute the scrip and when it is brought in to be spent, you will promptly buy back the scrip at a discount of 50 percent of the value.

The deal is a good one for the restaurants, which frequently offer big discounts anyway, and if they can generate traffic and build clientele at no other cost to them, it pays off in future business. For you it is good because you can spend the scrip now, and do not have to pay out the cash until someone actually spends it.

Restaurants may ask you to put up a float, say $500, which you continually replace as the scrip comes in and uses up the $500 security. But if you are spending $25,000 of scrip then you are well ahead of the game.

Hotel Rooms

Now you can pretend to be Hilton himself. Like unused airline tickets (but those are harder to deal with), hotel rooms that were vacant last night are lost forever. Contact several hotel owners in your area and in areas where people from your area may like to visit and explain your situation. You want to offer scrip that you will redeem at a 50 percent discount after it has been spent at that hotel on some of your real estate transactions. They can exclude certain times of the month or year from the offer.

If you live in California, pick several areas, nearby and distant, to make your deals. You might lock up one hotel in Reno, another in Vegas, a third in Puerto Vallarta, and a fourth in Hawaii. Your scrip could actually be good at any of them.

It could take years for $30,000 worth of hotel scrip to come back to you, and even when it does it only costs you 50 cents on the dollar.

Advertising

How to be a "Madison avenue" ad man via scrip. This can be a difficult item to get into, because it might require more work and effort than you want to expend. However, advertising is one of those perishable items I mentioned before, and you can make deals with radio and television stations to "sell" their off-hour times at a major discount from the normal rates. If you want to actually buy blocks of time and exchange that time for your scrip or desired property, you can do quite well. It would not be unusual to buy "off time" for $100 a unit and sell it for $500 a unit. (A unit here is a segment of time, which would depend on the market—in New York City a unit might be a 10-second spot, whereas in Bell Glade, Florida, a unit could be a two-hour program slot).

Jewelry

Jewelry is one of the alltime high-mark-up items on the market. The retail markup on the raw material to produce, manufacture, and put an expensive piece of jewelry in the store can be several thousand percent. A Cartier-designed diamond-and-sapphire ring could have a pricetag of $50,000, with a broken-down per-item price of the diamonds, sapphire, and gold of less than $10,000.

Make a connection with a fine jeweler and you will be surprised what kind of a "commission" you can make when you start bringing him customers by printing scrip that can be redeemed at his store.

Designer Apparel

Put an important name on it, and the price doubles . . . or triples . . . or more. Make a connection with a distributer of designer apparel, or, better yet, get to know a designer in your area and explain to her that you are a real estate investor who will bring her new customers if she agrees to pay you a nice commission.

Country Club Memberships

Newly formed clubs often initiate a major drive to add members. The initial fee to join can be negotiated by almost any enterprising person. If you tell the club managers that you want to offer their memberships as a part of your real estate transactions and that you may be instrumental in bringing new members to their facility, you can generally get 50 percent off the initial membership fee.

Furniture

Furniture is another high-ticket item. If you get a city occupational license to be an interior decorator, you will get major discounts at local designer showrooms and many furniture stores in town. With this discount in hand (usually 50 percent and sometimes higher), your scrip can have some real meat to it if your prospective seller is in the market for furniture.

The following example shows how this item can turn into a profit situation.

As a down payment on his apartment, you offer Abraham $30,000 of scrip to be redeemed at any of five major furniture outlets in the area. You know that you will get a 50 percent discount at those outlets, so the $30,000 down payment will cost you only $15,000 . . . only Abraham's wife goes wild and decides to refurbish their whole home at a cost of $100,000. Abraham and his wife add $70,000 cash to the total bill and expect you to pay the other $30,000. Only wait a moment: as the bill was $100,000 and you get a 50 percent discount, the net bill is only $50,000. Abraham paid you $70,000 so after you pay the $50,000 to the furniture store you get to keep $20,000 plus full credit for the $30,000 as the down payment on Abraham's property.

Non-Real-Estate Rentals

Rentals of just about anything can carry a nice commission for you. You cut a deal with a construction equipment leasing company to pay you 20 percent of every deal you bring to them, and you plan to offer scrip that will be good at their establishment to prove your interest in working with them. You offer Werner, a condominium developer, $20,000 worth of rental equipment, spread over an 18-month period. Make your scrip good in increments of $1,000 per rental and you may discover that Werner rents equipment at $4,000 per increment. If your commission is $800 per usual rental contract, the most you will be out of pocket for the full $20,000 of credit against something Werner is selling you would be $4,000, the other $16,000 being commissions paid back to you from Werner's rentals.

The above 12 examples should get your mind working. Work several of the deals together and use them to replace cash in your transactions. Use them as a sweetener or whenever necessary to nail down that deal you want to make.

The Secret Bonus with Scrip

A bonus with scrip: not all of it will come back to you. Some of the scrip you exchange may be lost, or not spent within the redemption time. That adds to your overall benefit when you use this form of exchange.

Create Value Where Nothing Existed Before

As you can see, with a few contacts here and there you can start printing your own money to be used with your other transactions. Later on you will find some examples of rather creative exchanges that can be made, but take a look at a rather simple one that makes use of two different exchange items.

An Exchange Example with Real Estate and Barter

You want to acquire Frank's duplex apartments. He is asking $125,000, which is a fair price, and he owes $70,000 to a local savings and loan. There is a second mortgage of $20,000 which can be assumed if the lender (Frank's mother-in-law) approves.

You anticipate that you will have to spend $5,000 in immediate repairs and cosmetics on the duplex prior to trying to rent out the side where Frank is presently living. The other side of the duplex is rented for three more months, and with a fixed-up building you hope to get more rent than Frank has charged. Part of your offer will be to dispose of a nice tract of land you own, which has a value of $20,000.

You offer the following:

The 6 Conditions of the Offer

1. To assume the existing first mortgage of $70,000.
2. To assume the existing second mortgage of $20,000.
3. To give Frank five acres of land near Boulder, Colorado.
4. To give Frank $15,000 worth of your scrip with the following restrictions:
   a. Good for 24 months.
   b. Maximum of $5,000 good in five different hotels.
   c. Maximum of $5,000 of meals at four local restaurants.
   d. No limit on furniture at the Mart (up to $15,000).
5. You agree to start immediately with repairs and repainting the building and will put up $5,000, which you can use for those expenses and for which you do not get credit at the closing.
6. Closing to be in three months.

There are several closing techniques imbedded in the offer as shown. Take another look at the six steps to the offer and see if you can spot what they are.

The first is a subtle question of form: you do not use the word "exchange" but, rather, make reference to the fact that you will "give" Frank the five acres, and will "give" Frank the $15,000 of scrip. While we talk about exchanges, and the whole essence of your reading this book is to learn about exchanges, use the words "give" and "get" whenever possible.

The second is the limitation on the use of the scrip—first, the limitation of the time period to only 24 months, and then a maximum that can be applied to hotels and restaurants. "Why," Frank is quick to argue, "I want thirty-six months' duration and no limit on hotels or restaurants." Good for Frank, he found something to counter that wins something for him but does not hurt your final deal at all; in fact, it might even help it, because now you might have up to three years to redeem some of the scrip.

Where to Find Barter Organizations and Clubs

Let your fingers do the walking. The very first place to look will be the local Yellow Pages. Check under "Barter" and also under "Exchanges." If you find nothing, look under "Clubs—Barter or Exchanges." Still find nothing? Then check the Yellow Pages of a larger town in your area. Go to the local library or central phone office and look through several directories until you find a barter club or exchange organization.

In a few out-of-the-way areas of the country you may still come up blank, so call the local Board of Realtors and ask if they have a real estate exchange organization, or if they can recommend someone experienced in exchanges. Contact that club or person, and if there is a barter organization around, they are apt to know how to make contact with them.

How Barter Clubs Work

Barter organizations work much like an international bank. They act as the currency exchange for all transactions that flow among the members of the barter organization. Here's how one such organization I belong to functions.

I became a member the day someone offered to acquire a property I had up for sale, offering me as a part of the deal $10,000 worth of Barter Center scrip. This scrip was deposited to my account, and for $150 I became a member of the organization.

I got a list of other members who would deal with me, accepting payment on their goods and services, which ranged from accounting services, barbershops, chiropractors, dentists, fur storage, gemstones, and so on. In addition to what was on the list, from time to time I could buy restaurant scrip from the main office. Each time I would "buy" something, I would have to pay an additional cash payment to cover state tax and 15 percent of the original purchase price to the Barter Center office.

Over the past few years I have bought and sold through the center and have generally been satisfied with the results. The key to using a barter organization like this is to deal with excess product or service you have that is perishable. Better to build up barter credits than to have that product or service go unsold and the profit you would have made lost forever.

Rules for Dealing with a Barter Club

1. Check the references of the organization with some of its members. Ask these questions: (1) How long have you been a member? (2) Are you pleased with the results? (3) Do you feel you have gotten good value for your membership?
2. Keep good records of what you do. Some barter organizations keep poor records. The IRS will want to know what you did in barter each year.
3. When you get any kind of scrip and anticipate using it, call ahead and make sure that the establishment still honors the scrip. Restaurants and other establishments can change hands overnight, and the new owner may decide not to honor the scrip. Also, find out if there are any restrictions. You do not want to show up with a dinner party of 12 to find out that the scrip is good for only two people, and sorry, not tonight because it's Sunday.
4. Do not own too much barter scrip or credits at any one time. Unlike a commercial bank, there is no insurance to cover your "deposits," and you will not earn any interest on the savings you have in the "bank."

Start Your Own Barter Club

Barter is big business and can be a very good profit maker—if you know what you are doing, and if there is a place for that business in your community.

When you consider that barter is the very essence of all marketplace theories, it is not strange that most of the people I know who operate barter organizations follow the "barter or die" philosophy. By this I mean they get so entrenched with the concept of barter and exchange that they don't spend money at all. They make money, but don't spend it.

The best way to start any kind of new business is first to work for the competition. What you will discover is that the barter organization works like a club, and the whole idea of making money, at the organization level, is to have a lot of members who recognize the value of barter and who use it as a tool to increase their business.

Remember, when I do a deal with the Barter Center I pay them 15 percent off the top of the deal—in money, I mean, real money. Every deal then, earns them a fee in much the same way. Having a million members who do no deals is no good, so the management must be dedicated to generating not only new members, but educating members who have a product or service that barter works.

The Pros and Cons of Barter Organizations

The Advantages
If you have unsold product or service in your overhead that if sold would have been all or mostly all gravy (pure profit), barter is ideal for you.

This applies to almost all suppliers of products and services, unless there is such a demand for what you have to sell that you have a waiting list now with people holding fistfuls of cash to get what you have.

If you are starting a new business, need to generate more clientele, or need to advertise, barter is a good way for you to go.

When you have a product you need to sell and someone offers you some barter scrip, and if the accommodation to make the deal requires you to take the scrip, then barter is already working for you.

People who have barter credits become willing spenders of that "cash." They can be sold things they would not buy with real money, simply because of the monopoly syndrome. You remember the game where you get $200 just to pass go. Well, earning barter credits is kind of like this. Because it is often viewed as **extra** money that would not have come in were it not for the exchange or the barter of surplus services, time, or product, the easy come, easy go philosophy works. You can take advantage of this if you need to build up some credits in a barter center by offering a product for sale to barter members. Going, going, gone . . .

The Disadvantages
There are some problems with barter clubs. One is that management of the barter centers can lose track of the original need of the membership: more members making more deals offering more products and service.

While this should be a positive situation, and could be if the management would just see it that way, they do not, and too few members seem to be doing too many of the total transactions. This causes imbalances, and before you know it the members who have the best products or services to offer get loaded down with credits, and have to withdraw their products and services from the system until they can spend down their credits.

When you consider that the problems with barter centers is a lack of **service direction** from the management, it would seem to be an ideal business for someone to get into who had **service motivation.**

Look Ahead

I encourage you to look into this fantastic tool as a method of adding value to your real estate transactions. You can start your own scrip with a few restaurants, hotels, a couple of furniture stores, and a travel agency on your side. You do not have to own any of these; just spend a couple of weeks working at making them believe that you want to bring them business, and you are in business dealing for yourself.

Warning! Any deal you work out with any merchant or company should be in writing, have a termination date (which is put on the scrip), and is authorized and approved by the proper and responsible party.

Tax Consequences of Using Barter

If you take barter in a deal, the value of that barter is treated as though it were cash. If you have a capital gain and a tax to pay because of that gain, the cash portion of the transaction will become taxable. If your gain were $50,000 and you accomplished a 1031 exchange that included $15,000 of barter scrip, $10,000 of cash, and the balance a qualified real property in exchange, your tax liabilities would be on the fifty percent of the transaction that was **cash** or **cash equivalent.** The pro rata accounting, then, is important as to how much of the deal does qualify for a tax-free exchange. Many exchanges are accomplished not for the tax advantage, but because the transaction is better than nothing at all (which means keeping the property you own).

Open your eyes to all that goes on around you. Never overlook a stone worth turning over, and make sure that when you see opportunity, you ask if she has a sister.

9

Getting the Most Out of Your Real Estate Broker

Real estate brokers and salesmen are worth their weight in Butterfinger candy bars. They can provide you with valuable information and bring you properties that might have slipped past even the best "comfort zone" system. When you find a real estate agent who works with you, you have found a major building block for your investment team.

Real Estate Agents: The Good Ones Are Great

As a Realtor for over 25 years and as owner and broker of my own real estate firm for most of that time, I have seen every kind and category of salesman. I have wetnursed them through their problems, bailed them out of their catastrophes, been disappointed at their failings, and marveled at their moments of brilliance.

There are smart ones, overanxious ones, those you can do business with and, naturally, those you should stay away from.

The purpose of this chapter is to open your eyes to the reasons for using a broker or salesman and to show you how to select the one for you and how to get the most out of him or her when you start to build your real estate fortune.

Why You Need a Real Estate Broker

First of all, rest easy that I am not biased toward real estate professionals. If anything, I am supercritical of everything that pertains to the real estate business and its so called "hotshot" professionals. That includes but is not limited to brokers and salesmen. I also am very critical of the auxiliary elements: the lawyers, the title insurance and property inspection companies. Good ones exist, just as do beautiful sunsets and white Christmas mornings—and in about the same proportion to the other kind.

For now let's hone in on the real estate broker or salesman. The key phase to keep in mind when you select a broker or salesman is: "willingness to work." You need to find a real estate professional who will work hard to help you meet your investment needs while keeping his own greed to earn a commission at bay.

Other qualifications, such as experience, background, good reputation, good references, and that sort of thing, are important, to be sure, but none of that means anything if the person is not going to work to help you attain your goals . . . or if his judgment is clouded by the fact that he has already spent the commission he expects to make on your next buy.

Remember, Insiders Deal Best with Insiders

In any profession or business, those who are already in prefer to deal with other insiders. This is natural. So take advantage of it, and do not shy away from brokers or salespeople. The real estate industry in the United States and to some degree Canada is made up of people of varying levels of professionalism. Some states have very strict licensing laws and requirements: Florida and California, two states with an overabundance of licensed brokers and salespeople, have tough examinations that must be passed. Many states have continuing-education requirements to ensure that up-to-date practicing professionals stay on basic information.

The National Association of Realtors is a professional guild that maintains a code of ethics and rules governing brokers and salespeople who qualify to become members of the association. Local Boards of Realtors link members of the National Association together and provide many helpful services to the Realtors in that area, including multiple listing services for all the properties listed exclusively by the Board's members and distributed to them in book form.

Through the local listing services the prospective buyer or seller reaps the advantages of the insiders working together to help one another sell property. The clan of Realtors unites through these mutual listing services, continuing-education courses, and social engagements to establish the foundation for most conventional real estate transactions.

I must promptly admit that Realtors do not constitute the whole of the real estate brokerage profession. Many real estate firms have chosen not to belong to the local Board of Realtors, and therefore have not joined the National Association of Realtors, even though they would be qualified to be a member. The reasons vary: some Realtors deal with their own property only; others with a unique kind of real estate transaction such as exchanges; then there are those "brokers" who would not qualify for the National Association of Realtors at all.

The point here is that you need to look beyond the label "Realtor," and find out as much as possible about the reputation the person and firm you will be dealing with has within the clique of local insiders.

In the original selection process of your real estate agent, you should ask about their experience. Have they ever used a wraparound mortgage? Do they belong to a real estate exchange group or club? What do they know about options or leasebacks? If they have not done any of these things it needn't remove them from your list, but should alert you to roadblocks you may have to deal with later on.

Once you find the right kind of person, put him or her on your team, then look around for another to add to your stable. While you may settle down with one or two brokers or salespeople later on, while you are getting started you should not limit your team members. It is a good idea, however, to set some ground rules on how you want to work with each of them. An easy way to make sure they do not present the same property to you is to request that each present only exclusives to their own office.

Agents Expand Your Base by Finding Opportunities

Keep your comfort zone small; once you know it like the back of your hand you can start to expand the geographical boundary and add new categories of property you would like to invest in. This will give you more mileage out of the brokers and agents working for you.

Opportunities not grasped are profits never made. You are not here to be an observer. You are here to make money, to profit through real estate investing. That means you must find properties and make offers, make offers, make offers—above all, make offers until you have made the kind of deal that will work for you. Your broker and salesperson can help you do that, so let them.

Getting and Keeping the Edge with Agents

This is the nitty-gritty part of dealing with real estate brokers and salespeople. Deriving the maximum benefit from real estate professionals is not difficult, and you do not have to have an in-depth knowledge of the profession. What you do need is to follow some simple steps that will give you the edge and let you keep it.

The 5 Steps to Maximum Benefits from Your Agents

Step 1: Show them where they will benefit. All real estate salespeople like to make money. This is one of the strongest motivations for any person who works on commission. If they are good at their job the sky is the limit as to what they can earn. The work is hard, takes long hours, and involves frustrating transactions where weeks and even months can go into one deal that falls apart at the last moment. No deal closed, no commission paid.

All good real estate agents must learn to establish their priorities and devote their time to transactions and clients who are going to be productive. How you first approach the agent will cause him or her to categorize you as a worthwhile cause or a waste of time. In fact, everything that goes on during the first two or three meetings with a good agent will affect whether he or she establishes a priority of working for you or not.

When a salesperson says, "Mr. Jones, it was wonderful to meet you and I am sure I can help you in your quest to exchange a pig farm in Uruguay for a penthouse apartment in Boston. Give me a few days, I'll call you," she may not have any intention of ever calling. It could be that Mr. Jones rushed things a bit in disclosing all his equity is tied up in a bacon ranch in South America.

Nothing Motivates Like a Commission in the Wind

If an agent senses—and some can smell it through 26 inches of concrete—that there is a commission to be made through dealing with you, you will get action, loyalty, and devotion.

Go slow. Let the agent know that you are an investor looking to buy, or a property owner who wants to sell. You do not have to disclose your investment techniques at the first meeting. You do need to take the upper hand. Remember, you are interviewing for a salesperson to represent your interests; you are not applying for someone who must accept you and your property.

If you are a buyer, then act like a buyer. Explain that you want to buy several properties and that you plan to be in the market for some time to come. Let the agent know that you will acquire properties and that you would appreciate their help.

Step 2: Be sure the agents understand your goals. Once you have selected the agent you can relate to and whom you feel comfortable with, go over your goals and make sure they understand exactly what you want to accomplish. Again, do not disclose the methods you plan to use: you do not want to "turn off" the agent, and, more important, you do not want to become married to one plan. You must remain flexible.

As your goals change, discuss them with the members of your team. Ask for their advice. Each person will have a different viewpoint and bias. You do not have to follow everything they say; in fact, that will to be impossible because you will get conflicting views on most major situations. Yet all of this, and most particularly the conflicting viewpoints, will help you formulate strong and decisive goals and clear pathways to achieve them.

Step 3: Help your agents become creative. Sorry, but 99 percent of all real estate professionals are conventional in nature, and that means they have next to **zero imagination.** They work a limited area of town, deal in specific properties, and for the most part are not exposed to different kinds of deal making. It will be up to you to express your interest in using creative ideas to achieve dramatic results. You will have to acquaint yourself with creative techniques, many of which are contained in this book.

Some of the very best real estate people, who will work their tails off for you, are newcomers who are full of energy and hungry to make a deal. Connect one of these with an experienced broker who will take the salesperson's hand from time to time and lead you both to your goal, and you have a real winning team.

You will move the real estate agent into creative activity by expecting and introducing creative ideas. If you are making an offer that contains an option or an exchange, and the salesperson has never had a situation like that before, make sure that the agent has a good grasp of the reasons why you are using this technique in the offer being presented and how to overcome objections from the other side of the deal.

You may want to give your agents a book or two on creative deal making (after you have read them yourself). Several good books available outline different kinds and techniques of creative deal making that your broker or salesperson should know how to use. Get recently published books, to make sure that you are reading current information.

Step 4: Discover their energy zone. If you want to keep your people on their toes and working their hearts out for you, show appreciation. One good way might be a gift of a book such as mentioned above. But the best way is to let them know that you sincerely appreciate the time and effort they are extending on your behalf: simple thank-you note, or "That's great, Charlie," or remembering their birthday with a nice card or flowers. Everyone wants to feel they are good at what they do. Everyone likes to think that their "trying hard" is seen, respected, and appreciated. A smile and warm thanks will light more fires under the members of your team than you can imagine. Do it.

Step 5: Make them a part of your team. Of course, you must make them a member of your team and let them know what that means to you. This is a personal approach to bringing people close to you and make them feel that you are letting them in on some of your secrets. It can turn them into staunch advocates of your cause. Care must be taken to ensure that you do not become known in the industry as a wannabee investor, one who uses up everyone's time but never buys or sells. This does not mean that you have to become the exclusive property of any broker or salesperson. That is entirely up to you, and you should not be intimidated into making that decision. However, it is a good idea to limit yourself to contacting a few brokers. You have no way of limiting the number of brokers or salespeople who contact you, nor would you want to at an early stage of your investing game. The whole idea is to have a real estate broker who will think of **you first** when they see the kind of deal developing that may fit your goals.

The 3 Key Factors in Dealing with Real Estate Pros

1. They have access to information you need.
2. They can make your life easier and more profitable.
3. They work for free—until the deal closes.

Special Things to Know When You Are Buying

Real estate is a double-edged sword. There are buyers and there are sellers. Each generally depends on the other for the game to be played . . . at least in conventional real estate. For every seller there must be a buyer. However, when you start to introduce the elements of creative real estate transactions such as exchanges, options, wraparound mortgages, sale–leasebacks, and that sort of thing, buyers can become aggressive sellers, and sellers active buyers. You needn't look for a "buyer" or "seller" to play the game, as I have stressed many times thus far in this book. The best way to stretch creativity to its maximum is through exchanges where you are not dependent on the other side (buyer or seller) and it is **you** that causes things to happen.

As you select a member of the real estate profession to represent you, or are thrust cold turkey into dealing with an agent you don't know and may quickly learn not to like, you can reflect on the aspects of the profession and the people in it I have already mentioned. Keep in mind that not all good agents are good at all aspects of the real estate game.

From the salesperson's point of view there are four stages of brokerage; some people excel in only one stage and are absolute failures in the others.

The 4 Stages of Real Estate Brokerage

1. Listing
2. Obtaining the contract
3. Closing the sale
4. Buyer brokering

Each salesperson has limitations as to the type and location of property he deals with effectively. The best closer of condos under $150,000 may never be a success in trying to close homes over $500,000.

This is important, because when you are buying you can be exposed to two or more different types of agents, who may not even work for the same company. One is the lister, who may or may not have a partner working with him, and the other might be your own team member. Real estate brokers and salespeople can have personality conflicts, not just between themselves, but with you as well. Unless you are careful, such conflicts can ruin your prospects of making a deal.

Take a Deep Breath—Then Scream

You can feel like doing that sometimes. As a buyer, a seller, or an agent who is listing or closing the sale, frustrations are the major enemy to deal making. They are generally caused by one or more of the seven deal-breaking factors.

The 7 Deal-Breaking Factors

1. A broker or salesperson who tries to force the deal
2. Personality conflict between the brokers
3. Personality conflict between the buyer and seller
4. Personality conflict between the brokers and the buyer or seller
5. Parties who are more interested in winning than in dealing
6. Parties who will not make counteroffers
7. Inability by anyone to make a decision

In each of these situations it is the broker's fault if the deal falls apart. The real estate professional is there to absorb the heat of the transaction. Conflicts can and do occur all the time. Many brokers or salespeople become so involved with their clients that they start to make decisions for them: "My client will not take three hundred thousand for that property, so it is a waste of time to present that offer." Boy, do I get riled when I hear that, and I hear it all the time in varying degrees and versions. No one—including the seller—knows exactly what he will accept until the signed offer is gently presented.

Why You Should Explain the Strategy of Your Offer

Rather than just making an offer and sending your agent to present it, it would be helpful for you to go over your reasoning. Don't simply offer $352,000 without explaining your reason for coming up with that figure. For example: "Look, Jack, Bev and I have agonized over this home for a couple of days now and in looking at the list of similar homes which have sold in the last twelve months, and in reviewing all the homes in the area on the market today, we feel that the property is not worth more than $365,000. Naturally, we would like to get a good buy, and are prepared to offer $352,000 because we think we can afford that price. We can be somewhat flexible on these following items . . ."

Now doesn't that sound much better than this: "Uh? Oh, yeah. $352,000 sounds like a nice round figure, doesn't it?"

The Best Buyer's Agent Keeps the Deal Alive

Back and forth, back and forth. That's the name of the game. As long as they are negotiating with you, they may not be dealing with someone else. The agent is at his best when he keeps the game going. Yet I have seen many agents present an offer, and when the seller counters at a higher price than that offered, the agent has all but put an end to the deal by going back to his buyer saying, "This guy is being very unreasonable. . . ."

A good closing agent knows that everyone is unreasonable, in the eyes of the other person. Buyers want to get the deal at the absolutely bottom figure or for the best terms. The seller wants to get the most and best terms. "Well Bob, I'm glad you accepted my deal at $387,000, but now that we have closed I want you to know I was ready to go all the way to $400,000."

"Charlie, it's sure good, then, that you came up to $387,000 because if you had held out one more day I would have accepted your $352,000."

Remember what I said a few paragraphs earlier: **the agent's job is to absorb the heat of the deal.** This means keeping all the frustrations and antagonism and conflict that might actually exist between the parties from coming to the surface. When the seller tells the agent, "Tell that s.o.b. to take his offer and stick it," the agent should never use those words to the buyer, no matter how sincerely they were expressed. Keep tempers cool and the deal remains alive right up to the moment the contract is signed—or someone else buys the property out from under you.

The 8 Things to Know If You Are a Seller

1. To repeat: become an aggressive seller.
2. Make sure your agent knows why you are selling.
3. Make sure your agent understands your timetable.
4. Never think an offer is ridiculous.
5. View every offer as a potential deal that needs to be massaged, worked, cajoled, and finessed into what you will accept.
6. Keep your cool.
7. Be open to creative ideas . . . however much you know, you don't know it all.
8. Know when to stand firm.

Presenting Your Exchange Offer Through a Broker

Here's the scenario. You have found a property you like. It may have come to you because of a FOR SALE sign in your comfort zone, or a team-member agent might have suggested you acquire it. At this moment you only know of the property, and it seems to fit your criteria.

Get all the data you need to make strong decisions. Once you find a property that seems to fit your requirements, do not delay in getting everything you need to make a decision to acquire the property. To obtain the right kind of information—which the broker or listing agent can get for you—follow this checklist:

The 25 Important Things to Get from the Listing Agent

1. **Date the property was constructed.** Older properties may require major expenses to upgrade. Knowing ahead of time can allow you to make valid comparisons to competitive properties.
2. **Date of any improvements or remodeling.** Sometimes improvements or remodeling actually cover up still-existing or potential problems. Get documented details on improvements of any kind: building permits, plans, explanation of work completed.

3. **Length of time owned by current owners.** This can be a key to their motivation. If they are long-term owners, their motivation may be more sincerely expressed as a solution to a desired goal, while short-term owners can have a strong motivation to sell, often because of economic reasons rather than of attainment of a goal. If you can discover the real reason for the property being offered, you can plan your offer accordingly.

4. **Amount present owner paid for property.** This is usually public knowledge. The listing agent may balk at giving you this information, but the law allows the listing agent to provide you with any information available to him that is public knowledge. If he resists, ask your own agent to get the data—or go to the courthouse and get it yourself. Knowing what the sellers paid does not give the whole picture, however, as expensive improvements may have been made, adding to the seller's equity. Knowing where the seller stands is a gauge to where he will go.

5. **Whether there is existing debt (which is assumable).** What mortgages can you assume? This may be important to you for financing and will show the economic pressure on the owner and a possible motivation to sell. If he has just been transferred or fired, heavy debt service can be a compelling reason to sell.

6. **Debt that is not assumable.** Even the listing agent may not know this, because sellers often do not tell their listing agents everything. If there is secondary financing to be paid off, it is likely to be recorded against the property. A check of the records at the courthouse will clear this matter up and give you more insight as to the seller's real equity and motivations. If the property is listed on the market at $400,000 with a first mortgage to be assumed of $100,000, you may be misled to believe that the equity is $300,000, when you could discover that there are three secondary mortgages that total $255,000 each at 14 percent interest with a balloon next March. The real equity is now $45,000 and the motivation is desperate. Your thoughts of an exchange just went out the window and the seller's solution leeway is growing smaller each day.

*   7. **Reason the owner is selling the property.** There are generally three reasons: the one the agent tells you, the one the seller tells you, and the real reason. Start with one and they all will eventually unfurl themselves.

8. **Is the mortgage current?** Unless the seller has been ultrahonest (few are), the only way you will discover this is to get an estoppel letter from the mortgage lender, which tells you if the mortgage is in good standing and is current. Ask the seller anyway, but rely on the estoppel letter. If there has been a foreclosure action against the seller, it will be public knowledge if it has gone to the point of actual foreclosure. Keep in mind that lenders will do almost anything to avoid foreclosure, and will send threatening letters for months before the lawyers finally act.

9. **Real estate taxes.** After you acquire a property the real estate taxes may greatly increase. In most areas of the country, tax assessors are notified of the sale (some areas require the buyer or the seller to send actual notification of the sale along with the price). If there is a sudden jump in prices being paid

in an area, the likelihood is that property values will be reassessed. If it is an income property, a doubling of last year's tax makes a substantial difference in the bottom-line cash flow; you may not want to buy the property. Get the answer to potential tax increases first, decide to buy later.

10. **Electric bill.** Some properties seem to soak up utility bills. Find out what it is, and why it is high or low if it seems to deviate from the norm. Local utility companies will give you information on all utility costs.

11. **Gas or oil bill.** See Number 10. Converting from one fuel to another might seem expensive at first, but depending on the area, lower natural gas bills or oil that is cheaper than electricity can make it worthwhile. Check out the basic situation so you needn't continually do comparisons for each property.

12. **Yearly maintenance cost.** This goes for all kinds of property. Do not overlook insurance, city requirements (such as mowing vacant lots), and, naturally, additional maintenance costs for income properties.

13. **Building code violations.** This is critical: some may have to be corrected at a great expense; others may be "grandfathered," i.e., the city allows older buildings to function without meeting the new code. Should you plan to remodel the structure, it could trigger a requirement for you to correct the violations.

14. **Pending code violations.** A new law may have been established that is not yet in effect. Your intended purchase may meet the code now, but as of next month will be required to have fire sprinklers or some other expensive item. Ask your agent to find out, and communicate the answer in writing so you have someone to sue if there is a problem because they reported back to you incorrectly.

15. **Known or suspected damage.** Most states protect the buyer to a great extent, so generally you have cause for action if either the listing agent or the seller knew of known or suspected damage and didn't tell you **when you asked.**

16. **New construction, roadway changes, or pending construction.** A new highway, bridge, hospital, or airport being built across the street or nearby—or planned construction—can ruin your investment. Ask and doublecheck.

17. **Other construction or demolition.** Same as Number 16.

18. **Tax assessment of this and abutting properties.** Get an idea as to the values of all the property in the neighborhood.

19. **Comparable sales in the area.** Find out what has been moving and at what price. You might find a steal that way, or keep from buying something overpriced.

20. **All sales in the past 12 months within several blocks.** This is a general look at what is going on in the area. Additional information for your comfort zone.

21. **In the general area, what is now on the market and how long it has been there.** This is part of trend information—what is offered, how long has it been

on the market without selling. This might affect the amount you offer, if there are alternative properties to select from.

22. **Size and dimensions of the land.** General information that is essential to make final decisions and comparisons to other properties on the market.

23. **Plan of building, showing square footage.** You will want to get this as soon as you can, to make decisions about the property and what you can do with it.

24. **Rental properties: copies of leases, rental income, and expenses for past four years.** This is essential information for any income property, so you can get the bottom line. A review of the leases can show you a real problem or an absolute gem.

25. **The seller's intentions after the closing.** In a straight purchase this is not as important as in an exchange. In the usual listing relationship the listing agent will not know what the seller plans to do, because most listing agents do not counsel their clients, so they have no idea of the clients' goals or investment plans. When you present an exchange offer, the more you know about the desires and goals of the seller, the better you can deal with objections. Say the seller has confided to his agent that he wants to sell so he can take the proceeds and retire to North Carolina. If you knew this ahead of time you might plan your exchange offer so that you can actually help the seller obtain a property in North Carolina using something you have as an exchange. "Mr. Seller, I am interested in acquiring your property, and I need to accomplish a real estate exchange to do so. I understand you are interested in moving to North Carolina, so if you would give me an idea as to what you would like to own there I will attempt to acquire it, via exchange, so that you and I can do a deal."

The actual statement might be a series of conversations through your agent and his listing agent, but the result could be that you move into an exchange through a North Carolina broker who facilitates the deal by bringing in another property.

Start with a Simple, Straightforward Offer

Chapter 2 contains several sample offer forms that you can use as a basis for your own offers, if there is nothing locally that serves the purpose. It is always best, however, to use a form the agents find most comfortable, so adapt to their forms, if they work. Avoid having a lawyer draft a long legal-looking document when you can use a standard form, which your lawyer has checked to ensure that it gives you adequate protection.

Have Your Backup Package Ready to Go

Assume that you are offering a vacant residential lot, which you feel is worth $55,000, as a part of your $80,000 down payment on a home for which the seller is asking $280,000. The property has a first mortgage of $180,000, and you also ask the seller to hold a second mortgage for $20,000 to round out the deal. Your offer would have these outlines:

You give the seller cash	$ 25,000
Assume the first mortgage	180,000
He holds a second for	20,000
You give him your lot	55,000

When your agent takes the offer to the seller, you should make sure that you have provided him with a property package that "sells" the lot . . . aerial photos, clear legals and descriptions, property comparables, and so on, just as though you or your agent were making a cold-turkey call on a prospective buyer of that lot.

Be Sure Your Agent Is Familiar with Your Property

If the property is local or not too far away, your agent should visit it. Take the agent to the property, and make sure that he can convincingly talk about it and the benefits that give it value. If you have an overpriced lot or other property that you are asking the agent to include in your exchange offer and he is aware of your overevaluation, the deal is doomed. You should be able to justify the value of your property, either through comparables or market studies.

For example, if the lot you are offering is worth only $35,000 and not $55,000, it's the same as though you are offering $20,000 less for the home. It is much better to illustrate this as a reduced offer than to simply try to pass off an overpriced lot as your way to match his value. Price your properties fairly and have the backup material to support the values. If your overevaluation is spotted by the agent or the other party, both will lose confidence in you.

Why Your Agent Should Plan to Show Your Property

Part of the technique of closing on exchanges is to get the other party to keep an open mind about this kind of transaction, and not reject it simply because it is creative or unusual. One of the best ways to do this is for the agent presenting the offer to be ready to show the property to the seller as soon as possible. If the seller can be asked to meet with the presenting agent at or near the actual property being offered, the showing can occur along with the presentation. If the lot you are offering is close to the agent's office or convenient to a restaurant where the parties can meet to discuss the offer (without you), so much the better.

Why a Joint Presentation Works Well

Because some agents are better at listing than selling, a joint presentation by your agent and the listing agent, or it could be two agents representing your offer, can work to your advantage. Whatever the combination, it is critical that the two agents understand their roles and have gone over both the offer and the subject properties being offered in the exchange, prior to making the presentation. When your offer is handed to the seller is the wrong time for one agent to be surprised at the terms. This can create problems, and a confrontation can occur on the spot. A smooth, well-orchestrated presentation follows a meeting where the listing agent was counseled first by the buyer's agent as to the nature of the offer and the goals the "buyer" wishes to obtain, and where there is some flexibility in the offer.

Negotiate to a Final Point—Never Start There

Everyone wants to make gold stars. You know what I mean? Those little stars you got as a kid in kindergarten for being quiet at naptime or drinking all your milk? Well, in adult life it is much the same, only we score our gold stars by pats on the back. The listing agent wants to be appreciated for helping his client gain some in putting the deal together. The agent presenting your offer wants to win, too, as does the seller. And, perhaps most of all, you want to win because you started this whole scenario by making the offer in the first place. But anticipate the natural tendency of people to want to **win,** and be sure you have some flexibility built into the offer to allow that to happen.

Have Some Throw-Away Provisions in the Offer

One of the best ways to help the other side win and affect you minimally is to have some provisions that you will allow to be changed or removed such as these:
- This offer is subject to approval of the buyer's lawyer within 10 days following acceptance by the sellers.
- Closing to occur within 120 days.
- The deposit to be held pending the inspections and approval of all building permits will be in the form of a promissory note in the amount of $20,000.

Each of the above contains elements that can be altered without altering the result of the transaction. Sometimes all the seller wants to do is to **win** at something, and if the main terms and conditions of the agreement are acceptable, it is much easier for the agents to obtain a closing of the contract on small items.

Expect a Counteroffer

When you make an offer you should expect a counteroffer. Sometimes the deal goes through immediately, but most of the time one or more elements of your offer are rejected; then it is up to the other party's agents to produce a counteroffer. In the exchange of property it is important to keep the lines of communication open, and as long as you are working back and forth on an offer there is hope for it ultimately to conclude successfully.

Any Kind of Counter Is Productive

As long as it is in writing. You made your offer in writing, so expect that your agent will bring back something in writing. At times no deal is really possible, and the counter is apt to be as impossible for you as yours was for the seller. You will succeed only by making offers and by not assuming ahead of time whether they will be accepted or not.

Start Closing the Gap

Opening up the idea of legs often closes the gap in real estate exchanges. I get into legs in greater detail in Chapter 13, but for now, the idea is to show the other party that it is not absolutely necessary that they "take" your property to do a deal with you. "Look," your agent might suggest, "accept this deal subject to our finding you a property in North Carolina you like and making a three-way exchange. Is that okay?"

You may not find a property in the exact place he wants, nor a property he would buy if he had the cash instead, but moving closer to his goal might be more attractive than keeping a property he doesn't want to own. If that part of the exchange is small enough (valuewise), some kind of accommodation exchange might be made. Take another look at how the example on page 313 was structured. The offer included $25,000 cash, a $55,000 lot and $20,000 second mortgage which you were going to give the seller. If he balked at that but agreed to take the lot, your agent could point out that the $20,000 note and mortgage should be easy to exchange as a part of a down payment or purchase price of a property in North Carolina which he wanted to end up with. Exchanging paper is much easier than property, and if he were to find a property in North Carolina he wanted, there would be a good chance the seller of that property would take the $20,000 mortgage as a part of the deal. But to "sell" this deal, your agent must understand the concepts and accept the idea that this kind of creative deal making goes on all the time. All you are doing is taking proven techniques and applying them to your situations.

Generating an Offer from the Other Side

There are times when you would be better served if the initial offer came in from the other side. If you have partners, for example, getting everyone at your end to agree to make an offer can be more difficult than getting them to agree to a deal that solves their problems. Making the offer is often the critical step to making a deal, and your agent can be essential in getting the ball rolling.

One way this is done is through exchange clubs, which I will discuss in detail in the next chapter. In real estate exchange clubs, the brokers and agents use what is called a preliminary exchange proposal, or a **miniform.** This looks kind of like an offer, but in reality is nothing more than one broker giving a memo to another broker that he thinks something like this or that offer might work. In the example that follows I am suggesting to Mike Dodeals a deal between the owner (my listing) of an Ocala horse ranch and the owner (his listing) of a resort in the Canary Islands. Would he present the miniform to that owner and see if he can generate an offer for exchange along the terms and conditions of the miniform offer?

How to Expand Your Broker Network

In a short while—using this book, working with your team, and having some in-the-field practice—you will become more knowledgeable about real estate exchanges than most of the brokers and agents in your area. Once you are comfortable with the knowledge you possess,

PRELIMINARY EXCHANGE PROPOSAL

FROM: ___JACK CUMMINGS___   ISSUED AT: ___BROWARD EXCHANGE CLUB___

ADDRESS: ___2669 East Commercial Blvd.___   DATE: ___March 3, 1992___

CITY: ___Ft. Laud___ STATE ___Florida___ ZIP ___33308___   PHONE: ___(305) 771-6300___

TO: ___Steve Engels___

REFERENCE YOUR LISTING:

> Steve, about your hotel on the ocean, Pier Pointe,
> 108 Units - In Lauderdale-by-the Sea...

I HAVE THE FOLLOWING IDEA:

> Why not exchange that property for my listing of
> over 700 acres in North Floirda.

[X] Let's get together and brainstorm the possibilities.   [ ] Will you please send and initiate the offer be-

[ ] At the break or end of the meeting.   cause _____

[ ] I'll call or write within the next 3 days to discuss.   [ ] Attached is a copy of my package.

[ ] Will you please let me see or send me a copy of   [ ] Attached is a copy of my "back up" material.
    "back up" package as soon as possible.

[ ] I will send you an offer by_____

REPLY NEEDED BY ___Next Monday latest___

REPLY COMMENTS:

Jack Cummings
Counselor

	YOU	WE
OV	10,500,000	5,500,000
Loan	6,500,000	0
Equity	4,000,000	5,500,000
Steve your guy pays Boot		1,500,000
Balance	4,000,000	4,000,000

_____
Counselor

you can put together a short lecture course, not to exceed two hours, including a 15-minute break in the middle. Offer this lecture to local Boards of Realtors as a free educational program. You can extend this course to large real estate offices and spend a couple of hours each month standing in front of real estate agents proving that you are now an insider.

I know that many of you cringe at the prospect of being so presumptuous as to think that, after getting through this book and doing some homework on your own, you could pass yourself off as an expert on exchanges. Well, you don't have to be an expert, all you have to do is help the real estate industry open their eyes to the fantastic tool of real estate exchanging. When you have some real-life examples of what you have done in exchanges, they will not only listen to what you have to say, but will want to make some deals with you.

Opening doors is what expansion is all about. The more doors that open to you before you knock, the better off you will be.

You Can Network by Writing Articles

Local newspapers and journals are good places to start. Real-life experience is what you want to talk about: how this or that worked for you, how you got started, and so on. The key is to select a topic that will show someone else how they can reach their goals. If you are writing for a real estate journal, you would want to show the agents how they will get more listings, make more sales, and therefore earn greater commissions. If it is for a newspaper catering to a retirement market, you might decide to write about an exchange or two you did that helped someone retire or attain that dream house they always wanted—perhaps someone who could not "sell" their home in upper New York State, until you showed them how to exchange out of it into a property you had in Florida.

Be positive. Everything you write about should be positive. It does no good to be negative in anything you do. Negative thoughts stay with you unless you decide that there will be nothing negative in your life. You will be surprised how that one single decision can change your whole outlook on life and, most interestingly, on yourself.

Become a Person Magnet

People like to be around cheerful, positive people. Even if what you have to say is not that important, you can be an uplifting person who makes others feel good. With kind pats on the back, a smile, and a "Good to see you, Charlie" tone in your voice, you will find that people like dealing with you. When people like to deal with you, much more gets done.

By becoming a magnet that attracts people—agents who come to you because you are positive and uplifting and agents who are out to make deals—you will be in the position to pick their brains. Getting information from people about what they know, what hot deals are out there, and where the trends are leading is a part of your learning process that continues until the final diploma. You can get and keep the edge without resorting to pressure and mind games.

10

Real Estate Exchange or Barter Clubs

Why join a real estate exchange club? The simple answer is: to make more contacts, expand your horizons, and make bigger and more creative exchanges. The sound business reason is that you can increase your exposure to investment opportunities.

The Real Estate Exchange Club Is Your Best Choice

There are two kinds of clubs to consider: **real estate** and **barter.** The first is most viable for you; real estate exchange clubs are generally made up of brokers and agents who get together on a frequent schedule to make exchanges and other kinds of real estate transactions. These clubs provide a foundation for many of the real estate exchanges that take place in your community. In addition to the local exchange organizations, there are regional or statewide groups that serve the same purpose.

The most important function of these groups is not the volume of exchanges that occur during the meetings, but the ability to meet other insiders who are also interested in real estate exchanges. Most of these groups provide an ongoing education and updated information on tax laws and creative techniques. Sometimes, just having someone to bounce an idea off is the single element that allows you to go out and close a deal that has been evading you.

Many Insider Clubs Are Closed to Outsiders

While many of these real estate exchange clubs have been closed to outsiders, there is a growing trend to open the doors and let in investors. I have done a complete flip-flop on this, and while I was once in favor of keeping the "insiders" clean of investors, I now believe the mixture of brokers, agents, and investors to be the best for everyone. But some clubs still are restricted to licensed real estate brokers and salesmen.

The 7 Benefits to Having a Real Estate License

The quickest way to become considered an insider is to get a real estate license. That does not mean you have to become a real estate agent, unless that field is of interest to you. As you will see, there are many good reasons to get a license; qualification to become a member of a "restricted" exchange club is just one.

1. **A world of information opens up to you.** Access to real estate databanks, county records, deed information, building and zoning codes and restrictions, and a host of other information, while public and available to anyone, could be quickly available to you through a real estate office computer hookup. Other Board of Realtor services that are available to Realtors could also become very valuable to you in your investment plans.

2. **Each deal is money in your pocket.** You get a break on commissions when you buy, sell, or exchange. Real estate commissions vary from deal to deal, as they should, but generally commissions range from 5 to 7 percent of the selling price for improved property, and up to 10 percent for vacant land. Commercial deals and other properties priced over half a million or so often drop as the values go up. Your share of the overall commission after splits within the office might be 50 percent or more. If you were to buy a $150,000 home with a 7 percent commission and receive 50 percent of the commission, your portion would be $5,250. This could go a long way toward the down payment on that same property if you were the buyer. Real estate agents often use their commission as the sole down payment to acquire a property which makes for neat cashless investing.

3. **You have your own private training center.** Real estate courses are available to you. Most Boards of Realtors and many businesses closely connected to the real estate profession offer seminars and courses. These are an easy, inexpensive way to increase your knowledge of real estate, from the inside out.

4. **You get insider scoops on what's going on.** You can get real insider information before it becomes public. New listings can be picked up from the "in-house computer" the day after they are listed, and sometimes several weeks before they are printed in the listing books. This can give you a great headstart on finding property in your comfort zone.

5. **You get exposure to other people's success and failure.** You develop friendships with fellow insiders to brainstorm with. Even if you do nothing but look and listen you are using one of the very best techniques to advance yourself and your investment plans. Learning from the mistakes of others can save you a lot of time, heartache, and money, so brainstorming with people who have been through the mill can be rewarding in many ways.

6. **You can camouflage your investment activities.** As an agent you have a good "front" for your personal investment interests. There is nothing wrong with real estate agents also being real estate investors. In fact, the more you back up your confidence in real estate by investing in it, the better you are as a real estate agent (should you go that way). As an agent you have direct access to the property, and you will be able to ask questions that principals never get to ask or never get answers to.

7. **You get a quick way to the inside.** When you have your Realtor's license, you qualify for "insider only" memberships open just to the professionals.

Exchange clubs are among the "professionals only" associations and organizations that would be open to you.

Getting a Broker or Agent to Front for You

This is the least acceptable way to get access to the exchange clubs you get only secondary information anyway. However, if you want to have some access and do not have a license yet, find a member who will let you know what is going on. You will not get all the benefits discussed, but you can still have access to the opportunities as they come up.

Dealing with Insiders Once You Become One of Them

Real estate exchange clubs vary considerably as to the style and attitude of their membership. The most important factor of doing business in exchange clubs is to learn whom you can best do business with. With this in mind, you can calmly observe events as they occur. Do not jump to conclusions as to which member is the "live wire" or the most professional. Maintain as neutral a posture as you can when first making acquaintances within exchange clubs (or any kind of club or association for that matter).

Watch Out for Overpricers

The reasons for not making hasty judgments is that people can be very deceptive about what they say they do and what they actually do. In real estate exchanges, more than almost any other kind of real estate transaction, your time can be grossly wasted by members who constantly start deals that are based on information that turns out to be wildly distorted.

Frank offered me a sailboat in exchange for several time-share apartments I owned plus some cash I would have to pay. As I was in the market at the time for a sailboat, I entered into an agreement with him subject to my inspection of the boat. To see the boat would require me to spend the better part of a day to drive several hundred miles to the marina where the boat was docked, but I believed Frank when he told me the value of the boat was $20,000 and that it was in good condition. "Needs to have the bottom painted, that's about all," he had said.

The directions he gave to me turned out to be wrong, and the name on the boat was spelled incorrectly. As there were only a couple of marinas in the general area, and armed with the name of the dockmaster at the marina, I eventually found the boat.

"Sure," the dockmaster began, "sure does need a bottom job, along with a top and side job." He laughed, spit some tobacco juice into the water next to the boat, and continued. "But for $5,500 she's a potential winner, don't you think?"

A $14,500 hike in value, the wrong directions, and a complete distortion of the condition of the boat taught me never to believe anything Frank says. Yet he does close on deals every now and then, probably with people just like him who have grossly distorted their values and descriptions.

Build Your Reputation by Fair Evaluations

Property owners have the right to price their property as they please. Frank could have said the boat was worth $150,000; he would have been wrong only in a greater degree; equally, he would not have found a buyer. Many exchangers rationalize that they overprice their property as a defense against other exchangers who also overprice. A high price justified by previous sales data, comparable sales, market studies, or valid appraisals is one thing. Prospective buyers can offer less and motivated sellers can accept less. But avoid a distorted evaluation of your property, and be cautious with members of exchange clubs who overprice as a normal practice. Your value to the exchange club and your opportunity to participate in more transactions will grow as you develop a reputation for being realistic in property values and in your assessments of what you can do.

Knowing Whom to Deal With

First of all, you never want to absolutely rule out anyone. Even the "overpricers" can come up with a deal now and then. The key is to get to know the members so that you know who is apt to be giving you the straight scoop up front, and whom you have to watch like a hawk. To establish a priority of whom you **want** to deal with is not going to be that difficult, as you will naturally gravitate toward people who are positive and who will be helpful to you early in your membership term. These people can well be the foundation for your success in doing business with the membership. Take a look at the following eight ways to pick an exchanger.

The 8 Criteria in Selecting an Exchanger You Can Deal With

1 Get feedback from other members.
2. What kind of property does someone deal in?
3. Other exchangers' reactions to him.
4. Does he make offers but never follow through?
5. Is he an overpricer?
6. What kind of deals does he actually make?
7. Is he negative?
8. Gravitate to people you like.

Because these eight steps are very important, take a brief look at each one:

1. **Get feedback from other members.** Feedback from fellow members is critical to your learning about people. Naturally, you must be discreet about this and not appear to be conducting an investigation of a murder. General conversation about who is doing deals, which member can you learn the most from, and that sort of thing will lead you to the topics you want discussed.

2. **What kind of property does someone deal in?** If he is like Steve, a member of the Ft. Lauderdale exchange club who deals in low rent properties, near to or actually in slums, you might discover that he is or is not the kind of person you want to get to know well. (Depending on the kind of property you want to deal with). Each professional who is successful at what they do will

have some specialty. This does not mean that they cannot bring you an opportunity outside that specialty, but direct your attention to the person's best side and profit from that.

3. **Other exchangers' reaction to him.** How the other members react to property presentations from this person can give you a good idea as to their business acumen. A true professional will be courteous of others, and will not present negative thoughts or conjectures that will disrupt another member.

4. **Does he make offers but never follow through?** Some members will not want to be outdone and will make offer after offer just (this must be the reason) to give the appearance that they are being productive. The problem is, they rarely follow through with anything. One guy I know is always making me offers. We make appointments to go see the property and he never shows up; or if he does it is hours or days later, and then it is to offer some reason why the deal is not going to work. He is a nice guy, does this to everyone, and is generally thought of as a waste of time, both his and everyone else's. Yet he does do a deal here and there, and because he is so likable people put up with him as long as he can be accommodated within their own schedule.

5. **Is he an overpricer?** All you have to do is to check out a couple of properties a person offers. If you have access to computer data of property values and sales information, this is easy to do and can save you a lot of time later on.

6. **What kinds of deals does he actually make?** Beware of talkers who never back up their words with deeds. Some members talk about multimillion dollar deals, but all you see them doing is exchanging water filters for second-hand cars. Look at the actual "closed deals" and that will give you the best picture of all. Not the entire picture of course—you are starting out with a blank slate and you would not want to be judged by the deals you have done—but the deals that do get done show where a person is coming from and going.

7. **Is he negative?** Eliminate the negative people—period. There are many points of view about doing business with negative people. Some say you can make a fortune dealing with them if you understand where they are coming from. Others stress the need to avoid them at all cost because they will try to drag you down to their mental outlook. Make an effort not to associate with negative thinkers and doers. There are so many positive people you can associate with that you simply do not **need** to be around negative people. (Mind you, I am talking about people within associations and clubs. When it comes to actual deals, you can profit equally by buying a property from a positive person as from a negative person.)

8. **Gravitate to people you like.** It is important that you have a rapport with the member you plan or hope to do business with. This is far more important in a closed group than in dealing one-on-one with a person you will never see again. If you have a personality conflict with someone, it is a good idea to avoid that person, because the conflict will grow and your relationship and reputation within the organization can suffer gravely. Learn to recognize different types of members.

The 3 Kinds of Members

1. Those who deal with their own properties
2. Those who deal with clients' properties
3. Those who deal with both their own and clients' properties

It dawned on me that there are also those who don't deal at all—but that is a negative thought, so forget I even mentioned it. The importance of these three kinds of members is that the first one and the third one are apt to be the easiest to deal with. The member who is there to get an advantage over "outsider investors" by dealing on the inside is just like you. He can make a decision without having to ask anyone else (with his own properties) what they think or want to do.

Working through principals is a key to doing business in exchange clubs. Of all the exchanges I have made with members of my clubs, the best results have been where I was doing business directly with the member on his or her own property.

Finding the Other Party's Hot Button

Everyone has a hot button, something that motivates and provides some extra incentive to make a decision or to act. Hot buttons can either be logical business factors or purely emotional factors. I have seen people make exchanges because of a sweetener tossed in that triggered that emotional "Okay, let's do it," when the sound business factors had remained unchanged. Making a deal with anyone, anywhere, can boil down to your ability to find that single element that closes the deal.

A recent transaction I was working on at the same time I was writing this chapter illustrates the point. Vinny's hot button was to make the deal on his terms, to prove something to his mother. It took me a couple of meetings with him in presenting counteroffers and attempting to get counters from him to narrow the gap and discover that hot button. Once I knew it, the negotiations shifted to counters that allowed him to "win" points toward that goal while counterbalancing the deal in other ways to make it acceptable to the other side.

Toys—Even Big Boys Like to Play

Some sellers are motivated by toys—**big** toys, like sports cars and fast boats, or to a lesser degree, computers, sports equipment, cars of any age and condition, and holiday packages and travel bargains. If you are dealing for a property and know that the owner has a weakness or a hot button for something along these lines, it would be a good idea to anticipate this by bringing in a third leg for part of the deal. This would mean you would first lock up an exchange on a "toy" and include it into your offer. More on legs in Chapter 13.

Be Careful of Dealing with "Open Listings"

In the real estate industry, an open listing is little more than information. For example, the agent calls an owner to see if he wants to sell or exchange his property. The owner says he *net listings?*

might, and after a brief conversation the agent has made notes that the owner would consider $250,000 for the property, or might take a home or vacant lot in exchange, if, of course, it was just where the owner would want to be. The agent also confirms that the owner will pay a 7 percent fee to the agent in the event a satisfactory deal is closed. That is about the most basic of "open listings."

Armed with that information, the agent shows up at the exchange club and offers you that property. A few questions about the property show you there is not much depth of information to be obtained, and no assurance exists that the property can be delivered or that the owner will really be interested in an exchange.

If the property interests you it might be worth giving a minioffer, letting the agent go back to the owner to determine how interested he might be. But you should not spend much time in analyzing the property, unless the agent can provide you with detailed information and demonstrate to you that he has some control over the listing, and some in-depth knowledge of what the owner wants to do.

Use Exchange Clubs to Make Yourself a Known Investor

In your early days of investing in real estate, the more you can do to put your name out as an insider, the faster you will begin to be treated like one. Exchange clubs, with all their faults and problems, are an ideal way to add to that sphere of reference that makes you an insider. If you discover that there are no clubs in your area, or you decide not to obtain a real estate license as a precondition of membership Chapter 11 will tell you how to start your own club.

Why You Should Join a Barter Club

Barter clubs differ markedly from real estate exchange. First of all, they handle things and services rather than real estate. Chapter 8 introduced you to some of the ways in which barter can be incorporated to your real estate transactions and how, through barter clubs, you can build a portfolio in barter items.

As you can add barter to your real estate transactions, you will find that you can also add real estate to your barter deals. For example, if you want to set up a third leg to obtain a "toy" to stroke the hot button of a property owner, you might go to one or more of the barter club members to make an exchange in that direction. If you need a car, then find out what the car dealers would take from you in exchange. It might be that all you need to do is build up some barter credits so you can "spend" the credits to get the "toys" you need to sweeten the real estate deal.

I recently exchanged with an autobody and paint shop a week's holiday at Disneyworld for services at their shop. The transaction was nothing more than my giving them the right to use a time-share week I own in the Disneyworld area. My "rental value" was $850 for the week, considerably less than a two-bedroom suite at a hotel in the area would have set them back; but it was still more than I would have netted out if the resort had rented the unit and taken their usual 20 percent fee. The deal was good for the autobody shop and me as I used the credit to paint and fix up a car to use in another deal.

The barter club charges a fee when you "sell" goods or services to barter club members, and in turn allows you to "buy" from other members, using the sale proceeds as credit.

For example, Billy is planning a big family birthday party for his parents and wants to bring in family members from around the country. He will need hotel rooms, a party room, food caterers, rental cars, a bartender, and beverages, just to start. He calls his barter club and discovers that most of what he needs is available through other barter club members. But does Billy have any credits at the club? Not yet, but what he does have is an unsold condo out west of town. It is fairly priced at $50,000 and has a $35,000 mortgage on it. Billy tells the barter club he will sell it for $15,000 in barter dollars.

Susan buys the condo, using barter dollars she had built up through her interior decorating business, plus a fee to the club for their services. The fee to the barter club is paid in real money. Billy now has credits to spend for his family party and, as he makes his deals with the hotel, the restaurant and so on, he also pays a fee to the barter club.

On one transaction, I sold property to a member and took credits that I spent over several years on a variety of items, ranging from car phones to light poles to the lights to go on top of them for a used-car lot I developed. All good value, each coming from a deal that would not have occurred were it not for barter and exchange.

There Are Many Ways to Skin a Cat

You only need one way at a time, and you should always look for the easiest and least complicated way to put any deal together. Using exchange and barter can appear to complicate a transaction, but in reality it can make it far easier because it will often be the case that without it you would not have a transaction at all.

Approach real estate exchange and barter clubs with the attitude that you will get contacts out of these organizations, and, if you keep your eyes open, some opportunities. Build on that and success will be yours.

11

Starting Your Own Exchange or Barter Club

If You Can't Find One, Start One

There are hundreds of people just like you who would like to have a strong base on which to build their investment plan. They, like you, want to reduce their investment risk while expanding their opportunities. Just like you, they recognize that exchanges are "in," and that by using real estate exchanges and barter transactions it is possible to start the process of building your fortune now. One good way to accomplish this is to do so through an exchange and barter club that you form.

The Goal: Generate Business for the Members

The idea is to gather a group of **real estate investors** and business owners who, by joining together, can benefit each other. By belonging to a synergetic group, greater things can occur, because of the joint effort, than if the individuals worked on their own.

The original premise of the organization of an exchange-barter club should be the simple but important goal that the primary purpose is to generate business for the members. This kind of club is not a local philanthropic organization, nor is it designed to support charity. This is a professional organization of investors who meet and do business together so that they can, in a very capitalistic way, profit through that association with the other members. The term "profit" includes all the benefits available, not just monetary profit.

This chapter gives you an outline of the steps necessary to set up your own exchange-barter club. To put the plan into effect can take time, effort, and money, and your ultimate rewards will be harvested in the long term rather than immediately. Because of this you may want to bring in a partner or two to get started. Together, you and your partners can share the investment of time, effort, and money, and reap the benefits.

Check Out the Local Situation

Find out what clubs may exist for real estate exchange or barter groups. Call the local Board of Realtors and ask them if they know of any real estate exchange groups. Does the Board have one? Can they recommend any Realtors who are knowledgeable in real estate exchanges?

Contact those people to find out if there are any exchange or barter clubs around. Make a list of all such groups you find and then continue by gathering as much information as you can about the other clubs in the area. Follow the checklist provided below.

The Information Checklist

1. What are their membership requirements?
2. What does it cost to join, and what is the annual membership fee?
3. What are the rules and regulations?
4. What are the methods of transactions? Is there a fee per transaction, and how is it calculated?
5. Can they send you a membership roster so you can check their references?
6. What is the history of their organization?
7. When and where do they meet?
8. For barter organizations: Request a list of current services, products, restaurants, scrip, etc. available to members.

All it should take is a phone call to discover the right person to supply new-membership information and their "membership package." Drop that person a note requesting this information, if it is not included in their membership-application package.

The most important of the above data, initially, is the membership roster. You should call a dozen members and ask the following questions:

Questions to Ask Members of Other Clubs

- How long have they been a member?
- Have they done any deals or benefited from the association, and if so, how?
- Are they pleased with the club?
- Would they consider joining a more professionally organized club?

Now You Are Ready to Start

Rules and Regulations

I have provided a base set of rules and regulations on which you can build. You will want to modify these rules and regulations to fit your needs, and to balance your emphasis with that of other local clubs in the area, if there are any. A description of a sample club follows.

Sample Rules and Regulations, Worldwide Exchange-Barter Network (WEBN)

```
Goal:  To build a network of investors and professional people who
can profit through exchange and barter with each other.
   Association:  The Worldwide Exchange-Barter Network (WEBN) is an
international organization dedicated to real estate exchange and
barter on a worldwide basis. The local chapter is operated by (your
name) as a private corporation for profit. The local WEBN will col-
```

lect membership fees and transaction fees. Membership fees shall be $100 per year, with transaction fees paid by the "buyer" in every transaction. The buyer's fees are 15 percent of the "sale" or exchange on barter items, and 4 percent on real estate. These fees are not commissions, but a handling fee for the processing of the transaction and the service charge for maintaining membership and other membership benefits which accrue to members. Of these fees, the local WEBN will retain 80 percent, with 20 percent sent to international headquarters.

Membership requirements: To be interested in participating as a principal in exchange or barter between other members. If acting as an agent for others, to do so only as an exclusive agent for the nonmember. Membership will be subject to an annual review of a board of no more than seven members and no fewer than three members, and all members must abide by future requirements for education and standards of ethics. Initial joining fees and annual fees are subject to change.

Unique business opportunities: Unlike other real estate exchange and barter organizations, WEBN is not a closed organization designed to keep investors on the outside while the agents are on the inside. WEBN is a network designed for members who are principals and agents and who act exclusively for their principals. WEBN is a deal-making place.

To facilitate the needs of all its members, WEBN urges all business owners in the area and all real estate investors to examine the benefits that can be obtained through membership in the WEBN. Remember the goal: to generate business opportunities between the members.

Wanted, but by no means limited to the following, are members who own or control all types of businesses that deal in a product or service. We encourage real estate investors to join as a way to expand their market.

How does WEBN work? Once you are a member, you will receive an orientation booklet explaining the exciting world of exchange and barter. You will be able to "sell" your goods or services through the club in one of two different ways, each designed to build credits to your account so that you can in turn acquire other goods or services from the other members. The first way to sell your goods or services is by **scrip**. WEBN prints up "money" that can be spent only at your place of business. To some degree, you may limit the amount to be spent at any one time, or have blackout periods (if a restaurant or hotel), and the scrip is not good for tax or tip. WEBN distributes this scrip to its members, who "buy" the scrip with credits they hold at WEBN. They will be charged an additional 15 percent. The dollar amount of scrip sold will be credited to your account.

The second way is for you to be an **open member**, which does not require you to have scrip printed for your business. For an open member, the transaction is made directly between members, and the transfers of credits are made over the phone. The selling member will collect a cash payment of 15 percent, in addition to any required sales taxes from the buying member. The cash payment of 15 percent will be sent to WEBN and the transfer of credits finalized. If real property is the subject of this transaction, the handling fee is 4 percent to the buyer. Time-share units, either ownership or use thereof, are not considered real property for the calculation of fees.

Open members: A member who is trading in the WEBN as an open member must establish the credit maximum per transaction, and other limitations within which they will exchange or barter. For example, an accounting or any other service firm may establish maximums per contract and limit a contract to 24 months. In this way, the accounting or bookkeeping firm may elect to establish a maximum credit for up to two years, which could be applied against the actual charges (if in excess of the maximum exchange or barter credit).

Single-use services (even though they can be repeated many times) or product sales can limit the amount of barter credit which will be accepted for each transaction by a percentage of the price, as well as a maximum per transaction. All non-real-estate transactions offered (either through scrip or by open members) will not be restricted more than the following.

Gross Sale Maximum	Exchange of Credits Cannot Be Less Than
$100	40%
200	35%
500	30%

For example, a service company can agree to accept barter payments, provided they do not exceed the percentages indicated above. If there is a sale of a $100 item, then at least $40 would be accepted in the form of barter dollars, and the balance paid in real money. Barter company fees would be based on the barter dollar portion and not the total transaction.

Naturally, the idea is to provide services and products at a full 100 percent barter; however, some items or services may not be available on that basis. The minimum percentages to which a member can limit his exposure are indicated above.

Transactions in excess of $500 may be limited to any amount. All limitations must be printed clearly on the scrip and in the case of open members, provided in writing to the local WEBN.

Printed scrip: When a member offers scrip, WEBN will require authorization signed by the member and payment for the printing. The member may restrict the scrip as follows:

1. Limitation on amounts that can be spent at any one time
2. Blackout dates
3. Not to be applied with other discounts
4. Establish a termination date when the scrip can no longer be used; said date must be at least six months from date of issue

In the use of scrip, the using member must abide by the limitations printed on the scrip, and understand that tax and tip cannot be paid in scrip or by credit card and must be paid in cash. In the event of an overpayment in scrip due to the denominations issued, no change will be offered, so members are advised to carefully examine the bill when presented.

Universal credit: As the WEBN grows and additional local networks join, the credits can be "spent" in any of the network locations and with all participating members. The local WEBN will mail monthly statements showing credits contained in the member's "WEBN bank," and lists of open members with the limitations on credit use at those businesses.

Violations: Failure to honor scrip or provide services or products as per the **open member agreement** will cause a loss of membership and a freeze of any credits held in the WEBN bank by the local WEBN.

A Place to Meet

All you have to do is to find a place where you can schedule meetings. Many restaurants provide meeting rooms for breakfast or lunch meetings for private business groups. The best approach would be to contact several such places that are convenient to local traffic and main highways. Explain that you would like to have a weekly breakfast meeting. You will expect to charge the members that attend a nominal charge for the breakfast, but you are a new group so you do not know how many people you will have. Select a quality location that will give all prospective members a good feeling about the organization. Plan to start small and grow.

Build Your Originating Team

To make the program work, you cannot be expected to pull it off all by yourself. You need to build a team so that the success becomes a team effort. You are the leader, so you determine who is on the team and what role they play. There are three stages to building your team.

1. **Incorporate.** This is essential to ensure that you are the leader. You will want to form your own company that is the local WEBN (or whatever you want to

name it). One member of the team will be a good real estate lawyer, so get his help in incorporating. The legal work will cost you several hundred dollars and the accessory material needed to validate the corporation will cost another couple of hundred. (The accessory material is stationery, business cards, and a phone listing.)

2. **Select the team members.** Essential team members will include at least one person from each of the following professions. Where possible, they will be members of your investment team.
   - Legal. This is your top real estate lawyer.
   - Accounting firm. The accountant you use.
   - A top mortgage broker. A good idea to have two.
   - A title insurance or escrow company.
   - A local real estate exchanger.
   - Owner of a local advertising firm.
   - President of a local commercial bank.
   - President of a local savings and loan company.

3. **Delegate responsibility.** Make sure these people realize that they will be in a position to benefit from their association with this organization. They will be asked to provide educational seminars or speakers to some of the meetings, and can participate in the newsletter, as well as become active members in the exchange and barter programs offered.

Plan Your Membership Drive

Your membership drive could take several approaches.
   - Targeted membership
   - Blanket approach
   - Brochure
   - Newsletter
   - Organized follow-up

Examine each in some detail.

Targeted membership. Your phone book and whatever homework you have already done should present not only the prospective members but everything needed to set up the mailing lists. Prospective members and prime barter members will be the following:

Potential Prospective Members
   - Known real estate investors
   - Accountants
   - Advertising media (print, radio, TV)
   - Air-conditioning sales and services
   - Airlines
   - Art galleries
   - Automobile repair and paint shops

- Bookkeeping services
- Carpet sales companies
- Caterers
- Cruise line companies
- Hotels
- Painting contractors
- Photographic services
- Physical therapy and massage
- Printing firms
- Restaurants
- Schools
- Small life-insurance firms
- Taxi and limo services
- Television sales and services
- Wallpaper sales and installation
- Yacht rentals and sales and services
- Real estate professionals who are recommended to you through the local Board of Realtors as being knowledgeable in exchanges, as well as selected associates from the larger real estate firms in your area
- Membership rolls you obtained from other exchange or barter clubs

Blanket approach. This is directed at less obvious targets in a blanket way. An ad in a local newspaper would be one approach. You might obtain publicity from some of the smaller business publications in your area by sending them a press release on the new club. In addition to helping you get started, they may also discover that being an active member themselves will add to their advertising, as this kind of participant frequently deals in barter.

Brochure. This is the key factor to obtaining membership. The promotional brochure contains all the material I have shown you thus far and is the membership presentation. Plan at least two meetings where there will be a program designed to educate the members to some of the aspects of the organization, show them how they will benefit, and so on. Your team members should be on hand for both of these meetings, to add something to the program and to set themselves out as the foundation on which the program is to be built. The brochure should be professionally done, but need not be in color. A good computer program can give you a newsletter-quality presentation that a good printing company can then print up for you.

Newsletter. This is the second print element that will kick your program off with a bang and give you a good shot at being an instant success. The newsletter serves as a promotional piece for the WEBN as well as an educational piece. This newsletter should contain examples of barter and exchange deals and list some of the kinds of goods and services that are or could be available. If you have lined up several members by the time you write the newsletter, you can discuss real examples and real goods and services.

Organized follow-up. Effective follow-up is the key to any effort. Without follow-up, leads and interested parties will not be converted to members. Always follow a plan. When people call, make sure you have a checklist of things to mention while you are talking to them. When you have meetings, make sure someone is ready to take membership applications. An example of a membership application checklist is shown below:

Sample Membership Application Checklist

    DATE:_____
    1. Name of person in charge: _____
    2. Company name: _____
    3. Address and phone number:_____
    _____
    4. Product or service available on barter or exchange
    _____
    _____
    5. Scrip to be offered: YES_____   NO_____
       Total amount of scrip to be offered: $_____
       Date scrip is valid:_____
       Scrip limitations:_____
    _____
    6. OPEN MEMBERSHIP: YES_____   NO_____
       Product limitations:_____
    _____
       Credit limitations:_____
    _____
       Date open membership is valid:_____

What to Expect from Your Own Club

First of all, you will be an innovative insider—instantly in for notoriety. Boy, try to say that fast. Working at barter and exchange and all that goes with it can be exciting, and can put you in the driver's seat for opportunities, as well as for building your portfolio.

Great Zanders—Exchanges on the Run

A Zander is something the likes of which you have never seen. It generates enthusiasm, excitement, anticipation of something big about to happen. A Zander is a fast-paced real estate and barter exchange that takes place quicker than the speed of a tobacco auction. It is an event, a happening, a marvel of emotion where thousands of dollars of property, products, and service are exchanged in a few minutes before your very eyes. Great balls of Zander.

How a Zander Works

A Zander is done on a Zander Board. A moderator begins with a property, service, or product at the top of the board. Eight offers can be made directly to the top of the board. These offers would be illustrated in Boxes A through H. Then, exchange offers can be made to the items in boxes A through H that were originally offered to the "top of the board."

Zander Board

A	B	C	D
E	F	G	H
1	2	3	4
5	6	7	8
9	10	11	12
13	14	15	16

How a Moderator Runs a Zander

Alex has a two-bedroom condominium apartment in Miami that he wants to exchange, and the moderator decides to put that property on the top of the board. Generally working in front of a group of exchangers at one of the exchange clubs (yours?), the moderator questions Alex about the apartment and gets the basic facts of the property so they can be put on the board. The apartment is worth $80,000 and has a first mortgage of $50,000 with an equity of $30,000. As with most exchanges in Zanders the most important element of the exchange is the equity. Mortgage amount is the second most important factor. Total price is a combination of the two. But the moderator does not stop with this basic information. He wants Alex to explain why the property is being offered for exchange, what does Alex want to accomplish, and where and what are his hot buttons.

In short, the moderator is interested in pulling out the truth, if that is possible, while at the same time enticing prospective members of the group to become "takers" for this property. The key at this stage is not to find the exact property that Alex might exchange for, but to put up to eight other properties on the board that can become legs for Alex to pass through into something he might accept.

The condo information written on an overlay and projected so everyone in the room can watch the Zander develop and, if they want, fill in their own Zander sheet.

The Zander Builds with Different Legs Offered In

Eight investors indicate they are "takers" of this condo and offer to exchange the following for the equity:

A. Bob offers two vacant lots in Ft. Myers, Florida, worth $30,000 free and clear of any debt.
B. Frank offers three time-share weeks in Key West, Florida, plus $5,000 cash.
C. Al offers a waterfront home in Ft. Lauderdale worth $195,000 and will balance with $165,000 in paper.
D. Lee offers $35,000 (retail value) worth of water filters in an overtrade for the $30,000 equity.
E. Dan offers a 36-foot, 1979 Morgan sailboat, free and clear.
F. Jack offers $20,000 worth of books and $10,000 cash.
G. Patti offers an oceanfront apartment complex valued at $595,000 and wants $50,000 cash and $515,000 paper.
H. Mike offers $9,000 of local restaurant scrip, $11,000 of hotel scrip, and $10,000 cash.

The board now looks like this (Note that "K" stands for "thousand"):

Zander Board

> Alex: 2-bedrm condo in
> Miami—$30K equity
> $50K mtg $80K V

A (Bob): 2 lots in Ft. Myers, F&C $30K	B (Frank): 3 time-shares, Key West + $5K cash	C (Al): Waterfront home—$30K eqty +$165K mtg	D (Lee): Filters $35K overtrade
E (Dan): 36' Morgan sailboat, F&C	F (Jack): $20K books $10K cash	G (Pat): Ocean motel— $50K cash $515K mtg	H (Mike): $9K food scrip $11K hotel scrip $10K cash

At this point the moderator closes offers on the top of the board and now opens offers on the letter boxes, so any member of the group can make offers to exchange what they have for anything in any of the letter boxes. To help keep things straight, in the bottom right corner of each of the numbered boxes will be the letter to or number for which the offer to exchange is directed.

In the beginning, the moderator will accept offers only against the letter boxes. When there are no more of these, offers can be made against the numbered boxes.

But first, the moderator goes back to each of the parties who have offered on the top of the Zander and has them describe their offers in detail. Bob will discuss the lots in Ft. Myers and will answer any questions members might have. What is built around them? Exactly where are they? How long has he had them? What are the selling prices in the area? All answers can be verified later on if any of the members are interested in a subject property. In these questions and the verification of the answers members of exchange clubs begin to trust or doubt their fellow exchangers. If someone asks, "What is the average price of homes in that subdivision," and Bob says, "Minimum of $300,000 and up," and a quick check shows that the average price is really $150,000 maximum, Bob's word has fallen to an all-time low.

Once Legs Are Offered, Side Deals Are Presented

When the moderator is satisfied that everyone has given a good accounting of what they have to offer, he will open the board for additional offers.

Here's how the Zander develops.

There are three different offers to exchange for the sailboat:

1. Val offers $40,000 of vacant land in Naples, Florida, that has a $10,000 mortgage against the sailboat.
2. Jim offers a 1988 T-Bird and three Disneyworld time-shares against the sailboat.

3. Craig offers two lots in the Bahamas, free and clear, against the sailboat.

There are two offers against Mike's package shown in Box H:

4. Vince offers a tract of land in Maine that is free and clear for the package.

5. Bill offers two years' prepaid rent in his office building on Oakland Park Boulevard for 1,200 square feet of office space for the package.

Assume that there are no more offers being made against the letter boxes at this point, so the moderator opens the board for offers against the number boxes. This means anyone can offer to exchange for Boxes 1 through 5.

Zander Board

Alex: 2-bedrm condo in Miami—$30K equity $50K mtg $80K V

A (Bob): 2 lots in Ft. Myers, F&C $30K	B (Frank): 3 time-shares, Key West + $5K cash	C (Al): Waterfront home—$30K eqty +$165K mtg	D (Lee): Filters $35K overtrade
E (Dan): 36' Morgan sailboat, F&C	F (Jack): $20K books $10K cash $515K mtg	G (Pat): Ocean motel— $30K eqty -$50K +$10K cash	H (Mike): $9K food scrip $11K hotel scrip
1 (Val): Land Naples $30K eqty $10K mtg E	2 (Jim): '88 T-bird + 3 Disneyworld time-shares E	3 (Craig): 2 lots in Bahamas, F&C E	4 (Vince): Vacant in Maine, F&C H
5 (Bill): Pre-paid rent 1,200 sq. ft. office, Oakpark Blvd. H	6	7	8

The Moderator Controls the Zander Board

At this point the moderator will go back and allow each of the last five offerers a time to give a very brief description of their offer. He will go through a shortened version of the same questions and answers that were asked of Alex when his condo went to the top of the board. Any other participants in the Zander may ask questions about the offer or the property included in the offer. The job of the moderator is to keep the session brief and use his experience and enthusiasm to draw in more offers. About two minutes might be taken per offer, so not more than 10 minutes will be taken to give everyone a chance to get more details on the property at this point.

Now the moderator allows offers to be made for exchange against the last five offers (or in essence, all offers made against the letter boxes).

In this Zander, the following offers are made:

6. Jay offers $5,000 cash and $25,000 equity in a $50,000 condominium in Hilton Head, South Carolina, against Box 2.

7. Chuck offers a $15,000 second mortgage owed him, plus a 20-foot Mako fishing boat for Box 2.

8. Sylvia offers $15,000 in WEBN scrip and $15,000 cash for Box 2.

9. Jack offers three one-acre lots in a Beech Mountain, North Carolina, ski resort that are free and clear for Box 2.

10. Norma offers a $30,000 equity in a Canary Island condominium that has a $55,000 first mortgage, for Box 2.

11. Sandra offers $30,000 equity in a beach condominium that has a $60,000 first mortgage, against Box 4.

12. Kevin offers an IBM XT computer plus a new IBM laser printer, software galore, and $10,000 cash against Sandra's offer in Box 11.

The corrected Zander Board is shown below.

Zander Board

> Alex: 2-bedrm condo in
> Miami—$30K equity
> $50K mtg $80K V

A (Bob): 2 lots in Ft. Myers, F&C $30K	B (Frank): 3 time-shares, Key West + $5K cash	C (Al): Waterfront home—$30K eqty +$165K mtg	D (Lee): Filters $35K overtrade
E (Dan): 36' Morgan sailboat, F&C	F (Jack): $20K books $10K cash	G (Pat): Ocean motel— $30K eqty -$50K $515K mtg	H (Mike): $9K food scrip $11K hotel scrip +$10K cash
1 (Val): Land Naples $30K eqty $10K mtg E	2 (Jim): '88 T-bird + 3 Disneyworld time-shares E	3 (Craig): 2 lots in Bahamas, F&C E	4 (Vince): Vacant in Maine, F&C H
1 (Val): Land Naples $30K eqty $10K mtg E	2 (Jim): '88 T-bird + 3 Disneyworld time-shares E	3 (Craig): 2 lots in Bahamas, F&C E	4 (Vince): Vacant in Maine, F&C H
5 (Bill): Pre-paid rent 1,200 sq. ft. office, Oakpark Blvd. H	6 (Jay): S.C. condo $25K eqty $25K mtg + $5K cash 2	7 (Chuck): 20' Mako sf boat + $15K 2nd mtg 2	8 (Sylvia): $15K barter scrip + $15K cash 2
9 (Jack): Beech Mt. lot, 3 acres, F&C 2	10 (Norma): Condo Canary Islands $30K eqty $55K mtg 2	11 (Sandra): Beach condo $30K eqty $60K mtg 4	12 (Kevin): XT computer + laser printer + software +$10K cash 11

The Zander could continue until all the boxes were filled and more added or stopped at any time the moderator feels activity is dropping off. For this example, let's stop here.

Sweeteners Are the Final Touch

At this point the moderator will pause and ask if any of the people who offered wish to sweeten their offer. Any participant to the Zander Board can add something, increase their cash, or whatever they feel would be a sweetener to their offer. Dan, Box E, might add 20 hours of sailing lessons; Jack, Box F, might add another $2,000 in books; Frank, Box B, might increase his cash by $500, and so on.

Any changes made (none actually made on this Zander Board) would be noted on the projected overlay, and anyone could update their sheet.

How a Dozen or More Exchanges Are Instantly Made

Now for the conclusion of this Zander. Alex is at the top of the board. In reality, he has his choice of anything below him . . . anything.

His first line of selection would be to take one of the letter boxes (A through H). If there was nothing there that interested him, he could bypass them and go to one of the number boxes, for example, Box 7, and accept the 20-foot Mako and the $15,000 second mortgage that Chuck had offered on Box 2. If Alex did that, then the whole sequence of events that ends with Box 7 would be perfected. Here's what I mean. Look at the following sequence of events:

> Alex at the top of the board.
>
> Box E is a 36-foot Morgan sailboat offered by Dan to the top of the board.
>
> Box 2 is a 1988 T-Bird plus three Disneyworld time-share apartments offered by Jim against box E.
>
> Chuck's Box 7 is offered not to the top of the board, but to Box 2.

Alex goes directly down the line to Box 7 and becomes the owner of that box and everything in it. Chuck does not take over the top of the board—and what is in that box—because that is not what he wanted. But what does happen is the names in this sequence slide up one notch. The new names on the board would be adjusted as follows:

> Top— Dan: Condo at the top of the board
> E — Jim: Box E, Morgan sailboat
> 2 — Chuck: 1988 T-Bird plus time-shares
> 7 — Alex: 20-foot Mako sportfishing boat plus $15,000 mortgage

Dan is now at the top of the board and can keep it or take anything below him, with the possible exception of Boxes E, 2, and 7, because they have obtained the exchanges they want . . . although Jim and Chuck still have the option of accepting other offers that have been made against the boxes they now hold.

Assume that Dan, who is now at the top of the board, decides that he would rather have Box 12, which is Kevin's offer of computer equipment and $10,000 cash. Take a look at the sequence of offers before this exchange is completed.

> Top— Dan: Condo at the top of the board
> H — Mike: $20,000 mixed scrip plus $10,000 cash
> 4 — Vince: Vacant land in Maine
> 11 — Sandra: Beach condo subject to $60,000 mortgage
> 12 — Kevin: The computer equipment

When Dan takes Box 12, the names shift up one: Kevin will now get what he wanted, Sandra what she wanted, Vince the scrip and cash, and Mike the top of the board.

The new sequence is:

Top— Mike: Condo at the top of the board

H   — Vince: $20,000 mixed scrip plus $10,000 cash

4   — Sandra: Vacant land in Maine

11 — Kevin: Beach condo subject to $60,000 mortgage

12 — Dan: The computer equipment

As Deals Are Made the Top of the Board Switches

The lines of offers remain on the board, and there now remain additional opportunities. If Mike decides to stick at the top of the board, the remaining letter boxes that have outstanding offers on them, or subsequent offers made on any other boxes other than the top of the board, can now be considered.

Vince, for example, decides he wants Box 5, which is the prepaid office rent offered by Bill. That deal is made and the final board update is shown on the following page. Names of owners that are underlined are members who have made an exchange thus far. Can you see any other possible exchanges left?

All this would take less than 25 to 30 minutes from start to finish, and nine different exchanges have been made. Nine investors were able to go to contract on nine properties and services, to move off something they owned that was not taking them closer to their goals, and to obtain something else that does. (See page 191.)

Zander Board

> Mike: 2-bedrm condo in
> Miami—$30K equity
> $50K mtg $80K V

A (Bob): 2 lots in Ft. Myers, F&C $30K	B (Frank): 3 time-shares, Key West + $5K cash	C (Al): Waterfront home—$30K eqty + $165K mtg	D (Lee): Water filters $35K overtrade
E (**Jim**): 36' Morgan sailboat, F&C	F (Jack): $20K books $10K cash	G (Pat): Ocean Motel— $30K eqty -$50K $515K mtg	H (**Bill**): $9K food scrip $11K hotel scrip +$10K cash
1 (Val): Land Naples $30K eqty $10K mtg E	2 (**Chuck**): '88 T-bird + 3 Disneyworld time-shares E	3 (Craig): 2 lots in Bahamas, F&C E	4 (**Sandra**): Vacant in Maine, F&C E
5 (**Vince**): Prepaid rent 1,200 sq. ft. office, Oakpark Blvd. H	6 (Jay): S.C. condo $25K eqty $25K mtg + $5K cash 2	7 (**Alex**): 20' Mako sf boat +$15K 2nd mtg 2	8 (Sylvia): $15K barter scrip + $15K cash 2
9 (Jack): Beech Mt. lot, 3 acres, F&C 2	10 (Norma): Condo Canary Islands $30K eqty $55K mtg 2	11 (**Kevin**): Beach condo $30K eqty $60K mtg 4	12 (**Dan**): XT computer + laser printer + software +$10K cash 11

Standard Rules and Terms in Zander Exchanges

1. Participants to a Zander should be able to provide a full backup package on the property, product, or service they are offering. Basics such as mortgage information, leases, exact address, legal description, and condition of the property or product should be available. Additional information such as photographs, surveys, appraisals, and other "sales" material would be helpful to conclude the transaction as soon as possible.

2. It is generally understood that any transaction is subject to the transfer of good title, and in the case of real estate the taker may qualify that he expects a warranty deed and not a lesser type of deed transfer.

3. Cost of transfer is usually handled as it would in any exchange or sale of the subject property, product, or service. Sales tax and other transfer tax would be paid as per application of the norms or by law, unless otherwise stated between the parties.

4. If the product or property is not readily accessible for inspection, the transaction can be put on hold until the property is inspected and approved. In general, as long as the property is as was represented by the owner (or his agent), the deal would be expected to close as agreed. This is a point where members of exchange clubs begin to know who is being realistic about the property they offer, and who is responsible to close on transactions properly represented. Each participant expecting to make an inspection of another property should do so as soon as possible—the day of the Zander is ideal.

5. Unless otherwise stated, no commissions are paid between the participants of the exchange. If you are represented in a Zander by an agent, your obligation would be to that agent only. If you are the participant in the Zander Board no fee is due from or to you. This is called YKYIKM— "You Keep Yours, I Keep Mine,"—and is often shown on listings within exchange clubs.

Tips to Make Zanders Work Faster

Control. Participants in Zander Boards must have absolute control over the property or items they are offering. It is much better if they are the actual owners, so that decisions can be made on the spot.

   Stay on the topic. The moderator's job is multifaceted, but the most important aspect is to keep the Zander moving and on the specific topics. Many "sidetrack" questions can come up while a Zander is in operation that, if allowed to be answered, will drag out the Zander and not add to the process in any beneficial way. The question "Would you take . . . " is the first path to be avoided by anyone other than the moderator. Prospective takers need not ask that question, because it may not be a critical question. Because the Zander Board allows instant pass-through of the benefits and ownership of the box on the board to participants several steps away from the offering member, what is important is what the "taker" has to offer.

   Suggest alternatives. This is another key factor for the moderator or any other participant in the Zander, to speed the flow of events. It is possible for people observing the Zander to see alternative moves or make suggestions that can open the board to more possibilities, and those suggestions should be made. For example, if someone who knew that Norma (Box 10 with the Canary Island condo) actually owned three condos at that same project and that they were in effect free and clear (she was putting a mortgage on the property in her offer only to match the equity), that might spark additional interest in her package. As it was, no offers were made to her during the Zander.

   Suggestions of soft paper can be made, where the person making the offer holds the mortgage shown in the offer at a low interest rate or with a moratorium of interest for a period. Or a lease-back situation could be suggested, where the property is exchanged, say Al's waterfront home in Box C, but leased back for six months by Al to give a prospective new owner time to get his or her act together.

Everyone dealing in a Zander should be looking for ways to make it work better and faster. The moderator should constantly be on the lookout for these suggestions, and when they seem valid and to the point, should permit them to be expressed.

Roundtable session. This is the time after the Zander for everyone to sit down and put it in writing. The moderator should check on each roundtable session to make sure that the participants are working things out. Only hot irons can flatten out wrinkles, so the deals are best made, put into writing, and executed while everyone is around to make final adjustments to the deals if needed.

Follow-up Zander Boards. When deals require inspections and that inspection has to be accomplished at long distance, or by busy people who don't have the time to do it now, whole lines of transactions can be left in limbo, and once the sequence starts to fall apart the whole Zander Board is in jeopardy of collapse. This is another of the tests that members of exchange clubs or investment groups go through to prove their worth to the other members. If, after a couple of Zanders, you get to be known as the guy who works his way to the top of the board, then never takes the proper steps to close deals, your reputation in the group will slip to zero. At the same time, you should avoid making offers on property presented by known and proven "zeros," because they are apt to be a waste of time, unless you know the property, product, or service and are sure that it can be delivered as promised.

When you are doing a Zander, you will increase your finesse by following these techniques for success in Zanders.

1. **Property package.** This is where your property package really comes in handy. No matter what you have to offer, have some written information about it. Back up your values and benefits with a professionally compiled property package.

2. **Lobby prior to the Zander.** This means you take your property package, aerials, the actual product, descriptions of the services, etc. and presell what you have, to get participants thinking about what you will put on the Zander Board long before it goes up.

3. **Prior to selection of offers ask these questions.** Is there a property package? Can they accept right now without inspection? What is the full debt information? Can they sweeten the deal, and if so, how?

Dealing with Different Zander Board Forms

I have shown a Zander Board I like, mainly because it allows you to keep good track of what is going on. However, some exchange groups use different forms and present them in different ways. The result is nearly always the same, however, and the idea is to create a possible flow-through of immediate legs in the transaction. Once you have grasped the concept of my Zander Board, you will be able to follow any other Zander.

Using "Legs" to Build Exchanges

In the previous chapter, on Zanders, you saw the importance of exchange legs. In essence, each sequence of the Zander can generate another offer on your property, or an offer on a property already offered to you. Each subsequent property, which either becomes a taker for your property or to which you can jump because of the sequence of legs, is another option you have in moving closer to your goals. Each option or alternative transaction is a **leg** for you to build on. The more legs you have, the stronger your position becomes in creating the best deal for you.

Building High-Priced Legs

Zanders are a good way to develop legs, but they rarely work for more expensive property. You need to know how to build legs when the equity goes above $40,000.

This chapter will show you how to find and hold on to legs as both a buyer and seller of property. As you will shortly see, legs can help you sell your property, as well as give you added opportunity to acquire what you want.

Aggressive exchangers know that exchanges work as a "selling" tool as well as a "buying" tool and that the alternative leg can make a transaction fall into place that otherwise may not have closed at all.

How Legs Work for Both Buyer and Seller

Legs help close the exchange. Often, the very act of creating a leg causes the other party to take the first property offered. An example: Bob offers Harry a waterfront lot in the Bahamas as a down payment on Harry's house. Harry turns down the lot but gives Bob some time to obtain a leg to some acceptable property. Bob gets three or four legs, each of which wants the Bahamas property. Harry, seeing that there is activity on the lot, whereas the only activity there has been on his house is Bob's offer, reconsiders Bob's original offer and takes the lot in the Bahamas. Legs can help establish value.

Legs create alternate choices for both parties to select from. This is the real worth of legs. In some cases, as an aggressive buyer you can obtain the leg using tools and techniques other than direct exchange. Suppose there is a duplex apartment house you want to acquire, and you know the owner will take a vacant lot in a recreational area like North Carolina or the Florida Keys as a down payment. You own a condo you would like to sell, so you offer that in exchange for the duplex. The duplex owner turns down your condo, so you start to look for a leg (a lot in North Carolina or the Florida Keys) that he will accept. You find several lots in each location that will do the trick, but none of the owners wants your condo. However, you do find a buyer for the condo if you will sell it for nothing down, holding a second mortgage on the condo. Now you can get the lot, by exchanging the second mortgage you would get on the sale of the condo for the lot you need to make the exchange on the duplex.

Legs give **time** to close by allowing a contract to be executed "subject to" obtaining another leg. Time is the single factor that will make you successful (if you have enough of it) or cause you to make mistakes (if you don't take enough of it for research). In the real estate game, haste does indeed make waste.

With legs, you can decrease equity in one property to bring a deal closer to filling the needs of one or more principals to the deal. If you are offering a free and clear property worth $100,000 in exchange on another property, and the owner of what you want indicates that he would do a deal but cannot accept more than $50,000 of exchange, you have several options open to you. The first would be to divide the property you offered in the first place. However, that is not always possible for many different reasons. A second and more plausible situation would be to find a taker for your property and then exchange part of the property you get in that transaction back to the owner in the first deal. You might have a buyer for your property, if you would hold $50,000 in paper and get a $50,000 equity in another property. If you can move the property taken as a leg to the first, then that transaction could work nicely.

How a Buyer Can Create a Leg

Frank has owned a vacant commercial lot for several years. It is on a busy highway location and has proven to be the good investment he thought it would be when he bought it, but the value has leveled off and he has decided now is the time to cash it out and reinvest in an income-producing property. However, even though Frank has priced the lot fairly at $150,000, there are no ready buyers.

Frank has $100,000 cash to add to the value of the property in a possible exchange. He looks around and finds a property that he feels will help him attain his goals.

The property is a small 7,500-square-foot strip store complex. It is divided among six tenants who are paying good rent for the area and the building. Asking price is $550,000. This property has a first mortgage of $140,000 at 9 percent interest with 12 years to go. This mortgage has a monthly payment of $1,593.31 principal and interest. Deducting the amount of the mortgage from the asking price indicates the owner has a $410,000 equity, assuming the price is realistic.

Frank's Offer

Frank offers to acquire this property as follows:
- He will assume the first mortgage of $140,000.

- He will give the seller a cash payment of $50,000.
- He will give the seller the vacant lot worth $150,000.
- He will give the seller a second mortgage on the apartments for the balance of $210,000 with interest-only payments at 9 percent per annum for 12 years.

The offer was well thought out and would work nicely for Frank. This exchange should qualify as a 1031 exchange, allowing Frank to escape any immediate tax on any gain he has in the vacant lot, and the debt service to which this offer obligates Frank can be covered by the income of the property (not shown here). The second mortgage works too, because Frank knows that at the end of the 12 years the first mortgage will be retired (paid off) and it should be relatively easy to refinance the property at that time, assuming that Frank still owns it then.

The seller likes most of the terms of the offer, but suggests that the second mortgage be cut to 10 years. However, the owner concludes, he is not interested in taking the vacant land in exchange. Ouch, thinks Frank. No exchange makes for no deal. So where does he go from here?

One thing he could do would be to look for another property, which Frank decides to do, but at the same time to see if he can make a deal on the strip store. He wants to try to set up a leg for the strip store owner. "Accept my deal, with the modifications that you like," Frank tells him, "based on my finding another exchange or deal that includes my vacant lot that would be acceptable to you."

The owner, who does not see a line of buyers standing outside his door, agrees to give Frank 60 days to get another deal that allows Frank to exchange the vacant lot on another property acceptable to the owner of the strip stores.

Frank is flexible in the original offer on the strip store and has some room to sweeten the deal if necessary. He can add cash to the deal and does not mind making payments on a second mortgage that is now only 10 years in duration.

Let the Other Party Direct You to a Workable Leg

The owner tells Frank of some types of property that would be acceptable to him. Here is the list:

- Sport fishing boat up to $25,000 in value
- Free and clear vacation home in North Carolina
- Small income property—annual apartments or triple net lease
- Holiday package of some kind
- A good investment that is not vacant land

Often a Leg Comes from a Previous Offer Turned Down

Frank recalls some previous offers that had been made to him when he was trying to sell his lot. He decided to massage a couple of them to see if he could make them acceptable to the strip store owner, even though Frank himself had not been interested.

One such offer came from a used-car dealer who wanted to lease the lot with an option to buy. The rent he wanted to pay was not that attractive to Frank, and the other terms presented had killed any possibility of a deal between them.

Building an Acceptable Leg for the Other Guy

A few phone calls and two meetings later, however, Frank had a prospective deal worked out. The car dealer agreed to a lease that included a four-month moratorium on rent, then annual rent that increased from $15,000 for the first year to $18,000 for the second and $21,000 for the third, with a cost-of-living index thereafter. The car dealer insisted on an option to buy the lot. Frank structured the option so that it was not exercisable until after 15 years, with a price to be determined by multiplying 11 by the then-annual rent, said price not to be less than $300,000.

Frank went back to the strip store owner and explained the deal to the car dealer. Frank showed that this was as close to the kind of deal he wanted as he was going to find, and under the circumstances it was a pretty good deal. After some back-and-forth negotiations, Frank even sweetened the deal by agreeing to add another $6,000 in cash to the original offer if they would make a deal right then and there.

The strip store owner didn't accept the deal as presented, but after a few counters on some fine points, a transaction was structured.

How a Seller Can Create a Leg

Billy wants to sell his 12-unit apartment complex that has an adjoining three-bedroom, two-bath house with extra room, to add up to four units behind the house. His asking price for the whole package is $560,000. There is a first mortgage of $270,000, which is payable interest only at 10 percent per annum, payments made monthly of $2,250. This mortgage balloons (comes due and payable) 124 months from now. Billy has $240,000 in equity in the apartment complex, which has been on the market for six months without any acceptable offer being made.

To expand his market potential Billy has his agent run an advertisement in the local newspaper in the exchange column. In addition to this, a flyer is sent to members of a local real estate exchange club offering the apartment property in exchange. The advertisement reads:

Annual Apartments for Exchange

> 12 beautiful apartments plus home and room to expand. $240,000 equity, asking price $560,000. Make offer, owner will trade for ? Call Jack Cummings, (305) 771-6300, Agent.

There were many calls and several interesting offers. Each offer became a leg for Billy to have as an alternate property to sell or exchange. In addition, the offers presented different opportunities for Billy to consider taking instead of selling.

Collecting Legs and Determining Their Value

The word "value" has a double meaning here. First of all, you need to ascertain if the person proposing an exchange is serious. There is no need to take time to study a property offered to you if the person making the offer can't deliver the deal as proposed. This is one of the reasons you need to be careful of working with agents who have little or no control over the property they offer. If the principal behind the agent has not authorized the proposed exchange, then you could be spinning your wheels.

Ask yourself whether you can trust the other party. At one time or another, in real estate exchanges at least, trust becomes the critical factor. I have stressed the ethical worth of the other person before and will once more. If you have a bad feeling about the other party and think he or she is giving you unreliable or misleading information, and you choose to continue the negotiations, be warned that you may get burned.

Once burned, you can shy away from that person. In the real life of one on one, investor against investor, your caveat should be "Trust only the facts you have checked out yourself."

You can do some simple steps to cause the real value of the property, product, or service to surface. Start with a real property.

How to Check the Value of Real Estate

A valid real estate appraisal commissioned by you through a well-respected appraisal expert with a list of references a mile long may be a simple approach, if you want to pay the price for the service and have the time to wait for the work to be completed. Loan officers might ultimately require such a validation of value prior to approving a loan, but for the investor who needs to get a quick answer, appraisals are usually not the answer. If the other party (owner or his agent) presents you with a completed appraisal that the owner has had made, I would take it as information, and not necessarily the validation of value, because, to the discredit of appraisers, it is too easy to get a tailor-made appraisal that will overstate value.

What to do then? Assume that you are offered a single-family home across town as a down payment for your property, or perhaps a vacant tract of land in another state, or a seven-unit apartment complex in Chicago, while you are in Honolulu. What do you do? Follow the Three Steps to Establish Real Estate Value.

1. **Be sure you get full information.** It is foolhardy to attempt to discover anything about value unless you have complete information on the property. The most basic information you must know is this property information checklist:
   - Legal description
   - Street address
   - Subdivision name
   - Zoning and permitted use
   - Detailed description of all improvements
     1. Date constructed, date of any improvements, and condition of those improvements
     2. All inventory included and condition and approximate value thereof
     3. Idea of replacement cost
   - Land size and any unique characteristics that might affect its value
   - Leases (if any)
   - Contracts that must be maintained
   - Problems known by the owner or his agent

2. **Check comparable sales in the area.** This is easy for your agent to get for you, because in most cases it is nothing more than running off a computer search of the subdivisions involved. A general computer search for all property sold will give you some idea of trends, and that too can be helpful. Pick out properties that are as close as possible to the property you are looking at acquiring. If the property is vacant, the job of making a comparison between what you are interested in and what has sold is easier. Remember, however, that location is the key to all real estate, and unless you are looking at very similar circumstances, comparables can be misleading. Nonetheless they are a basis and can help you balance out the other methods of assessing value.

3. **Find out what is on the market.** As in the second step, if the property is exactly the same, which can be the case, then comps of "solds" and "available on the market" give you a direct basis of value. In tract housing or in apartments that have the same floor plan and similar building location, the best point of value is a recent sale. Naturally, there may be factors that cause a specific sale to be higher or lower than a realistic value, but once you know those facts you should be able to narrow down a fairly good value range. What you are looking for is range and not exact value.

Building Legs Even If You Don't Want the Property

The 4 Factors to Consider

1. Would legs be easier to sell?
2. What price would make the leg sell quickly?
3. Should you keep the leg?
4. How long can you tie up the leg?

Take a look at each of these elements in some detail:

1. **Would legs be easier to sell?** If you have a white elephant, or because of market conditions, your property is not going to sell quickly or at all, accepting one or more legs that you tie up for a while can position you so that if any of them sells you have gotten rid of your own property. Billy knows, for example, that if he gets six bona fide offers to exchange for his apartments and each of the properties is realistically valued, he has increased his exposure to the market by 600 percent. If the offer leaves Billy room to negotiate, he can actually aid the sale of the leg by modifying the terms or discounting the price of the leg.

   Suppose one of the six offers was a $130,000 condominium apartment with a $30,000 mortgage. The condo owner was going to pay $140,000 cash to Billy's equity ($240,000) to acquire the apartments.

2. **What price would make the leg sell quickly?** Billy knows that there was a $40,000 buffer in the original price of his apartments to give him some negotiating room, so now he can turn around and attempt to utilize that buffer by discounting the condominium on a quick sale. If the condo was

fairly priced at $140,000, then at $100,000 it should move quickly.

3. **Should you keep the leg?** Considering the play in the deal which Billy has, he might try to get the condo owner to sweeten the offer somehow, and actually keep the condo or use it (and his $40,000 cash) as an offer on something else that he would like to own.

4. **How long can you tie up the leg?** The time you can get to make your legs work is critical. As an aggressive seller you will want to establish as many legs as you can, and have control over them for as long as possible.

   Let's say you get three offers that look good, even though they are not for you. If you can "perfect" the offer—get it in writing subject to your being able to exchange or sell the property offered to you within a certain period of time—you can establish control. The period of time should be as long as you can get the other party to agree to. Ask for a year, and work back from there.

Be Receptive to Creative Techniques Using Legs

All real estate investors should appreciate the value of legs and learn how to use them to expand their portfolios and options. As you expand your investment portfolio and develop confidence in your ability to see the opportunities within your comfort zone, you will automatically start to see potential legs develop.

Every time you put a property on the market and have a prospective taker make you an offer, that situation can develop into a later leg. Even though you may not be interested in the offer (as occurred on the Zander Board) those takers can become stepping stones to another property. Keep good records of all prospective deals that come your way, and review them from time to time to make sure you are not overlooking another path to follow.

 **Nine Creative Techniques**

That Are Magic to Exchanges

An artist with skill needs only white, magenta, cyan, and yellow to establish a million hues. The real estate investor armed with a few solid investment techniques can mix and match methods of buying, selling, and exchanging to produce hundreds, if not thousands, of different investment proposals, each one designed to work for the needs of the investor with respect to the exact situation he is faced with and the unique property he is attempting to buy, sell, or exchange.

Building Your Own Creative Techniques

Look at the following nine creative ideas. These are your colors to paint your own picture of success and financial independence. I will explore each in detail to show you how and why the technique works, and when it would be ideal to use it. As you read through this chapter, try to see how you might have used these techniques to put together a deal that has escaped you up to now, and how you can use them tomorrow. Let these nine build your rainbow and its pot of gold.

The 9 Creative Exchange-Making Techniques

1. Paper Exchanges
2. The Pyramid Exchange
3. The Double Exchange
4. The Future Exchange
5. Exchange Options
6. The Mixed-Bag Exchange
7. International Exchanges
8. The Prepaid-Rent Exchange
9. Lease-Back Exchanges

Paper Exchanges

One of the easiest exchanges to accomplish is a paper exchange. This is where you offer a or unsecured, for part or all of the equity in the property you wish to acquire. Paper exchanges are the foundation of all cashless forms of investing.

Robert's paper exchange. Robert has found a small apartment building he wants to acquire. He has a little cash but wants to keep that as "working capital" to pay for fix-up expenses for the property. The seller of the apartment building is asking $120,000 and there is an existing first mortgage of $75,000 on the apartments, giving the seller an equity of $45,000.

Robert offers the seller a personal note for $30,000 dollars, payable interest only at the going rate for seven years, and $15,000 cash. The cash, Robert anticipates, will come from a new conventional second mortgage, or from refinancing the existing first mortgage.

Albert's second-mortgage transaction. Albert offers Charles a second mortgage secured by Albert's holiday home in Hilton Head as a down payment on the office building Charles wants to sell.

Mark offers a first mortgage. In another type of paper transaction, Mark offers Betty a first mortgage secured by a vacant tract of land he owns in return for 100 percent of the value of a property she has for sale.

These transactions involve the exchange of a mortgage or other form of debt agreement. This is a form of secondary financing, and each of the above examples offers the "buyer" different opportunities. Take a look at each.

In Robert's offer the seller of the apartments would get some cash, which is the enticement to hold the unsecured mortgage. Because the note given to the seller is unsecured, the lender will be more inclined to refinance the whole mortgage, or at least give the needed $15,000 in the form of a second mortgage.

An unsecured note is not as valuable to the seller as would be a mortgage or other security behind the debt, because if Robert were to fail to make payments it may be very difficult to collect on an unsecured note. On the other hand, if Robert has a good business track record in the community and can demonstrate confidence in himself and the deal, it is possible that he can sell himself and his proposal to a motivated seller.

One key to this deal would be if Robert were going to fix up the property and would promise to put up money in an escrow account, which would be "spent" only on improvements to the seller's property.

"Look," he might begin, "as I plan to spend at least $15,000 in improvements right away, I'll set up an escrow with the closing agent that can only be spent on your property. That should prove my intentions."

The technique of putting up spending money in that way works wonders in many other deals, where you want to save your capital for improvements or other needed expenditures that will increase the value of the property just acquired. Sellers may be satisfied that you are risking equity, even though they are not getting direct benefit from those funds. The fact that you are spending the money on their former property is a form of security to them in the long run. Naturally, the seller is better off if the paper you give him is secured by the property, and is not an unsecured note.

Paper Has Risk

Exchanging paper with anyone has a certain amount of risk to both sides of the transaction. The seller must consider the risk of not being able to collect on the debt owed and the buyer runs the risk of taking on more debt than he or the property will support.

In the transaction between Albert and Charles, the paper is secured by Albert's home in Hilton Head. Charles is relatively secure if the total debt-to-value ratio is low, and if Albert has at least 25 percent equity remaining in the Hilton Head home. In Albert's offer Charles gets no additional cash, only the second mortgage as down payment.

Mark's deal with Betty is a 100 percent exchange of values and might have started out with Mark actually offering Betty some of the land, which she turned down. If Mark anticipates an increase in the value of the property he owns, putting a mortgage against it and giving that mortgage to Betty allows him to keep the land while pledging it as security to acquire Betty's property.

Each of these transactions can be combined with one or more other techniques and modified in many ways.

Finesse in Paper Transactions

One of the most important aspects of using paper in any offer is to remember that because you are creating the debt, the terms and conditions of payment can become very flexible. You do not have to follow conventional "bank" terms. In the flexible terms of the debt you can meet, or at least get closer to, the values the seller has placed on his property.

Two Negotiating Points: Interest & Terms

The right terms make the deal fly. If you are the seller, the terms you structure can entice investors or other exchangers to your property and create deals where the market was flat. Interest rate and repayment terms are two flexible aspects of a paper transaction that are important negotiating points in adjusting and fine-tuning the paper.

Every mortgage represents a tradeoff between interest rate charged and repayment terms. Give me the right interest rate, and my pace and schedule of repayment, and I can pay almost any purchase price. Begin with the interest rate charged on the amount of the money lent.

The interest rate can close the deal. When you offer a mortgage in an exchange or other acquisition you are creating, you can adjust the "real value" of that mortgage by the interest rate you plug into it. Imagine two debts of $100,000 each, one with 8 percent interest per annum and the other with 12 percent interest per annum; these two rates will have different consequences for the people making the payments. The interest payment alone would vary between $8,000 and $12,000. That $4,000 spread could relate to a gain or loss of $40,000 in value in the transaction. This would happen if the buyer required a 10 percent return on his investment. If he has a mortgage with a payment of only $8,000 interest, he will have a cash flow of $4,000 more than with 12 percent interest.

At the same time, the seller of the property may rather have the extra $40,000 of value (reflected in the sale price) than the extra interest, which may require a reduction of the price. As a seller, do not jump to the conclusion that you will want the other side to pay you greater interest. You may want to show a minimum interest rate, while holding firm on the face amount of the loan. Adjustments in this area should be tied to your tax circumstances, which would be impossible for me to anticipate. This is one of the factors that you should discuss with your CPA team member prior to setting a value to your property.

"Invented" Notes or Mortgages

Because paper that is "invented" at the time of an offer or counteroffer is between the parties to the transaction, there can be a lot of flexibility in how the final mortgage, or note and mortgage, end up.

To limit the negotiation on the terms and conditions of the note or mortgage, you should draw the offer as though the note or mortgage already existed. If you wanted to use as a down payment on a property a second mortgage to be created by you on a property you own in Hilton Head, South Carolina, you might include wording such as this: " . . . as a part of this transaction, the first party will transfer to the second party a second mortgage secured by a single-family home in Hilton Head, South Carolina. The terms of that mortgage are . . . "

Remember that interest received is income to the person holding the mortgage, and taxes must be paid on income received. Because of this, a "seller" often will take a deal even though the interest is lower than their friends and advisors may suggest is the minimum. You have to keep everything in proper perspective in making offers.

Using the Best Bank in Town

Sellers are the best bank in town, because real bankers deal with other people's money, while sellers deal with their own—to satisfy their goals first. If you were going to a banker to get a loan, you would have to deal with him to get someone else's money. The banker's sole job is to make the most secure loan at the highest possible return to the bank. On the other hand, when you are asking the seller to hold paper or to take a note or mortgage in exchange for part or all of this equity, the most important factor is the achievement of the seller's primary goal: the disposition of the property.

To a motivated seller, the attainment of that goal outweighs most other considerations, and the banker who might turn you down at his bank will take your paper if he is selling his own property.

Interest is the boat, and the payment schedule is the fuel to loan values. When the payment schedule is introduced as a variable, payment terms become deal makers. Payments can be monthly, quarterly, annually, or on any schedule you can think of that will be accepted by the other party. It is not unusual to have different rates of payment during the term of the payback, or even to have a moratorium on payments.

Subordination with Secondary Paper

Buyers should consider the total effect of other financing terms that must also be met, when they are structuring new debt on a property. Subordination is where the holder of the mortgage (the person who collects on the mortgage) agrees to allow the security (the property) to be pledged to a mortgage in a superior position to the mortgage being held. If a first mortgage balloons (comes due and payable) in two years, offering the seller a second mortgage with 10-year terms would not be any advantage to you, unless the second mortgage provided that the holder of the mortgage subordinate to new refinancing of the first mortgage.

How Amy used subordination. Amy acquires Phil's home and, as a part of the transaction, gives Phil a second mortgage to balance the equity in the exchange. Amy assumes the existing first mortgage, which will be paid up in full in two years. To avoid having to pay Phil off to refinance the house with a new first mortgage, she has a **subordination** provision in the mortgage Phil is holding, which requires Phil to permit the security on the second mortgage to be used as security for another mortgage when the first mortgage is paid off. This is necessary because Phil's second mortgage would automatically become a first mortgage when the existing first is paid off, and Amy would not be able to refinance the property with a new first mortgage without paying off the second mortgage.

As a practical point, Phil should insist, just as you would if you were in his position, that there will be a limit to the amount of new financing that can be placed in front of the second mortgage. Assume the transaction was for Phil's property worth $100,000. Amy's deal is a first mortgage of $50,000, a second mortgage of $20,000 proposed, and her other property worth $30,000 to balance the exchange. Because the first mortgage balloons in two years, Amy wants to ensure that she can refinance the property to get the needed cash to pay off the first mortgage. Phil has agreed to subordinate his second mortgage to the new refinancing, but limits Amy to a first mortgage of $65,000. Without that limitation, two years from now Amy could, under the right circumstances, obtain a loan for over $100,000 on the property, and Phil's second mortgage could no longer have any value, as it would have little (or no) real security behind it.

Tip! A mortgage is not a first or second or third because that is stated at the top of the document. It maintains a position against the security as to the date it is recorded as a lien, with that property pledged as security for that lien. This is very important, because you can think you are getting a first or second mortgage because in bold print are the words, first mortgage or second mortgage. You must always check to see if any other liens have been recorded. This is one reason there can be a delay between the time all the documents are signed and when the actual funds of a loan are transferred or title deeded to the other party.

Limiting subordination terms. Phil's limiting Amy's potential refinancing to $65,000 is not enough. He needs to make sure that the terms of the new mortgage are reasonable. Many factors can come to play in obtaining additional security. For example, tying the loan to "institutional terms" makes sure that Bobby doesn't go to the loan shark down the street and get a loan that has horrible payback terms and interest rate that is sure to make him go into default. You do not want to be forced by foreclosing on Bobby to take over a loan with a heinous repayment schedule just to protect your second position.

Flexibility When You Create Paper

When you are creating paper in your offer or as a part of your property package, remember that you can be highly creative with the payment schedules. This is not a bank loan and you do not have to pretend that you or the other party are bankers. The payback you devise should fit the deal. It can, and should, provide incentives that entice the party who needs to be "sold," as long as those conditions work.

Repayment schedules can contain moratoriums where you have a period of time before they actually start: "During the first two years of this second mortgage, there will be a moratorium of principal and interest, so that unpaid interest will be added to the principal owed on the mortgage. Beginning on the twenty-fifth month following the closing of this transaction, monthly payments of interest only at the rate of 8 percent per annum [or whatever you can negotiate] will begin."

Payment schedules can provide for periods when the payments are reduced for specific times—"during the months of July, August, and September, the payments shall be interest only at the minimum legal rate of interest allowable"—or against the principal owed, such as might occur in an acquisition of an income property where the original value was established as a multiple of the gross income. If the subsequent income falls behind the levels anticipated (risky for the former owner), the principal amount owed can be reduced.

Creative repayment schedules allow buyers of property to have time to get into the new property so that ownership changes can take place. Reduced payments at first, or moratoriums of payments so that improvements can be made, cause income and property values to grow and, above all, soften the blow of meeting debt obligations.

Use paper exchanges whenever you can, by themselves in the form of pyramid exchanges or as a tool to work out the transaction that seemed to get bogged down in a mire of offer and counteroffer. Keep in mind that the best banker for you to deal with is the property owner who is motivated to dispose of his property. That person could be the other party, or in a turn of the coin, you. Learn the creative steps of dealing with paper. One of the more advanced is the pyramid exchange.

Pyramid Exchanges

A pyramid exchange is a type of paper exchange that works in a unique way to build wealth. Of the previous examples of paper transactions, two were pyramids. Only Robert's deal was not. All pyramid exchanges rely on the fact that the buyer will pay all or part of the equity in acquiring property A with financing from property B (or financing secured by several properties). The key is to keep property A as debt-free as possible.

Building on Robert's Exchange

Assume that Robert is unable to buy the apartment complex as he had originally offered. He counters by offering to assume the first mortgage of $75,000 and to give the owner a $45,000 first mortgage secured by a seven-acre tract of land he owns in North Carolina. Robert pegs the value of the North Carolina land at $75,000, which makes the $45,000 mortgage 60 percent of the total value and a reasonable risk to hold, if Robert's assessment of the value is correct.

To ease the payment schedule and give himself time to fix up the apartments and increase rents, Robert conditions the payments of the mortgage with a 12-month moratorium of interest payments. At the end of the first year he indicates that interest will begin to be charged against the loan balance, and that the first payment of 10 annual payments will be due at the end of the second year. Interest is to be 8 percent per year.

Robert agrees to put $15,000 in an escrow account to be spent on improvements of the apartments, spelling out clearly the details of what he expects to do and what is meant by "improvements."

Now that Robert has pyramided into this property, he can proceed to do the work intended to increase its value. In an ideal situation, by the time he finishes the work he can increase the rent roll of the building and move to the next stage of his investment plan, which would be (1) to keep the property; (2) to sell or exchange the property; or (3) to refinance and pyramid up to another property.

With time, a revitalized building, and an increased rent roll, Robert should be able to refinance the existing debt. If he can increase the mortgage to $100,000, he can pay off the old one of $75,000 and have $25,000 cash to apply against the mortgage on the North Carolina property, or to use as fix-up money for the next deal.

The next deal could be similar property, where, this time, Robert would offer a second mortgage, using the just-fixed-up apartments as security.

The 5 Tips for Maximum Leverage in Pyramids

1. Develop a well-planned presentation of the offer. Much of your success in real estate investing is in how you play the game. That means your team has to play a serious game from start to finish. All the work you do up to the moment the offer is presented to the other side is just training for the real thing. Keep in mind that the presentation lasts all the way through to the close. Both you and your agent should expect to work for the deal, and that means making every attempt to close any gap that might exist between you and the other party (buyer or seller). You cannot assume that the other side will share your enthusiasm about acquiring their property. You will have to find their hot button, and use creative techniques in such a way that you don't scare them. Bit by bit, you will learn how to handle the obstacles that will be thrown in your path.

2. Have the right kind of property package. It should show value and why the property is good security for the pyramid mortgage. The same property package that I discussed in Chapter 5 works wonders in showing the value of the property you are offering as security. Keep in mind, however, that you may have to stress different benefits to show security more than possible "ownership." You are not selling your property, only using it as security.

3. Show your strength. Nothing soothes the savage breast of a seller quicker than information about the buyer that indicates he is capable, honest, and honorable. Can you present that kind of picture? If you cannot, you need to work toward that end. No matter what your economic background, you should be able to present a favorable position. Work on that aspect of your total image; it is important.

4. Show the intended plan for the acquired property. If you have sketches showing what you plan to do to improve the property, let your agent or whoever is going to present your offer take them along. Detail, effort expended, and a solid plan that demonstrates not only that are you professional but that you recognize good value and know how to improve it will again hammer home the message that you can do what you have promised. One of the things you are promising is to pay back a mortgage you are using to acquire the property. Image is important, but demonstrating that the image is genuine is everything.

5. Play up the Greener-Grass Theory. Here's how this works. The owner of the property you are trying to acquire bought it a dozen years ago and paid $50,000 for it. You are now offering him $750,000 (or thereabouts) for the same property, and in a conventional transaction would ask him to hold a second mortgage of $200,000. Look at this from his point of view. He paid $50,000 and is now asked to hold a mortgage of $200,000. Something does not compute. After all, he is selling this property; he knows it is overpriced, he wants to walk away from this property and never see it, touch it, have to foreclose on it, ever again. No, sir.

"Look over there, sir," you or your agent says, "see that beautiful green pasture that is just on the other side of the fence? See how beautiful and valuable it is? Wouldn't you like to hold a mortgage on that property? I sure would. I wish I had the chance to hold a mortgage on that beautiful property on the other side of that fence . . . greener and all that. Wow."

Get the idea? It works because that is human nature.

The Double Exchange

The double exchange is a very creative method of using the "Greener-Grass" syndrome to its utmost benefit; with it you can make two deals at once. In the double exchange, you are able to pyramid from two properties you do not own to acquire the other. When the situation is right, you could actually acquire two properties at the same time without spending any capital.

In the usual circumstances, you will use this technique as a part of the total transaction, adding other equities to the deal to close between the two other parties. First, look at how the double exchange pyramids you into two properties with no cash invested.

A Nothing-Down Exchange into Two Properties

Ronny has found two ideal properties to acquire and fix up. One is a $100,000 duplex that has a garage that can be enclosed to make into a third apartment. There is a first mortgage of $50,000 on the duplex. The other property is an old home on the market for $100,000 that he wants to convert into medical offices. There is a first mortgage of only $65,000 on this property.

The zoning allows these conversions and additions, and Ronny knows that when this work is completed the values of each property will increase substantially. He calculates that the cost to do the work on both properties will be $20,000, nearly equally divided between the two. He has this capital, but nothing more to add as down payments.

Using the double exchange, he goes to the duplex owner and offers to assume the $50,000 existing mortgage, and as a down payment to give the owner a $50,000 second mortgage on the medical office building conversion. Showing the duplex owner sketches of the work he contemplates doing on the old home and a drawing of what the building will look like when completed, he adds, "Once this work is finished this property will be worth $200,000. There will be only $100,000 in the form of a first mortgage; the second mortgage would be secure."

Then Ronny goes to the owner of the old home and offers to assume the existing first mortgage of $65,000 and give the owner a second mortgage on the duplex he is going to convert into three apartment units. "Notice how we will improve this property," he or his agent says, going over the plans and sketches. "Your second mortgage of $35,000 will be secure."

To buy time and to show equity in the duplexes, Ronny agrees to close at the end of 90 days, during which time he plans to actually start work on the improvements in the property, spending his own money for this work.

What Ronny did was acquire one property using equity from the other. There is absolutely nothing wrong with this kind of deal; as with most creative forms of exchange and real estate investing, the presentation must be first-rate and professional.

Because a pyramid works with equity from another property, Ronny could have pulled cash out of the deal by refinancing one of the properties. In the above deal, when the medical offices are completed Ronny anticipates putting a new first mortgage of $100,000 to pay off the existing first mortgage of $65,000, and to replenish his cash. The second mortgage on the medical building (held by the owner of the duplex) would contain a subordination provision to allow the new first mortgage of $100,000, which was, after all, the amount of the mortgage which Ronny indicated would be ahead of the second mortgage when the offer was presented.

Using the Double Exchange with Other Techniques

In almost all of your exchange transactions, you will mix and match techniques to fit your needs and the demands of the transaction. There is no limit to the combinations of techniques, but keep the primary goal in sight. It is easy to become sidetracked into doing a deal for the deal's sake, rather than for your benefit.

In double exchanges, you satisfy one of the major factors at which sellers balk: secondary financing against their own property. Asking him to hold a second mortgage on his own property may not work, simply because he does not see any equity being put into the deal by the buyer. On the other hand, to offer that greener pasture down the street (the duplex) in the form of a second mortgage on a property about to be remodeled can be appealing, not only to his emotions of getting something rather than giving something, but also to his primary goal of selling the home.

An Added Bonus in a Double Pyramid

One of the advantages in doing a double pyramid is that you structure financing on a property that can make it more marketable later on. Look back at Robert's deal, where he offered a $45,000 second mortgage, secured by property in North Carolina as the down payment on an apartment complex. The mortgage was set up so that there was no payment for two years. This kind of financing could make the property in North Carolina a good buy for someone else. In fact, if Robert would agree to take something in exchange for his equity ($30,000 as he placed a value of $75,000 on the property and there is now $45,000 in financing) he could move off the North Carolina property and pass on the responsibility of the debt to someone else.

Take My Financing and I'll Pay Your Price

There is a trade-off between price and terms. Once price has been narrowed down, terms can make any deal fit. Most sellers arrive at a price they cannot, or will not, soften on. By working on the other elements of the deal you can close the gap by paying their price while making the deal more attractive to you through the terms. Time is the key factor, as time means money. Sometimes all that is necessary is to delay the closing, giving yourself time to start the work you want to do without having to pay the **ownership cost**. Reduced interest rates and relaxed payment schedules both play a role in making the property worth more, because you have the time to profit more.

If you are buying a $400,000 property and plan to remodel it, which will take 120 days to accomplish, the cost to hold that property for 120 days (after you close on it) could easily be $15,000 or more. See the calculations below.

Interest on $400,000 for 4 months	$12,000
Taxes on the property for 4 months	1,500
Insurance and other costs	1,500
Minimum cost to own	$15,000

Pyramid and paper transactions play a major role in all kinds of real estate transactions. The very best banker to go to for financing will be the owner of the property; he is the most motivated and is looking to solve other problems.

The Future Exchange

"I will give to you a penthouse apartment overlooking the Pacific Ocean in Puerto Vallarta in exchange for your property in San Francisco. The only catch is, I haven't built the building in Puerto Vallarta yet."

All kinds of exchanges can be made of property, products, and services that you do not yet have. Start with some very basic concepts of future exchanges and build from there.

A Sweat Equity Exchange

The easiest of all future exchanges to follow will be the service exchange. In a sweat equity exchange a future event is often all or part of the equity in the exchange. Bob agrees to paint your house if you let him use that work as down payment on the lot you want to sell. Jay agrees to serve as your CPA for the next three years in exchange for the down payment on a condominium apartment that Carter Builders has for sale. I agree to give you a home in the subdivision I want to develop on the land you exchange to me in trade for the home. Each is an exchange that has, connected to it, a future event. Be creative.

Where Future Exchanges Work Best

Future exchanges work best in situations where the product or service offered in the exchange is such that it can be used over a period of time. Restaurant scrip, as a good example, can be offered as a part of a transaction with ample time allowed for the other party to use up the scrip. If you know that the owner of a property entertains a lot or has a use for restaurant scrip, and if you can obtain scrip from an acceptable restaurant, you can include that in your offer. Keep in mind that even if you do not own a restaurant, you have the capability of obtaining the scrip through some other kind of exchange—like offering the owner of the restaurant something you have or can get for the scrip.

Personal services, yours or someone else's, can also be part of a future exchange—the limitation is only in the amount of services the person can absorb.

In real estate, the future could be an apartment in a building you are going to build, or are just finishing up now. You can exchange ownership or use, as would be the case if you offered prepaid rent as the equity. (This technique is discussed in detail later in this chapter.) As my offer to you, I will give you three years of prepaid rent in this office building as a down payment on your property.

Closing Future Exchanges

If you think it is hard to close an exchange contract on a tangible that someone doesn't want, see what happens when you offer a future event, product, or service in exchange. The odd thing is many times the exchange goes rather smoothly, once you have overcome some of the objections that always come up. I'll get to the objections in a second or two, but look first at the general philosophy of futures and their acceptance.

Imagination is a wonderful thing, and when you can spark imagination, paint a picture, or hint at the potential, you can have success with future exchange offers. Mind you, you have to have something to offer that allows for all these great things to happen.

People will take an offer that holds out promise, as long as they believe they will eventually get the property, product, or service offered. People, and you have seen this before, will give up a fistful of cash and a diamond-studded gold watch in trade for "what's behind Curtain Number Two."

The key is **you.** The other party must believe that you will deliver. "Look Mr. Jones," your agent explains as he is presenting your offer, "anytime within the next eighteen months you can select one or two of the apartments which will be constructed on your property.

Even though my prospectus anticipates that there will be price increases every four months, you will be able to select at the preconstruction prices that will be offered to the public for the first four months only. Naturally, your selection will be from any available units, as once an apartment is sold it is gone, so your early selection would be suggested. The value of the apartments you select will be deducted from the total purchase price and the outstanding mortgage you are to hold will be the balance owed to you. Let me show you some of the model apartments planned."

Overcoming Negative Factors in Future Exchanges

Four negative factors adversely affect your ability to do future exchanges.

1. Lack of confidence
2. Poor track record
3. Poor presentation package
4. Unrealistic proposal

Any prospective party who does not have **confidence** in your ability to perform under the terms of the contract will be a tough sell, unless you have anticipated this roadblock right from the start.

A lack of confidence will be exacerbated by the next three negatives. No track record at all is better than a poor track record. "Oh yes," the prospect tells your agent, "I read about that guy. Didn't he stick it to a land owner a year or so ago?" Not good for your image, to be sure.

A **poor presentation** is a sure sign that you are not a professional, and your deal can be dead in the water right from the start.

An **unrealistic proposal** is another problem that you can never recover from. Tie everything together, and you might as well have never seen (and fallen in love with) that property.

Okay, so how do you handle this? Remember the key words in future real estate exchanges:

☞ **Key Words:** Tie It Up Today at Today's Price But Pay for It Tomorrow

The condo or the house in the subdivision are both down the road in the future, but you get the price advantage if you accept this offer today. You are making a deal that is an alternate to all the other deals that are sitting on their desk right this moment. How many are there?

Lack of confidence. The direction you have to work at is building confidence in yourself. It will not come overnight, and even the best agent can do little more than shine up your image . . . the image you have to make on your own.

Poor track record. If you have no track record, don't worry about it. The idea is to impart the fact that you have confidence in yourself and in your own abilities. Point out that you don't want to start out with a problem, that you have a solid team behind you, and that you want to acquire property (to which the offer is directed) that will ensure success. If you actually have a poor track record and have failed at several attempts to do exactly what you are now attempting, then this method of exchange may not work.

Poor presentation package and **unrealistic proposal.** These go hand in hand and are sloppy ways to do business. Nonetheless, the unrealistic proposal is one area where you can recover if everything else is in good shape. After all, your first offer is slanted in your favor, as it should be.

Exchange Options

An option is the right to do something in the future, but if you don't want to do it you don't have to. For example, Kim has the option to buy an office building in Chicago for $500,000 cash anytime between now and two years from now. If the present value of this building jumps to $750,000 in six months with the prospect of increasing even more over the next 18 months, Kim's option has substantial value. It can be sold or exchanged to someone who might want to acquire the building, or kept as an investment for a future transaction.

The addition of an option to an exchange transaction is often used as a closing tool: something that is added at or near the end to entice the other side to make the deal. Options are kind of like the item behind Curtain Number 3, because no one knows for sure if the option will be worthwhile in the end.

An option is a one-way street, however; its advantage is one-sided. If you have the option to buy my house five years from now at a price (or formula) that we establish now, I will lose out if the value goes up above that option price, and you will profit considerably. Because you own the option, I have no control over what you are going to do. All options work that way, and unlike the contract that requires you to buy, the option lets you off the hook. Options lock up only one side of the deal—the person who must deliver the property if the other party says, "Okay, I'll do it."

You can be very creative when you deal with options simply because you can option anything, even things you don't actually own. You can option ownership or use, and you can set levels of use or ownership.

Charlie's Option Deal

Charlie wants to buy some land to build a strip center, and he has worked very hard to get the owner to accept his deal. Just when he is about to give up, he reaches down for one more technique, and decides to give the seller the option to buy back one of the "out parcels" anytime during the first 18 months after the closing, at a price that is established now.

This kind of offer works well when the reluctant seller can be sold on the idea of the option as a way to profit from the proposed development. If the land goes up above the "buy-back option price," the option was worth the extra negotiation effort. Charlie may give up some profit he might have made by selling the out parcel, but if he can't tie up the land to do the development, there won't be any profit anyway. As Charlie will still make a profit in selling the land back to the original owner, this technique doesn't hurt him at all.

Sometimes the option is used to entice someone to do something they didn't really want to do. Jack is trying to lease a used-car lot he owns, but the prospect doesn't want to lease. "I own all my car lots," he tells Jack. Not to lose a deal, Jack agrees to make an exchange: he will give the lot operator a favorable lease and an option to buy the lot if the operator agrees to a long-term lease wherein the option to buy cannot be exercised for at least 10 years. Each party gives in and the exchange of elements becomes the negotiating tool that closes the deal.

The option may never actually be exercised. In the first example there is no reason for the option to buy the out parcel to be exercised, unless the value increases and the option price turns out to be a bargain. The ultimate price of the used-car lot will be passed up unless values have increased to the point where that price is a bargain.

The Problems with Options

Making sure everyone understands the terms. Options can pose several interesting problems. The most common is making sure that the option is clearly detailed, and that all the parties involved know how the conditions are to be met. This is more critical than the actual sale and transfer of title, because if there are problems at that level they usually surface at the actual closing of title. However, because exercising the option will occur at some future date, it might be years down the road before you discover that there is not a clear understanding of how that event was to be dealt with.

The English language is full of double meanings, and in business not every term has a universal connotation. For example, the condition of a mortgage payment that is part of an option agreement could read: " . . . and at the option of the first party, the second party will release one acre of land from the Purchase Money Mortgage, for every $50,000 paid against the purchase price." There are two factors at play in that statement. First is the "purchase money mortgage," a mortgage held by the seller. This means that at the closing of title, a mortgage would be established where the first party can release land from that mortgage by making payments of $50,000 per acre. This provision allows the first party to obtain clear title to the land that is no longer pledged as security to the purchase money mortgage.

The second factor is that the phrase means that for every $50,000 paid against the purchase price (and not against the purchase money mortgage), there will be a release. Any cash or other value given to the "seller" at closing or later on will apply against a release.

Dates at which things are to occur to validate an option are often confusing (sometimes by design) and it is not unusual for a party to overlook an important factor in an option and, for that reason, to lose the option.

Interpretation of terms and conditions in the contract that have been hammered out by the principals can sometimes be mumbo jumbo to the closing agency who actually draws up the mortgages and other documents needed to effect the title transfer. It is essential that you not only review the exact wording of every closing document, but also compare them to the actual terms that were intended in the contract. Slightly differing wordings can sound similar, but may be miles apart in actual function, and the words "not payable" may be typed "now payable"! What a difference that could make.

Make sure you have control over the future. Another problem with options is that the future is an unknown quantity. Will the future event be possible? This is always a question with any event you contract for that has a future closing date. The longer away the date is, the more problems can occur which can create circumstances that make the closing difficult, if not impossible. People die, go to jail, get divorced, get sued; their property foreclosed on, taken by eminent domain proceedings, divided by courts, or is taken by the United States Marshal, the local sheriff's office, or through Internal Revenue Service proceedings. In addition to all that, some people just will not do what they said they would because they believe or want to believe they do not have to honor their commitment. You can sue, of course, when you have grounds and have not actually defaulted on your end of the deal.

Because of this kind of problem, it is a good idea to make sure of the condition of the title to any property you may eventually take title to or come into possession of (if through a lease or other form of ownership or use), within a reasonable time after going to contract. Make your deal subject to your verifying the quality and condition of the title and to the owners clearing up problems, if problems exist with the title. The older a title problem becomes the more difficult it is to clear it. Naturally, you will seek competent legal advice on this and any other matter when it comes to real estate contracts, and make sure your lawyers advise you on any potential problems you might have because of that specific deal.

Mixed-Bag Exchanges

Mixed-bag exchanges give flexibility. There is no reason not to consolidate several of your properties, products, or services into a "bag of exchanges." You do not even need to concern yourself that the other party is going to take all the items being offered. What is important is that the items offered work in the total picture of the exchange.

Sydney's Mixed Bag: A Simple Exchange

A simple mixed-bag exchange would be where you offered several items to the other property owner. Take Sydney's offer for Curtis's motel. Sydney offers a package of five items as the equity in the exchange. Sydney proposes that Curtis take the following as payment on the motel:

1. $120,000 equity in a home Sydney owns
2. Two free and clear time-share units in Mexico
3. $20,000 worth of appraised and certified rubies
4. $10,000 worth of barter scrip good at several local barter organizations
5. $25,000 cash

Of the above five items, the only one that is clearly acceptable is Item 5. Cash always works into a deal somewhere. The other items may be accepted by Curtis, or he may counter to remove them. In a creative exchange, the end result might be that not only do the initial items stay in, but others get added to sweeten the deal.

Assume that both these parties are represented by real estate agents. This indicates the likelihood of a fee to be paid by each principal to his agent. Curtis might turn to his agent and suggest that the transaction would be acceptable if the agent took the time-shares and the rubies as his fee. The agent might negotiate this a bit and indicate that some cash would be needed, or that it would be a deal if, in addition to the time-shares and the rubies, the commission were increased by the barter dollars. Curtis might counter for more time-shares, rubies, and/or barter dollars, in anticipation that those might be (and usually are) soft items that probably can be increased without putting the transaction in jeopardy of making it fall apart.

A Zander Can Help

Zanders often become a mix of items, with different people getting different things, or one person getting many things offered by participants in the Zander Board. Very large transactions can be put together by the use of a divisible property, product, or service where a multileg exchange is divided between different people with the divisible property being used to balance everyone's equity. Often the dividable property is accepted by all the other parties as an accommodation to the deal, because they are achieving a majority of the intended goals through the exchange. This use of a mixed bag of items can become very complex. The following exchange shows how a multiple exchange was worked out.

A Multiple Mixed-Bag Exchange
The Properties

    A. An estate in the Azores worth $850,000 free and clear.

    B. A commercial vacant tract worth $650,000 with $100,000 debt and $550,000 equity.

    C. Ranchettes in Texas, minimum values of $40,000 free and clear can be offered up to $1,000,000 in value.

    D. Oceanfront land in Mexico. By the front-foot, at $300 per front-foot. Maximum available $1,500,000 value free and clear.

    E. A home in Marbella, Spain, valued at $330,000 free and clear.

    F. A tract of land in Spain, valued at $190,000 free and clear.

This deal is compiled by you or an agent, not because all of these people came together but because one or more of the principals is attempting to satisfy his specific goals and, to accomplish that, has brought in the dividable properties in an attempt to work them into the deal and make the whole picture work. The dividable properties are C (ranchettes in Texas) and D (Mexico oceanfront land).

Look at the other property owners' goals.

The Owners' Goals

Property owner A:	Wants to move his equity to the States, where he can have more control over that value. The estate has served its maximum benefit to the owner and is doing nothing to advance his position.
Property owner B:	Wants to acquire Property E, the Marbella, Spain, home, and possibly property F, the vacant tract in Spain.
Property owner C:	Is open to taking a mixed bag of properties in exchange.
Property owner D and E:	Is open to taking a mixed bag of properties in exchange. He (owns both properties) turned down the offer from B to take the vacant land, but indicated that he would be interested in a larger tract of less expensive land, or even a big home.
Property owner F:	Wants to move his equity to the United States but does not want to add other property or cash, and wants only free and clear land.

All the Possible Takers

A: Azores—$850,000 equity   **takes**   C: Texas—up to equity
                                                     D: Mexico—up to equity

B: Vacant—$550,000 equity   **takes**   E: Marbella—$330,000 equity
                                            F: Spain—$190,000 equity
                                                Short—$20,000 equity

C: Texas—to $1 million   **takes**   A: Azores—$850,000 equity
                                            B: Vacant—$550,000 equity
                                            D: Mexico—up to limit

D: Mexico—to $1.5 million   **takes**   A: Azores—$850,000 equity
                                            C: Texas—up to limit

E: Marbella—$330,000 equity   **takes**   A: Azores—$850,000 equity
                                            C: Texas—up to limit

F: Spain—$190,000 equity   **takes**   C: Texas—$190,000

By simple examination and elimination of the matches through who will take what, you can quickly see that there are some properties which will not be considered, or which will consider only certain other properties. Because the idea is to meet as many of the goals and therefore make as many exchanges as possible, an attempt should be made to maximize the board. Quick eliminations suggest the following will match everyone. Keep in mind that there could be other matches that could be exchanged if the entire mixed-bag multi-exchange falls apart.

A Completed Exchange Where Everyone Wins

A: Azores—$850,000 equity   **takes**   D: Mexico—$850,000
B: Vacant—$550,000 equity   **takes**   E: Marbella—$330,000 equity
                                            F: Spain—$190,000 equity
                                            D: Texas—$30,000 equity

C: Texas—$580,000 equity   **takes**   B: Vacant—$550,000 equity
                                            D: Mexico—$30,000 equity

D: Mexico—$880,000 equity   **takes**   A: Azores—$850,000 equity
                                            C: Texas—$30,000 equity

E: Marbella—$330,000 equity   **takes**   C: Texas—$330,000
F: Spain—$190,000 equity   **takes**   C: Texas—$190,000

As you can see, each property owner has gotten something. This mixed bag of exchanges worked because several of the property owners took a package of different properties from different owners. The real key to this kind of exchange is having dividable properties (Texas and Mexico), which go to different owners to match out the equities. Deals like this, while not uncommon, will tax even the best exchanger, and can take weeks of searching for key properties that can become the catalysts.

International Exchanges

Mediterranean restaurant on the waterfront, the thought of an island rendezvous in Fiji. Just close your eyes. Dream of that erotic evening with the person of your dreams; could it be that this is the prelude to your deal of deals? Could it be that you have been lulled into the sensation that nothing could be better for you than that deal? Is it true that distance does lend enchantment to a deal? Are travel and the excitement of going places and doing things part of your hot button? If so, then you and people like you are ripe takers for international transactions. International exchanges are easier than you think.

International transactions are not just deals where you take a property in Rome and give up a property in Japan. No, indeed. The entire concept of international dealing has to do with what I call the **t.k.e. connections,** the taxes, knots, and emotional connections. These three elements govern the entire spectrum of international deal making. The more you understand the philosophy of doing business internationally, the greater your opportunity to come out on top in such a transaction.

Taxes

Take taxes first. The payment of or, better stated, the desire not to pay, taxes causes many transactions to be contemplated that would not have been anticipated otherwise. Income tax, sales tax, real estate tax, and so on, all play a role in this game of doing business around the world. Some people play the game clandestinely and hide their movements, hoping never to be found out. Many of them never are found out, and even those who are discovered face minor penalty.

Dealing honestly, with all the avenues of law and justice on your side, can still mean avoiding tax, and when you can avoid paying a tax, almost any tax, you can improve your profit. The bottom dollar is king in many parts of the world. Perhaps yours, too.

When it comes to doing business in any international venue, you should obtain the very best advice you can about the taxes you might be subject to, how to limit or avoid that tax completely, what tax could you be subject to on the other side of the fence (world), and what can you do to limit or avoid tax in any future transaction once you own property there.

Sound complicated? It is, and it requires careful deliberation **before** you make a deal, before you get stuck in some foreign nightmare that looked like a peaceful island with nothing but palm trees swaying on a moonlit night, as you sipped a cold beverage with your arms around a warm companion.

Knowing that **tax avoidance** is a key factor in international deals, and armed with the proper details that affect dealings between you and people of Country X, will give you the upper edge. It does not matter if the other party plans or anticipates that what they are going to do is legal: if they go to jail that is okay; if you go to jail because you become an accomplice to their illegal actions, then shame on you. Worse. Shame and nightmares to you.

Don't Go to Jail for Them!

Lawyers and other professional people in the United States have been active accomplices to criminals from foreign countries for years. Several clients of mine have confided that their bankers and lawyers here in the United States have been active in their business dealings that involved violations of laws in their native countries. One day these lawyers and other professionals may be on holiday in France, Argentina, or Brazil, only to find there is a warrant out for their arrest. I surely hope so.

Just do not let it happen to you. In fact, let this motivation—this drive that is so strong it will cause people to move to the very edge of jail to make a deal—work for you. Understand that there are people who will do almost anything to "get out of" something. That "something" is usually taxes.

Naturally, I cannot tell you everything you need to know about this subject. All I want to do, really, is alert you to the fact that the urge to do an international deal to avoid taxes is so strong that millions of dollars are made, and lost, because of it.

Knots That Tie People to Faroff Lands

Where did your family come from? I mean, way back, where did they come from? Feel a tie there? Is there anything to tie you to that part of the world? Any knots that cannot be untied? That's the way it is with many people. Like me, for example. I have family by marriage (worse that way, I'm told) who live in Spain. I have a knot that ties me to Spain, which for me has become more of a rationalization of why I invest in Spain than a reason (or is that a rationalization?).

If you are dealing with a person who has a tie that developed into a knot with the area where you own property, you can use it in making your transaction. This becomes what I call a "soft motivation," one that you should not call attention to directly, but that all the same is a factor you should understand and point out.

A client of mine had a property in Portugal, not far from Lisbon. It was a villa and estate of some 15 acres overlooking the sea. He lived in Florida but was a native of Martinique. The son of a diplomat from mainland France, as a child he had lived in Martinique. Later in his professional career he had lived in many places, and while in Portugal for 10 years, thus the owner of this villa, he had never returned to Martinique.

I proposed an exchange for land in Martinique. It was ultimately accepted.

Play your game as you see fit. Look for hot buttons, and ties that will direct people back to the home fires, even long after the fires have gone cold.

Emotional Connections

People get fed up, sick to death, anxious, distraught, divorced, and married, drafted, ill, and they die. People become incapable of paying off their debts, their rent, their car payments, or their alimony. People make decisions that have nothing to do with reality, ration, or reason. People act with a spontaneity that will surprise you or which will shock you, or they loll about unable to decide what day it is, much less decide something important. People do things that are insane and without explanation. They do things that are based on instant needs or long-term frustrations. They fall in love, become attached to the darndest things and people. People do all of these things because people are only human, which means they are full of faults and make mistakes of judgment and act without experience and forethought. They also act with intuition and careful planning and are capable of doing great and wonderful things. It's up to you to find, then use, emotional connections.

People do things, and more often than not they do those things correctly. In real estate investing you do not depend on someone else making a mistake to profit. But there are situations when you can profit from someone else's mistake or error of judgment. Are you ready to take advantage of that? Are you ready to reap the harvest of others' misfortune?

You may not have even thought about it in those terms. It is not like we are dealing with millionaires winning or losing, but in the long run it makes little difference. What we are dealing with, in the real estate game, is simple mistakes or errors of judgment or wrong calculations of timing that cause profits and losses to be made.

"Okay, you are transferred to California and you leave next Wednesday. I'll take over your mortgage and give you, let me see, a time-share in Cape Town for your equity. Deal?" Or, what about "I'm sorry about your husband, Frank. He was a great guy, too bad, and what a horrible way to go. Anyway, as I was saying, I can't give you any cash, but if you make the next two payments I'll step in and assume the mortgage. . . . "

Sure, that's hardball, but, look, if that is the only ball offered, it might fly, and if you are the only knight in shining armor around, your armor doesn't have to be that bright.

I Don't Want It But...

I want yours more than mine. There is a little of this concept in most exchanges, sometimes as a truth, often as a rationalization, occasionally in retrospect. International deals or transactions that fail are entered into because some emotional quandary or other occurs, often because people suddenly get frustrated to the point that anything looks better than what they are dealing with. People want to believe that the grass truly is not only greener on the other side of the fence, but doesn't need to be trimmed either. People honestly think that what looks like paradise will remain that when they move there. Sometimes they find it truly does.

International transactions seem to work well when any of the three factors—taxes, knots, and emotion—are present. Each lends a tempering focus to that faroff land, the haven from crime, worry, and taxes. Watch for those factors, and if you, too, are wishing for the island paradise, or the mountain hideaway, or Shangri-la, then wish a little harder and it may find you.

Prepaid Rent Exchange

Several examples of exchanges in this book have included prepaid rent as a part of the transaction. This is a very simple equity to add to any exchange and it can be an effective closing tool. Prepaid rent exchanges occur when you offer the other party prepaid rent in a property. The property could be the very property that person is exchanging to you, or another property you own.

Sal wanted to buy Oliver's home. Oliver was balking at the deal, complaining about the upcoming holidays, the difficulty of getting out of the house by the proposed closing date, and so on. Sal reexamined the deal and decided he could wait a couple of months to move in, as long as he could start doing some remodeling to the exterior of the home. In a counterproposal, Sal offered three months of free rent to Oliver in exchange for acceptance of the deal as presented.

Bruce was trying to acquire two vacant lots from a developer where Bruce could build two homes for resale. As a part of the transaction Bruce offered 12 free months' rent of office space in a building he owned. If the developer needs office space he would be a direct user. If not, a live-wire agent would attempt to work out the deal by exchanging the space for something the developer did want or could use.

A Creative Look at Prepaid Rent

Rodney Construction Company offered a 200-unit deluxe rental apartment building to the owner of a vacant tract of land where Rodney wanted to build. As a part of the transaction Rodney offered the owners a five-year prepaid lease in a penthouse apartment. They countered for eight years and the deal was made.

Prepaid rent transactions work well when there is a need for the space, and giving up the space to be rented does not adversely affect the taking party. It all boils down to the economics of a transaction. Rodney knows that in a large rental complex there is bound to be some vacancy on a year-round basis. Any new building takes time to rent up, so one apartment given up as a substantial part of equity in the transaction is a soft cost to pay.

Bruce had a vacant office that was a negative for him, so giving that space in exchange for two lots on which he could build two homes for ultimate profit was good business. Not only would he make a positive move (getting closer to his goals) but if the people who took the office liked it, they would likely stay beyond the year he exchanged to them.

In Sal's case the prepaid rent was not real cost because he did not have to move into the home, and he had the access he needed to make repairs and to remodel the exterior.

Take Advantage of This Soft Cost in Counters

Put yourself on the other side of the offer for a moment. If you are getting close to your asking price but are still not quite there, consider a counter where you get some prepaid rent as part of the transaction. This would be an obvious direction to go if you had a use or need for any property the other party could extend to you through prepaid lease.

Often, maximizing the results of your counteroffer involves knowing what the other party can offer to you that has a soft cost to them. Prepaid rent is just one of these kinds of soft costs, and a creative counter will take into consideration this factor. Other soft costs can include, but by no means be limited to, a product, property, or service that the person making the offer has at their disposal.

Lease-Back Exchanges

A lease-back is when a person sells or exchanges his property, then leases all or part of it back. As a financing technique this is one of the best methods of pulling out capital by getting rid of the actual ownership of a property but retaining the use of the part you actually need. Tax considerations can also make a sale or exchange, and then a lease-back be worthwhile. You should frequently ask your accountant, "Should I consider a sale or exchange with a lease-back on any of my property?"

A Basic Lease-Back Exchange

A basic lease-back exchange would be if I gave you the equity in my shopping center for your free and clear home in Acapulco, Mexico, and I agreed to lease-back the center from you as a part of the deal. This is not a 1031 tax-free exchange, but it could have benefits for both of us, depending on our circumstances. I may have longed to live in Acapulco and due to my situation I have little or no tax to pay on a sale of the center. For you, I become a taker for your home in Mexico (which you haven't used in three years).

Lease-backs are, all by themselves, a tax-planning strategy. There are sound reasons for using this technique that have nothing to do with exchanges of any kind. However, tying exchanges to this tool can be very productive for both parties in the right situation.

A sale of any capital property can be a taxable event for the seller. This can take place because of a capital appreciation of the asset and or a reduction of book value (or basis) through annual depreciation of that same asset. For example, Able has owned his publishing facility for nearly 12 years and his accountant has informed him that his tax basis for the property is $100,000. The current market value of this property is nearly $2,000,000. Based on this information and nothing more, if Able were to sell the property he would have a gain of $1,900,000 and a tax of over $475,000 to pay. If he had to turn around and pay rent of close to $200,000 after all expenses are paid per year, there would be no real incentive to enter into a sale, unless Able was strapped for cash and could not refinance to generate the needed cash.

A qualified 1031 exchange can produce a tax-free event for Able, but if Able is cash hungry the exchange will not solve the problem unless the other property has better prospects for financing (as could well be the case).

A lease-back sale is an ideal technique to use when you want to generate cash and do not need to own the property, as long as you have exclusive use of it. If you have a substantial tax loss that can be used to offset and therefore negate the gains tax, a sale with a lease-back can be ideal.

Keep in mind that the owner of the property you are exchanging into does not have to be the person who ends up with your property. Because of this, it is quite possible that in a situation where a **lease-back sale** would be ideal, that even more ideal can be **a lease-back exchange** if you play the cards right.

One of the major considerations in any lease-back deal is the annual rent that the previous owner must now pay to occupy his former property. In a straight sale the buyer must look very critically at the capital investment. This capital investment is usually made up of two factors: cash down, and mortgage obligations. The sale of a $2,000,000 property with 25 percent down would require a cash down of $500,000 and a debt service based on repayment of $1,750,000. For an investor to obtain a moderate return of 10 percent on his cash and to make payments on the mortgage would take every penny of $200,000 and even more if the financing interest were excessive. The tenant must also take into consideration the triple net provisions of a typical lease and add to his rent all the other cost to stay at this location (such as real estate tax, building maintenance, insurance, and so on).

This ultimate cost to the previous owner, both directly and indirectly, is the stumbling block to lease-back deals. However, in a lease-back exchange the party making the exchange may have a substantial tax savings on their side of the deal to enable them to offer lower rents while providing most of the cash the seller wants.

Assume that Able's building is free and clear, worth the $2,000,000 previously indicated; also that due to other events, Able has a substantial tax loss for his company that year and can take advantage of a sale without having to pay any tax on the gain. Despite the property being worth $2,000,000, however, Able would like to pay only $175,000 in rent per year. Because rent and value are connected (lower rents bring values down), no investor is willing to pay $2,000,000 at that rent structure.

Along comes Bill. He has a property worth $500,000 that only cost him $25,000 five years ago. He offers to give Able the $500,000 worth of property and $1,500,000 in cash. All he wants in rent is $220,000 triple net with a cost-of-living index to go into place at the end of the fourth year and with assurances that by the end of the fifth year the annual rent will not be less than $230,000 per year. Bill will lease-back the land he gives to Able for a term of four years for $45,000 per year. Bill wants an option to buy the land back at the end of the four years at a set price of $700,000, but if he has to will let Able delete that condition from the offer.

Able studies the offer and sees that for a term of four years his net rent will be $175,000, because although he must pay Bill $220,000, he will collect rent from Bill on the vacant land of $45,000 per year. At the end of the four years Bill's lease expires and if he does not exercise his option to buy, the land remains Able's to keep or sell or exchange. In fact, Able always had that option right from the first day, and Bill's lease-back with option might have encouraged a buyer at a reasonable and acceptable (to Able) price.

The offer is acceptable to Able because the cash is about what he needed, and the rent is exactly what he wanted to pay. He will take the vacant property because, well . . . the value checks out, and there were no other deals that looked as good. Most of Able's goals were achieved.

Bill goes (already checked it out beforehand of course) to his bank and shows the purchase of $2,000,000 with a triple net lease of $220,000 per year and obtains a loan from the bank for the required $1,500,000. Bill might even borrow more and put some cash in his pocket from this transaction.

Bill's tax situation is enhanced because he accomplished a 1031 tax-free exchange and saved on paying tax from his end of the deal. That plus the ability to finance the transaction by showing a real rent of $220,000 but with a counter lease-back of $45,000 was able to give Able the rental value that made it work for both of them.

As you can see, the use of this technique is highly creative and depends on a combination of circumstances that will never fall into place exactly as you first hope. Tax situations never do, because each deal and each person has different criteria and goals to be met.

How a Developer Uses the Lease-Back Exchange

It is a good idea to look at the use of a lease-back exchange if you are a seller of property that may appeal to a prospective developer. If you own a nice corner site that would be good for a shopping center you might approach developers with the following proposal:

Exchange to them your site, free and clear of any debt, provided they exchange to you land under another center they currently own, which they lease-back.

You accomplish a 1031 exchange, they get the free and clear land, which makes their life as developers far more comfortable, and at the same time you provide easy financing to decrease their equity in a money-making venture. They don't really pay you rent; the tenants of the center pay the rent.

Naturally, if you are the developer you can use this technique to acquire more sites. In this instance look for sites where the owner has a low tax base. This means that an exchange that will qualify for the 1031 provisions will be beneficial to the seller, and a conversion from nonincome property into income property can be very attractive.

In reality you have accomplished a form of pyramid using a lease-back instead of mortgage to establish the equity in the transaction.

Pitfalls with Lease-Backs

There are two major pitfalls with lease-backs, the strength of the tenant, and the value of the property.

1. The strength of the tenant. When you acquire any rental property you must view the property first, and the tenant second. In a lease-back, however, you have to consider the tenant first. Why is he doing a lease-back? Is his reason based on sound business decisions to save on tax, to generate the capital he needs, or is it that the property has been on the market for three years without a buyer and the lease-back is a way to attract an investor rather than a user. Check out the motives for making the deal, as well as the credit of the owner as a tenant. Unfortunately, I have seen several lease-back deals go sour quickly because the seller was more interested in getting the cash than in staying on in the property.

2. The value of the property. Now take a hard look at the value. Just because the owner says he will lease-back at $220,000 per year does not mean the property value is $2,000,000 or thereabouts. If the economics are structured to show an attractive rate of return, which in turn is based on the rent the seller (who can skip to Rio with your $2,000,000 the next day) is willing to pay, the deal and the value of the property may not be worth your effort.

Fortunately, for both pitfalls you can install safeguards. Nothing beats checking out what people say, and in business that is not as difficult as you might think. But do it carefully. Have your CPA go over books and records, get references and appraisals, and check out values in the area. Be sure to check the rental market to make sure that the per-square-foot rent the tenant is going to pay is not inflated. Cheaper rent works because you can use a tool that counterbalances the problem that can occur if your tenant (the former owner) skips town.

The best safeguard in lease-backs is to use the property given in exchange as a security on the lease. Take another look at Able's deal with Bill. If Bill had been concerned with the value of the property or with Able as a tenant, he would have come to a decision about the property first. What value, Bill would want to know, would make the purchase of Able's property a bargain (in the current market). If in this situation Bill calculated that at $1,500,000 anyone would love to own the property, Bill could insist that Able pledge the $500,000 property that Bill gave in the exchange as a cross-security to the lease, at least for its first four or five years. This additional security has no effect on Able's position, other than the fact that he cannot sell or exchange the property. But there would be no reason to do that because the rent coming in from Bill offsets Able's rent to Bill.

If for some reason Able goes into default on his lease to Bill, Bill accelerates the lease and takes the security, which is Able's land. Bill now owns the property with a first mortgage of $1,500,000 and can deal freely in the market with a solid property at a ripe price.

There is a major benefit to Bill in using this additional security back from the transaction. When Bill goes to the bank to obtain the money from the mortgage he gives the bank, the fact that Able is willing to secure the lease with a $500,000 property is very impressive. Not only does Bill have $500,000 of equity in the deal, but there is another $500,000 worth of property behind the lease. Never mind that both $500,000's came from the same property. Consider the property as if it were cash. In a lease-back, cross-collateral can consist of any asset of the tenant's becoming additional security to the lease and/or mortgage.

Eleven Pitfalls in the Real Estate Business

The real estate game, and in particular real estate exchanging, depends on person-to-person confrontation. You rely on people, what they say, and what they give you in the way of information and documents. You become a slave to their timetable when it conflicts with yours. You are trapped to wait for their return call because they were out when you called them, and you are frustrated that, of all the important things you needed to answer, deliver, sign and execute, or destroy, only half has been accomplished.

Surviving Pitfalls Means Surviving People

It is people who create all your roadblocks and pitfalls. If you let it get to you, your life as a real estate investor will be most frustrated, and you will surely become a neurotic wreck.

Dealing with pitfalls is an art; discovering how to deal with people requires the use of charm, patience, display of self-confidence, firmness (when firmness serves a purpose), a sympathetic ear, understanding, and, on rare but unavoidable occasions, a few well-chosen cuss words to serve as an exclamation point that your limit has been reached.

You Can Win with Patience While Losing at Investing

I am a firm believer that in most life situations, patience wins out in the long run. Not that you win every match, of course, but in personal relationships and one-on-one dealing, patience is the better avenue to follow than clock watching frustration. In real estate, however, patience may mean that you become the spectator to events that others make happen. In the world of investing, time is not on the side of the spectator.

Anticipation of problems and pitfalls is a key to dealing with them, because you will be able to nip the difficulty in the bud long before it develops to the point of being an impossible situation. If you know what can happen you watch for it, and don't worry about its occurrence (that would be counterproductive).

This chapter discusses 11 basic pitfalls: file them away in the back of your mind, and when one of these pitfalls confronts you, you will be forewarned and properly armed to deal with the situation.

The 11 Pitfalls

1. Overpriced property
2. Mortgages and leases of convenience
3. The phantom deal maker
4. Hot and black money
5. Your own accountant
6. Sloppy contracts
7. Nonstandard standard-looking forms
8. Owners who lie
9. Hidden loopholes
10. The lawyer—yours and theirs
11. The broker—yours and theirs

1. Overpriced Property

There are five factors about the price of real estate that most people do not fully understand. It is essential to recognize these factors before one can deal with the pitfall of overpriced property and to deal with each one in a different way. The five factors of price are:

1. Market conditions
2. Replacement cost
3. Location
4. Benefits
5. Ownership

You will agree, I hope, that the price of properties would be affected by each of the above five factors. Reviewing any property with these five factors in mind should give you some idea of the difficulties of pricing any property, because while each of the five factors will change, you will never find an exact, down to the very last detail, duplicate property.

Price, then, becomes a relative element in real estate that is unique to this kind of investing. Almost every other form of investing has its identical, duplicate, or a copy so close that differences are not important. Stocks and bonds and gems, or coins and stamps and so on, do not rely on all these same factors, although certainly the market conditions and the ownership aspects do play a role in the price of those items.

Concentrate on the five for a moment as they relate to real estate.

Market Conditions

I am sure you've heard the term, "buyer's market" or "seller's market." These terms refer to the status of the property you want to sell or buy as it responds to the market conditions. The market can be a "buyer's" and a "seller's market" at the same time, but for different kinds of property, or hot or cold in one solid direction for all property. These ups and downs of the real estate market lag behind or precede other events that take place in the economy, but are not uniform across the country. This factor makes it very difficult to predict the exact results of a future trend for any single location, based on a past trend elsewhere. While certain patterns do surface, the reasons for the impact of any trend are best viewed after they have occurred rather than in anticipation of them.

For example, when money gets tight around the United States, housing starts generally slump. This is a predictable trend that will generally hit areas that are overbuilt and have especially critical economic problems. But the key word is "slump." This does not mean that housing starts come to a halt, because so far they have not. I cannot remember, ever, when new housing construction actually came to a nationwide halt. But for some communities it did, and in some other communities at exactly the same time there was little or no change; and oddly, in others, the housing starts actually went up. Had you tried to predict the trend and anticipate the market conditions for your area based on the statistic, without benefit of other data, you would be doing nothing more than soothsaying.

This is where sleepers are born. Whatever the local circumstances, an improper view of market conditions can cause a price to be put on a property that is excessive. Mind you, a miscalculation on the part of the seller, who has not noticed that the "slump" is over or does not affect his area of town, can create a "sleeper" for you to snap up.

In general, the condition of the market shifts to the point that property is put on the market at an artificially high price. Brokers and agents are anxious to get the listing, so they hold out hope for the seller to get a high price, the sellers agree, and the price is set higher than the market would dictate.

☞ **Key Words:** Don't Let High Prices Stop Your Offers

Market conditions may reflect on the property and not the price, to the point that lowering the price does not produce a buyer . . . unless the price is reduced so much that investors recognize the bargain and step in to neutralize the situation. However, in counterbalance to a property that is overpriced, it is not unusual for a property to sit on the market, unsold— until a strategic effort is made to market the property more aggressively. Exchanging is one of those aggressive means.

Replacement Costs

Properties may be overpriced due to current replacement cost. Most sellers whose properties are overpriced are quick to point out that it would cost an extra $100,000 over their price just to replace what they have. This is a very good selling point, and can be true much of the time. However, even when it is true, the reconstructed property would be brand-new and exactly what the new owner would want it to be, not the tired old property that even the owner would not duplicate if he had the money to do so. Although age can make many properties more charming, it also produces obsolescence and shortens the time between enjoyment and repairs.

Generally, the final factor in replacement cost is the cost of the land under the improvement. It is, when all is said and done, the land that has increased in value the most. This is most clearly demonstrated where once-grand buildings are demolished to get at the former vacant lots so that newer, better buildings can be constructed.

Learning About Replacement Costs

By looking at newly constructed properties you can begin to develop a comparison of what it costs to build. Take a few days each month to go where such properties are offered for sale, even if they are out of your comfort and investment zone. Ask questions that build your understanding of what an addition would cost, or a larger pool or different carpets.

Ask the builder what it would cost to build that same property on your lot were you to buy one nearby. It should not cost much more or less on a neighboring nearby lot. Having a ballpark figure of construction cost enables you to make your own assessments of value, and to recognize a sales pitch when you hear it.

Rising costs of construction, the expense of getting permits, paying impact fees, and dealing with zoning laws, building restrictions, and the growing cost of public utilities is what makes for higher replacement cost. These are real elements, and more than the actual cost increase of the lumber or the carpenter is the value of the frustration you would go through to build the same property today.

This is the cause of an increase that has nothing to do with the other four factors, and you will ultimately have to weigh all of this when you consider purchasing something nearly new, something which is in need of a major fix-up, or starting from the ground and building for yourself.

You counter an overpriced property whose owner argues replacement cost by saying, "Yes, but then, I have to consider the fact that acquiring this property is different than what I would build."

The seller, astute and ready for all hardballs thrown at him, will aptly reply, "Isn't it fortunate that you do not have to settle for less, and can acquire it in this very property."

Location, Location, Location

I know, I know. It's stick-your-finger-down-your-throat time, but it is true. Location is the three most important things that affect property value. But consider that while a location is fixed, the value of the property at any given location can go up and down in value, depending on what else is going on at that location.

Consider a property that is three blocks away from where everything is happening. That property, even though of identical size, road frontage, and zoning, will have a lower value, and command a lesser price than its sister property that is right on the main highway in the heart of the commercial center of town.

There is more to it than location alone. This proves that location is the determining factor, right? Well, almost. What happens next happens all the time, all over the world. People, those little devils that can make or break everything from Savings and Loans to camels' backs, to say nothing about location, location, location, come along and mess up your good thing. All it takes is some project or other to disrupt the flow of things—a major building, a bridge, a new hospital or convention center. The locations remain the same because you can't move them. But what has happened is that the importance of the location has changed.

The importance of important locations. Investing in real estate centers on your ability to pick the next important location. You could make a horrible mistake by selecting the very best location in town (today), to wake up (tomorrow) only to discover that the city has decided to close the highway for seven years while they build a new one three blocks away, or that the convention center burned down and the new one will be built on the other side of town, or . . . well this list could go on for a long time.

So it is not exactly location, location, location after all. Instead, you need to look at what makes that location important.

Benefits

If you are starting to think of benefits as the reason to own or invest in real estate, then this book has been worthwhile. Nothing else really counts, except what you gain from the ownership of your property and how that ownership moves you toward the attainment of your goals. Goals, success, happiness, peace with yourself, financial independence, a good night's sleep . . . whatever success means to you, it comes from the benefits you can produce for yourself and the benefits you derive from the things and property you own. Weigh the benefits and see who values them most.

Benefits are relative to the ability to utilize them, and if your property can produce more benefits to someone else than it does for you, then the other person should realize a greater value to them. For example, if you own 200 acres of timberland in the state of Maine and your only benefit is the ultimate sale of the timber, that same property could produce greater benefits to the investor who can turn it into a winter ski resort. The same location, the same property, and the same benefits are available; but different owners have separate and different appreciation and use of them.

People who overprice their property often do so because they only see the benefits they are obtaining, without realizing their situation is unique, and that unless an exact or nearly exact reproduction of ownership occurs that could utilize and appreciate the same benefits, the value they have set for the property is excessive to other investors.

Helping the seller put this into a proper perspective can be a very difficult task. About the only thing you can do is point out that perhaps they should not try to dispose of this property at all, because the benefits which you or any reasonable investor would expect do not warrant that kind of price.

Don't forget about your goals. Sometimes reality sinks in when people place their own goals on the balance scale. They have become complacent, and all during the time they are enjoying certain benefits they are being sidetracked from their goals. What happens is that people begin to enjoy the benefits and forget that they have become stagnant in reaching their goals. This occurs because people's needs change, and the pursuit of goals must be a constant, active, and ever-changing thing.

Ownership

> **Owner has been transferred.**
> Must sell oceanfront home this week.
> Make offer now.

That's a bit strong, but you may have seen similar ads in the newspaper. If this is not just the brainchild of an ad agency, there is an owner who has a problem—and owners' problems create profit potential. It is called opportunity.

Ownership can be the key to the value. When ownership motivation is strong, the price that will be accepted is in inverse relation to the needs of the seller. The greater the motivation, the lower the final price accepted will be. Many real estate agents overlook the personal needs of the owner and price a property to get the listing, rather than solve the ownership problem. I have seen this hundreds of times in my 25 years as a Realtor, where the listing agent is "surprised" at what comes out when I present my offers; this is because I delve into the sellers' needs, and attempt to find their real reason for selling.

Are You Your Own Worst Enemy?

The seller is often his own worst enemy when it comes to selling his property, and will price a property above its market value because he has misled his agent. All real estate brokers and agents should explain to their clients that every property has a price range for the current market conditions. They should explain that, based on the comparable and replacement costs, the specific property will appeal to certain buyers more than others. The final buyer will be the one who can take advantage of more of the benefits the property can offer, provided that buyer is able to afford the price, or that the seller can accept the amount that person can offer.

Time is the judge. As always, Father Time will determine the value and the price. If the seller has enough time, then there is never an overpriced property, only one that is priced before its time.

2. Mortgages and Leases of Convenience

Mortgages and leases of convenience are documents that are created in name only just prior to the property's being offered onto the market, but in reality the mortgages or leases do not exist at that moment. They are a good tool which can be used in creative financing and deal making. However, unless you are careful, the same tool can be used to mislead the buyer as to the value of the property.

Keep in mind that creative secondary financing is one of the best ways to acquire or dispose of property, and has sound foundations in practice. However, either side of the negotiations can use these tools in a way that can distort values and disguise a horrible investment as a good one.

Why Keep It a Secret?

I have shown examples earlier illustrating that, when offering your property, you may not want to disclose that the mortgage or lease shown is in fact one of convenience. The positive point to this is simply that of negotiation. If the buyer believes the mortgage or lease is already in place, there can be little or no negotiation on that part of the total price. On the other hand, if the offering clearly states that the seller will hold secondary financing and/or will lease back the property, then both of those elements become entwined in the negotiation process.

What You Should Look For

The bad part of mortgages and leases of convenience happen when the other party has created in name only a mortgage which has payments that are greater than the property will actually support, as if, "to give the impression that a lender has confidence in the property and the reported value." A lease of convenience that calls for monthly rent well in excess of what a real tenant would pay clearly distorts the reality of that property.

You should never make an offer on any property where you have made a value judgment based on existing financing or leases without having the right to approve the documents. You need time to thoroughly review them as well as the people who either lent the money or are tenants to the leases.

The 5 Questions to Protect Yourself
1. Is there a direct connection to the seller?
2. Are these documents actually in place **now?**
3. Do you have every part of the document?

    4.   What is the tenants' credit history?

    5.   What is the payment history on the mortgage and lease?

If there is any connection between the seller and the lender or tenant, you will want to know what that is. Insider deals are not uncommon, so a relationship between the two parties may mean nothing; but if it means nothing, then there will be no reason you should not know. On the other hand, the brother of the seller might have entered into an excessive lease for other reasons . . . such as to help his brother out of a tight market.

Of course, knowing if the documents are in place now gives you the ability to open negotiations in those areas, as well as negotiations on price. If the coin is turned and you have offered your property with a mortgage and/or lease of convenience, and can support the reasons for the terms of the mortgage or lease, then do so openly and state that these conditions make you want to sell.

Get All the Facts

To review any document, you must make sure that you have every part of the agreement. This is critical, because subsequent amendments or letters of modification can surface later. The only way to ensure that you have the total agreement is to get an estoppel letter from the parties to the document. Estoppel letters would come from the lender, in the case of a mortgage, and the tenant, in the case of a lease.

The estoppel letter is simply an affidavit that states that the mortgage or lease is in good standing, and that payments through the date of the estoppel letter are current. The estoppel letter can also verify that the copy of the mortgage or lease attached constitutes the full agreement between the parties.

Without this form of insurance, you take a risk that some term or condition may have changed. The warranties of the seller that the mortgage, leases, and other contracts are as presented, give you legal recourse against the seller only once you find out otherwise; and legal actions to rescind an agreement or recover damages from a seller long gone can be wasted and very expensive energy. Get the facts up front.

3. The Phantom Deal Maker

I love this guy, because he reminds me of the little ghost in the comic strips named "Not Me." You may have seen him: he's the real culprit; he'll get in your way every time. When a mother asks a child, as she finds a broken plate on the floor, or a balloon tied to the cat's tail, "Who did that?" the child replies, "Not Me."

In this fashion, the Phantom Deal Maker really gets around, because just about anytime you are going to make an offer he has beat you to the punch. It works like this: "Your offer is a bit low, Mr. Cummings, and not nearly as good as another offer we are considering" (from the Phantom).

The Phantom also is the guy they expect to hear from later that day, or who is going to see his lawyer about drawing up a contract. The Phantom also bought several other properties down the block, and loves their property above all.

Dealing with the Phantom

You are bound to come across this guy sooner or later, so the best way to approach him is to ignore him altogether. I have seen other methods, such as inventing your own Phantom: "Well Mr. Seller, we have to run now, we have an appointment with the owner of a similar property a few blocks away to discuss an offer." Or try to bluff them out. "Okay Mr. Seller, because you are considering an offer from Mr. P, maybe it would be best if we looked elsewhere. If your deal with P doesn't work out you can give our agent a call and if we haven't found anything else . . . well, we might be interested." But neither of those methods work as well as just moving along as though their dealings with Mr. P in no way affect what you are going to do.

It would be okay, advisable in fact, to ask this question: "Oh, do I understand that because of Mr. P, you would rather not consider an offer from us?" That simple question should set things straight. Move on, Mr. P or not.

4. Hot and Black Money

It is a crime to accept illegally obtained money if you know that the funds were so obtained. If you discover later on that the money was of that category and do nothing about it, you could be subject to punishment as an accomplice to a crime.

The majority of hot and black money comes from the sale of drugs, illegal gambling, and other vices, and from the illegal transit of money from foreign countries.

In South Florida from the mid seventies to the mid eighties, it was relatively commonplace for much of this hot and black money to find its way into the real estate market. Slowly the banks became the target of investigations, and as money laundering through the banks slowed and law enforcement agencies began to crack down on illegal purchases of property, the drug and illegal money started to disappear from the open market.

I am not sure where those funds are now going, but I suspect that much of that money is currently flowing into Europe, where the tracking of the origin of investment capital is not a common practice.

Suspicious? Get It in Writing

A simple comment made by one of the agents in jest—"You have to wonder how an eighteen-year-old would have a million in cash to put down on this hotel. Must be drug money"—could hit the nail on the head and come back to haunt you at his trial. "Did you," the district attorney would grill you, "know that the million dollars in unmarked bills were obtained through the sale of heroin to seventh-graders at West Side Elementary School?" Wow, good-bye money, hello jail.

If you are suspicious as to the origin of a buyer's money, ask for two things from the other party: (1) a list of references, which you check out and get replies from in writing, and (2) verification that the funds being used to acquire your property, or the real estate being transferred to you, were legally obtained and that no violation of any law of any nation was committed.

If I could not get this from a party I suspected of dealing with hot and black money who wanted to acquire my property, I would not proceed with the deal. You will have to act as you feel prudent.

5. Your Own Accountant

Okay, so this guy is a member of your own team and should act accordingly, right? Well, he should, but unless you know how to deal with your team members, it is possible that not only your accountant, but your lawyer and every other member of your "team" are not doing you justice.

Roadblocks and pitfalls can come from your own team members through your acting on bad advice they give you. The problem is that it is generally your fault, because you have not given them the full details of the situation, or have asked them for a decision rather than advice.

It is one thing to ask your accountant to give you the breakdown of how the 1031 exchange will affect your year-end taxes, and entirely another thing to ask if you should exchange for the 200-slip marina that has been offered to you.

The 3 Kinds of Professionals Out to Get You

There are three kinds of professionals and they can all reside in the same person—like a Dr. Jeckle, Mr. Hide, and Professor Seek. Depending on the situation and their own experience, these professionals thrive on:

1. Giving the best advice and information possible to allow their clients to make their own decisions.
2. Volunteering, without being asked, to make the decision for their client as though it were their own deal, and stepping right in to help negotiate the deal.
3. Giving a categorical "No," when asked if you should do the deal, because they do not want to be held responsible, should things go wrong.

There is nothing wrong with brainstorming the situation with your team members and asking, "What would you do?" as long as it is followed up with "Why and why not?" But even those questions only elicit the answer of what they would do.

Getting the Most Out of Your Team Members

Getting all the pros and cons from many points of view is essential for any investor. It is through a member playing "devil's advocate" that you discover what information is lacking or flow to the final point where you are comfortable with the decision you can now make, either on your own or jointly, with your partners (not your team members).

Explain to all your team members that you welcome their candid opinions, and hope they will play devil's advocate whenever they are able to defend another point of view. That give-and-take will allow you to increase your own data base (between your ears) and to overcome many people's natural tendency to have their decisions made for them.

Do your part, by giving them all the information necessary for them to give you the advice you require.

6. Sloppy Contracts

Offers and counteroffers can become sloppy, and a sloppy contract can contain provisions or terms that are difficult to understand and enforce.

In the heat of a deal, a real estate agent might rush the offer, or a lawyer with other things to do may quickly dictate the provisions he wants in the agreement . . . and a ball can start rolling that will end up a mess somewhere down the road.

The offer is presented and the other side makes a counter. Sometimes the counter is a matter of crossing out this, adding that, and marking up the agreement with pen marks and initials of the accepting parties.

Compound this by another counter or two, and the whole offer can look like the third re-do of a handwritten manuscript. Everyone thinks they know exactly where the changes have been made, and everyone thinks they have a clear understanding of the final document. Which is the final document anyway? Even that can be hard to determine, with these modern copy machines turning out copies that look better than the originals.

The 7 Steps to Maintaining Clear Contracts

1. Make sure that the original offer can be read, and that every term and condition is clear. You do this by reading it several times. If a sentence doesn't appear to be clear or could possibly have two meanings, depending on what "it" and "they" refer to, rewrite it until it is absolutely clear. Good contracts use definite names rather than pronouns, to avoid that kind of confusion.

2. When a pen change is made on the original offer, the change should be neatly made so that everything is clearly shown. Make sure that new words added are understandable and the changes match the intent.

3. Make a dated **list of changes made** and attach it to the revised offer. The first list of changes made would list each change that was made to the original contract; any subsequent change in future counters, where changes are made to previous changes, would require a newly dated list of changes made which brings the final offer up to date.

4. Read each counter carefully and make sure that the list of changes is accurate and that no change has been made to the contract that you do not review.

5. Once excessive changes have been made on a contract that could make future changes difficult to read or understand, draft a new agreement that incorporates all the changes made so far, along with your new counter. Show clearly what the **new change** is and present this new agreement as your counter. You can also make the change on one of the old agreements, to document that the new agreement is an accurate summation of all previous changes.

6. Make sure that only the final agreement is used for the closing. The best way to do this is to have only a few agreements going through the offer/counteroffer process, and to destroy agreements that have been superseded by new offers or counters. (You can keep one of each for reference, but mark it so that it is not later assumed to be a firm and binding agreement.)

7. At the closing of the agreement when title is transferred, make sure that all documents, mortgages, leases, and so on have been drafted to reflect the provisions and conditions of the final agreement.

7. Nonstandard Standard-Looking Forms

In every community there are **standard forms** available for just about every legal document or agreement you can think of. These forms make life easier for the professionals who deal in the area of business for which the form was designed. One neat trick played by the truly dishonest is the use of nonstandard forms that look standard—if you discover someone using this tactic I hope you spread the word about it.

If you are a lawyer, accountant, real estate agent, or broker and are handed a form that looks exactly like a standard form you are used to dealing with, you may overlook some of the fine print. After all, you have seen that form a thousand times before and know it like the back of your hand, right? I love that phrase, because it is exactly the right analogy. Put one of your hands behind you and now describe exactly the markings on the skin of that hand. I doubt you will describe the back of your own hand accurately.

So how can you expect anyone to notice the difference between a standard form and a nonstandard standard-looking form unless they make a careful study of whatever form they are using.

This is so important that you must never assume that a standard form actually is one. Mechanical copiers can duplicate everything, including different-color print that might overprint the real standard form with wording such as "APPROVED BY THE GEORGIA LAWYERS ASSOCIATION."

A carefully altered form can be a considerably different document, one that you would not accept if you knew of the alteration.

Protecting Yourself

Read all forms carefully, and ask your lawyer to do so as well. Watch for changes that might not be easily recognized as alterations—replacing "buyer" with "seller," or "not" with "now." Simple changes can have a major impact on who does what, when.

Warning! Agreements you execute may be binding. The fact that the other party was slick enough to present you with a contract that you and your team members did not read carefully does not alter the fact that you executed it. You certainly had every opportunity to study the offer presented, and what is in black and white can be binding, unless you can prove that you were intentionally led to believe something different. I personally think this method of doing business is unethical, but I do not know of any law that would protect you in this kind of situation.

In real estate the following types of standard forms are used:

Typical Standard Forms for Real Estate Transactions

    Agreement to purchase
        Coops and condos
        Commercial property
        Vacant land
        Businesses
        Installment-sale contract
        Uniform real estate contract
        Exchange agreements of all kinds
    Deeds of transfer
        Quitclaim deed (individual)
        Quitclaim deed (corporation)
        Grant deed

        Special deed
        Trustee's deed
        Warranty deed
    Forms to secure debt
        Mortgage (individual)
        Mortgage (corporation)
        Deed to secure debt
        Deed of trust
        Promissory note
        Note
        Corporate note
    Forms to end encumbrances
        Satisfaction of lien
        Satisfaction of mortgage
    Tenancy forms
        Agreement to lease
        Agreement to rent
        Lease contract
        Lease with option to buy
    Assignments
        Buyer's assignment
        Seller's assignment
        Assignment of lease
        Assignment of option
    Miscellaneous
        Estoppel letter
        Insurance binders
        Mortgage commitments
        Option contracts
        Warranties

Nothing beats being careful. Which leads us to the next pitfall.

8. Owners Who Lie

Sorry, most will. Being told a lie or a distortion or misrepresentation of fact can result in major problems with the investment or the property. There is no way you can fully protect against a lie, except to make every attempt to verify every fact given you.

If the facts are material, then you should never take the unverified word of the owner or any of his agents or representatives. This statement does not mean that everyone will be telling you lies, only that what they tell you may be information they obtained from an unreliable or misleading set of facts and information.

This very afternoon, I had a meeting with the owner of a hotel who, unable to sell it, was crying the blues. "They all lied to me," he said, "and here I am; I can't sell it for anything; everything they told me turned out to be untrue. The income figures, the advance reservations . . . everything. They must have seen me coming a mile away."

Don't let them see you coming a mile away. Verify everything. Question items that seem out of the ordinary, and make it happen because you are sure—not because they assure you.

9. Hidden Loopholes

In any contract, there should be nothing that is more or less than the written word explains. Only, do you understand every word of the agreement, and the special connotations or time periods that can go into the determination of certain factors? Beware of hidden conditions that can hurt you.

Hidden Time Delays

If the agreement says that the buyer will close within 30 days from the date the buyer obtains all approvals and permits for construction or remodeling, and you as seller do not know what approvals and permits are involved, a hidden condition exists. Some approvals and/or permits may take years to obtain, and at the whim of the buyer may not be ultimately obtained at all.

Anything in a contract that contains a condition must be clearly understood by you, prior to your acceptance of that condition. Often, the conditions which contain the loopholes are phrases that appear to be more limiting to the buyer, such as, "Buyer must deposit an additional $100,000 within five banking days from acceptance of all inspections, and inspections are to be made as soon as possible by the inspecting authorities." The problem with this is the phrase "as soon as possible." This is up to the inspecting authorities; and exactly what inspections are meant by "all inspections"? It is possible that somewhere else in the agreement there is a provision that indicates the need for the property "to be inspected by the proper governmental authority to validate that no toxic waste had contaminated all or part of the subject property." A seller who does not understand what this means, and who knows that he has done nothing to contaminate the property, may let that condition pass. However, the hidden loophole is now that the buyer can wait until the government has inspected the site and has validated it free of toxic waste. This event can take months, due to local backlog and the necessary documentation needed prior to the inspection.

Logical Statements Can Set You Up

Logical statements, such as the toxic waste problem, set the stage for other kinds of hidden loopholes. For example, "This offer is subject to the Buyer obtaining a first mortgage in . . ." What amount is the mortgage to be limited to, how long does he have to get it and so on . . . all items not shown. Hence, the contract is left open, with the seller tied up until the buyer gets what he wants.

Even set dates that appear to be definite are often not, owing to other provisions in the agreement. For example, there may be a condition that "the Buyer will close on January 25, 1993" in one part of the agreement, but in another section there might be a heading such as "Survey." Typical wording in a standard form for this heading would be:

> The Buyer, within the time allowed for delivery of evidence of title and exam-
> ination thereof, may have said property surveyed at his expense. If the survey
> shows any encroachment on said property or that the improvements located
> on the subject property in fact encroach on the lands of others, or violate any
> of the covenants herein, the same shall be treated as a title defect.

This condition generally favors the seller, in that the seller is not asked to deliver a survey at the seller's expense. This paragraph is one that is often altered in the nonstandard standard forms so that "The Buyer" is replaced with "The Seller." But this substitution does not create a loophole. The loophole would be created if the paragraph were altered as follows:

> The Buyer, within the time allowed for delivery of evidence of title and examination thereof, may order a **boundary and topographical survey** of the subject property at his expense. If either survey shows any encroachment on said property or that the improvements located on the subject property in fact encroach on the lands of others, or violate any of the covenants herein, the same shall be treated as a title defect. **Delays for any reason beyond the control of the Buyer for either of the above described surveys to be completed shall cause approval deadlines of inspections and title approval to be delayed by the same number of days plus two.**

It is logical to argue that if the surveyor cannot get the work completed, then why should the buyer be put into jeopardy. But topographical surveys can take weeks or even months, depending on the kind of property in question. Boundary surveys are much easier and faster to accomplish.

Question Every Condition

None of this is dishonest; nothing there is deliberately hidden, because it is written clearly and in black and white. Only you skip over it because it "sounds okay." Question everything. What does this mean? Why? When? Who?

Set Absolute Deadlines

Three deadline dates are important, and these three should have some limiting factor. The limiting factor can be a specific date, or a date that cannot be exceeded under any circumstances. The three deadlines are (1) date of acceptance by the other party; (2) date of ratification of the agreement when all approvals, inspections, and intermediate conditions are met; and (3) closing date.

Keep in mind that most contracts have a provision that allows for reasonable delay to close should the title not be good, or for other events over which neither party has control. Under no circumstance should you enter into any completely open-ended agreement; with no definite date to close, the other party could tie you up indefinitely.

What if the Other Party Needs Time?

Most loophole provisions are designed to give the other party time, or an out, or both. If the question is time, then you should address the problem up front and build in provisions, if you are so inclined to do so, where the other party can "buy" extra time to close or review inspections or get permits, or whatever. But perhaps if the other party simply needs or wants an "escape clause" that will allow him to tie up the property for a period.

Many buyers require time to make sure of the acquisition and therefore an escape clause because they are not speculators, but investors who need the property for a specific purpose. If, for example, Greg wanted to buy a tract of land to build a mobile-home park and for no other purpose, he is likely to insist on time to obtain the necessary permits for that development. If for any reason he is not able to obtain them, then he would walk from the property.

Know what you risk before you decide what to do. As the seller of the property, your risk would be that property will be tied up by Greg. If you get nothing in return for the time and he walks away from the deal, you would have to weigh what Greg is risking to see if there is a good chance of the deal closing.

This kind of decision boils down to Greg and his past record. You can ask him to put money in escrow, which if not spent for the necessary permits to get the mobile-home permit will come to you. If he is unwilling to demonstrate that he is going to risk money to close on the property, then he is a bad risk for you. He is demonstrating a lack of self-confidence in his own abilities, and may well be nothing more than a speculator.

If you have the time and there is no one at your door, even this type of buyer or exchanger can be a welcome sight. But make sure you not only see what you think the contract says, **inspect what every nook and cranny of the agreement holds in store for you**. Do not become a victim of a hidden loophole.

10. The Lawyer—Yours and Theirs

Your own lawyer can be a pitfall for many of the same reasons that your CPA or accountant can, **plus a few more.** As with your accountant, you don't want your lawyer making decisions for you. Your lawyer should only be your adviser, your devil's advocate, and your counselor and not your partner (unless he is willing to risk some of his cash along with yours). The information the lawyer gives you should be designed to let you make the most informed decision possible.

Specialization Can Work Against You

Lawyers tend to specialize more than accountants, and if you have a specific problem or deal in a certain kind of property, you should always attempt to get team members who are experts in that field. This is most important with the team's lawyer, because of the implications of a real estate acquisition through purchase or exchange, and the later disposition of that property by some other means, can be terribly lasting . . . and very expensive.

Check out the lawyer as you would a surgeon. You don't want a foot specialist doing open-heart surgery on you, do you? Or how about a proctologist removing your adenoids? Most distasteful thought, isn't it? Well, if your best friend is a divorce lawyer, and the best in the business, do not assume that he knows anything about the problems that you can encounter trying to do a multiple exchange under the IRS 1031.

Non-real-estate lawyers may not have done a real estate transaction in years, so they are apt to rely on their legal assistants—who **can** be very adept and efficient if they are experienced in real estate transactions. But if they are just as fresh to this field as their lawyer boss, then you have a situation of the blind leading the blind—so you cannot expect to be told anything informative. Worse, because the lawyer may feel very uncomfortable with the task, he may suggest that it is a bad deal, to avoid messing up a good deal by mistake.

The Best Way to Find a Good Real Estate Lawyer

Go to a lawyer you know and ask him whom, outside his own office, would he recommend as the best real estate lawyer, experienced in real estate exchanges involving the kind of property you want to deal with. Adjust that question to fit your specific needs, of course, but make sure that you are not asking the lawyer to help you, other than to pass you on to two or more lawyers. Suggest that they pick from a firm where you will be dealing directly with the lawyer they recommend, rather than their giving you the safe choice of the biggest firm in town where you get handed to the newest, just-passed-the-bar lawyer.

Dealing with the Other Party's Lawyer

The other lawyer is someone you have no control over, but you can anticipate that most lawyers want to redo, revise, restate, reword, remove. Even simple, clear contracts meet this response. All of this takes time, and time can work against the deal. When the lawyer takes a week or two just to set up an appointment to review the offer, takes another week to review it, then wants three days to change it, and so on, momentum is lost. Brokers know this; they know that many transactions go down the tubes because of a break in the enthusiasm for the transaction between the two parties.

I know that my own lawyer has messed up more than one of my transactions because of his unreasonable delays. So I try very hard to make it clear to my lawyers that if they cannot respond to me quickly, they should tell me up front that they are too busy so I can go to someone else.

But consider that you are going to be at the whim of someone else's lawyer. What can you do? Here are eight tips for overcoming the other lawyer's roadblocks in advance:

1. **Know in advance who the lawyer will be.** This can be helpful, because it might be someone you know or know of. Check with your own lawyer and other team members to see if they know of this person. This will come in handy later when the offer is going to that person for review.

2. **Have two good copies of the offer for the lawyer.** Often fax copies are sent that are impossible to read, and that delays everything. Avoid this by having two extra original copies earmarked for the other party's lawyer.

3. **If an exchange is part of the deal, provide a full backup package of the property you are offering**. This is essential to the other party in any exchange and equally so for the other party's lawyer.

4. **Provide copies of IRS codes that may have benefit to the lawyer's client.** If there is a specific benefit to the other party by virtue of IRS 1031, or other sections of Internal Revenue Code that you are aware of or that your accountant can acquaint you with, make copies of those codes and include them in your "lawyer package."

5. **Make your resume a part of the package.** Do not assume anything. It is always a good idea to have a personal and professional resume of you and your track record, if it is impressive. If it is not, have a biography showing who you are and what makes you the right person for that property.

6. **Have your own lawyer set the stage.** Prior to making the offer, you might ask your own lawyer to alert the other lawyer that an offer is forthcoming. Insiders, remember: lawyers are the insiders of all insiders and deal much better with each other than with outsiders.

7. **Be ready to help expedite any phase of the offer/counteroffer process.** This requires care and finesse, but can help things move along nicely. It is all a matter of simple things. Make sure that your agent volunteers to pick up and deliver documents (within reasonable distances, of course) and that, if something needs to be retyped or additional information or data is required, it will be hand-delivered. Do not provide any pretext for the lawyer to pass a delay on to you.

8. **Keep your cool.** It can be very frustrating when nothing seems to be happening because of one or more of the other party's team members. Keep in mind that you may not be told the truth; it might be the other party, not his lawyer, who is causing the delay. It is a recognized practice to pass the buck. Remaining cool does not mean you relax pressure, only that the pressure comes from others and not you. Let your agent, your lawyer, or other members of the team press for action and an ultimate decision.

11. The Broker—Yours and Theirs

The custom in most parts of the world is that the broker, and the agents who work for the broker, work for the seller they represent. This means if you contact a firm that has a property listed and work through one of their agents to acquire the property, in the absence of any other agreement with you, they are legally the representative of the other party. This does not mean that they have a duty, under the laws of your state, to act ethically and conduct themselves in such a way that you are not deliberately misled. But by law they are not free to discuss things about their principal or the situation that need not be disclosed to you by law.

The Fiduciary Relationship

You can understand this better if you are the seller and you confide with your agent that the reason you are selling is because you have a mortgage coming due on another property and unless you can sell this property you will be in big trouble. You only have a month before the balloon. Armed with this information, it would be the agent's responsibility to help you list the property so that it can sell immediately. Time is against you, unless there is another alternative. So you list the property at a rock-bottom price (according to the agent), but you confide with him that you really have no choice and are desperate. Why, you'd even take $40,000 less if you had to, you tell the agent.

Along comes a prospective buyer or exchanger who can solve your problem by generating sufficient cash to meet your needs. He asks your agent who is showing the property, "How low do you think he'll go?"

Do you want the other party to know how desperate you really are? That you would take $40,000 less? I would think not.

Knowing that the agent represents the seller and you are the buyer, you can elect to hire an agent to represent you as a buyer's broker and pay him a fee.

Unless the broker is truly working for you, you cannot treat him as a full inside member to your team. Instead, look on the broker as an adviser who works with your team but is never told everything. It will be a "need-to-know" sort of relationship, which, while not ideal, will be the way it should be in those situations.

Exchanges are a two-way street, and you are better off being the aggressive party to the exchange. This enables you to have your cake and eat it, too, with respect to your agent. As an exchanger, you will have a property or a package of properties, products, and services to exchange. Your broker or agent represents that package and goes hunting for properties or other things for you to exchange into. Because you are a "seller" in this respect, your broker is bound to work for you, and because you pay him a fee, he will be representing you in dealings with the other side of the deal. The other side is generally represented by their own listing broker, so the deal evolves into the insider brokers dealing with each other. In those situations each side is usually paid a fee by the "seller" they represent.

If no other broker exists, then your broker or agent will be the only broker representing the transaction and will either be paid by you only, or, with your agreement and understanding, will also receive a fee from the other side.

The Other Party's Broker

This is another story altogether. When it comes to general real estate you are a buyer, and the seller has a listing broker as I just mentioned above. The conventional custom is to treat the broker as an adviser, and nothing more.

In real estate exchanges you enter a new and more creative world of real estate transactions, and the conventional "list-and-sell-houses" broker or agent can become a major pitfall to overcome.

Go slow and be positive—you will make a deal. This can be difficult if the market is hot, and when you have difficulty with the brokers in the deal you are faced with the problem of trying to go around the broker and get to his principal without him, or forgetting the deal. I do not advise trying to go around the broker because that is not a good way of doing business, and if you have an agent representing you it is possible he would be in violation of the professional code of ethics. There are five things you can do, however, that can help you get past a difficult broker or agent.

The 5 Tips to Overcome the Other Broker

1. Get to know him.
2. Deal through your own team-member broker.
3. Let them see how they are to be paid.
4. Explain that exchanges are big business.
5. Insist on your agent making the presentation.

Used together, these tips will help you make more deals. At the same time, go slow and build a strong base for your future transactions.

16

Getting Through the Closing Successfully

Major Preclosing Problems

A good proportion of conventional real estate contracts make a successful transition from signed contract to closed transaction. The proportion of real estate exchange deals that make it all the way from contract to closing is much lower, however. This is a sad fact within the real estate industry, and it discourages many real estate agents from getting involved with exchanges. It is hard enough to put the deal together, and even tougher to have to start all over if it falls apart. But the reasons for the difficulty to close real estate exchange contracts are clear, and for the most part, you can gain control over the circumstances. The purpose of this chapter is to alert you to the things you and your team members can do to mitigate the effects of common closing problems and make sure your closing ratio is higher even than that for conventional closings.

The 7 Major Preclosing Problems

1. Cold-feet-itis, or seller's remorse
2. Confusing advice
3. I've-been-suckered syndrome
4. Termite delight
5. Title problems
6. Money problems
7. Renegotiation time

Before we take a detailed look at each of these problems, take heart: you may never need to deal with these situations. The better you have prepared the initial parts of the deal, the fewer problems you will have once the agreement is executed and everyone is proceeding to closing. In my 25 years of buying, selling, and exchanging, I have seen more than my share of difficulties. They are all like a good Western novel. The stories remain the same, only the settings and the characters' names change. Some of the seven problems that I am about to detail will occur for the other party of the deal, because **you** will be creating the difficulty in closing. Pay attention to the circumstances and watch for them in the other side as well as in the mirror.

1. Cold-Feet-itis, or Seller's Remorse

Almost everyone who finally agrees to sell a property has cold-feet-itis, or what is more commonly known as seller's remorse. It is a natural feeling that what you own might be better than what you are going to buy or exchange for. This sensation usually hits two or three days after the transaction is signed by both sides, and might be nothing more than a couple of sleepless nights. A full-blown case of this can end up with the individual looking for a way out of the deal.

Recognizing the Early Symptoms

You usually know when this is going to happen long before the agreement is signed. The party who is too hyper, too excited, and too anxious is on a high. When that high comes down, seller's remorse sets in, in the form of fear, worry, or just the depression that can come with the mental exhaustion of making an important decision.

There are some very close connections between this problem and several of the other six in this list. It should be obvious that if other problems start building up, there can be a snowballing effect. More of a reason to nip things in the bud right away.

One of the best ways to counter seller's remorse is to anticipate it. Make sure somewhere in the presentation as it is nearing the final moment, or just after the agreement has been signed, your agent makes a statement similar to the following:

> Now that we are getting close to nailing this transaction together, I want you to realize that most property owners experience a strange sensation. It is natural and will likely happen to you. After the excitement of putting this transaction together, there is a moment of doubt: "Did I do the right thing?" I know that if you have that moment, you will be able to laugh about it and say, "You bet I did the right thing."

2. Confusing Advice

This is the closing problem that all brokers and agents dread: wrong or confusing advice that throws one of the parties into a tailspin. Advice from whom? It doesn't matter. It can be the hairdresser, bartender, lawyer, accountant, or next-door neighbor. The worst part about wrong or confusing advice is you may not be able to combat it.

I was the consultant on a large project for the sale of a major oceanfront hotel, in a deal that fell apart for this reason. The price of the hotel was $17,500,000. The person acquiring the property was hot to go and had done a considerable amount of homework; best of all, the property suited her needs to the T.

Hot, hot, hot one day, then cold as an ice cube the next. The cobroker was at a loss as to the reason, was intimidated by the prospect, and would not ask the reason for the sudden turnabout. I insisted, and the story came out that the buyer had been told that there were title problems and the sellers could not close "on time."

It was wrong information, so, hot under the collar, I called the buyer's lawyer. I learned that the buyer had not even spoken with the right lawyer and that the information was more misleading than incorrect, because the right lawyer was on vacation.

Should have been a simple matter to fix, but it wasn't; and so far, over a month later, the hot, hot deal is still cold as ice. Wrong advice is something you may never recover from, because it, like the partial lie, has the ring of truth.

Keep everything clear. Your only defense is to make sure that every sales tool that was used to create a fully executed contract is part of the seller's package, with clear copies made available to the lawyer.

For this and any of the preclosing problems, it might be necessary to go back to the step the agent or agents were at just before the final agreement was executed. What convinced them at that moment? A soft resell of that element may get things back on track again.

3. I've-Been-Suckered Syndrome

This is almost exclusively an exchange problem and rarely occurs in a conventional deal at this stage of the game. What happens is a bit like seller's remorse, only it is directed less at the property being given up and more at the property they will get. New information comes in, or the inspections show problems that were not expected, and the new owner begins to feel as though he has been had.

The basic cause of this is "oversell," something that overly enthusiastic real estate agents, or even the other party, frequently engage in. The attempt is to paint the best picture, but instead what is painted is a different picture. The remedy is to resell the basics of the property and point out all the positive factors. Keep in mind that if the oversell has been too grandiose, too elaborate, and includes too much fantasy and not enough reality, the new course established by the other party may not be alterable.

To keep this potential deal killer to a minimum, it is a good idea to make sure that your property package does not contain pie-in-the-sky statements. Income properties should not have pro formas of income and expense that create the illusion that the property is really worth $3,500,000, when the real down-to-earth, **truthful** numbers show a total value closer to $2,500,000.

Even the smallest untruth discovered will be a crack in the dam, letting through a trickle of doubt. Honesty on your part is not enough, however, as you must make sure that the agents have the right information to give out. What your agents say is reflected back on you, and if they inadvertently or deliberately misrepresent something, your deal can go down the tubes.

4. Termite Delight

In areas of the world where termites live—which is most of the world—they can reside inside your buildings, and unless you check you may never know they are there.

While the damage may be minor, having termites discovered in your property can be the straw that can topple a deal that is already on shaky ground.

In Florida, all standard contracts call for termite inspections, and there are provisions that place the cost for damage to the present owner, up to a certain dollar limit. Even though the dollar limit may be sufficient to cover the repair, the very fact that termites are discovered can throw doubt into the deal. Doubt is the father of worry and worry the sister of frustration, and frustration is the mother of revenge. When revenge sets in, watch out. And all it took to break that camel's back was a little ol' termite.

Get a Termite Inspection Before Closing

As the owner of a property, **get a termite inspection** on an annual basis to ensure that there are no termites active in the property. If you have a termite service that periodically sprays and checks for termites, they will (in most cases) sell you a termite insurance that will cover you for cost of repairs and removal of termites, should any occur, during the term of the policy. This should also ensure that there will be no termites found during the inspection period of your exchange.

When you have not taken care of the termites in advance and they **are** found, you need to attend to the problem post haste. There should be no argument about who pays for what, because it is your own fault for not taking care of the matter earlier. Now that they are there, get rid of them and repair the damage. The quicker you do that, the less of a problem you will have with the other party.

If you **are** the other party and the property you hope to acquire is loaded with termites and the owner is taking care of the problem quickly and completely, you can breathe easier—assuming that there was no major damage that cannot be corrected. On the other hand, if the owner is shopping around for a cheap solution, balking at repairs, or pointing a finger to the contract that reads, "if the repair cost of the damage exceeds $5,000, and the Seller does not agree to pay the excess, then the Buyer may pay the added cost or elect to withdraw from the contract," then you have a decision to make. Is the property worth the added cost or not? That shouldn't be too hard to calculate. But make sure that there are no other problems that you may not have had an "out" on. If there are, and you can escape from the contract you might have been bound to, then parachute away. Geronimo.

5. Title Problems

Get these solved before you close. When you acquire a property, you are given a deed or what would represent title to the property (may not actually be called a deed). This document transfers whatever interest the other party had to you. If the other party had good title, then it is possible that he has been able to pass good title to you. Only possible. If the other party did not have good title, whether he thought so or not, you can be sure that you do not.

The importance of this should be obvious. Here you go, exchanging a good property for one that is valuable, will serve your needs, and take you on a path directly toward your goal; but two years later you discover that it really belongs to someone else. That can really smart. So what can you do?

Handling Title Problems

As soon as you have an accepted contract, you go to your lawyer or title insurance company, who will close on the transfer and make sure they clear the title. What they must do is check the chain of title back to a statutory date (different for different states) to make sure that every transfer was in the clear, that no unpaid or unsatisfied liens remain, and that there are no improper transfers or improperly filed death certificates that could affect the validity of the title you are given.

Have a survey done and compare it to the legal description. Make sure you don't make the same mistake I did. Make sure there are no encroachments on the property, and that no building on the property encroaches on another property. Also, have the local building department verify that all buildings are within the proper setbacks and that no utility easements exist across the property.

Buy Title Insurance—But Know What Is Insured

In all states, to the best of my knowledge, you can purchase title insurance. This ensures that the title you get is good. Like many kinds of insurance, title insurance may have its own loopholes, in the way of exclusions from the coverage. Whenever you get title insurance, you should make sure you understand what the exclusions are. Question the lawyer or title insurance company in detail, about the reasons for the exclusion and about what possible claim could occur that would allow the insurance company to escape liability. See if there is not something that can be done to have the exclusion removed. Often these exclusions are based on information not given to the company, such as claims that are made based on facts that would have been evident were a recent survey presented to the insurance company. If that is all they want, and your contract provides for the other party to pay for that survey, then get it. If you are satisfied that there is little or no possibility of such a claim and want to take a risk of faulty title, then proceed. Most of the time, the insurance will give you good protection . . . better than you will have without the insurance, to be sure.

A thorough examination of the past title transfers will divulge most latent problems, which is why you are safest when dealing with a lawyer or title company experienced in that kind of property and that specific locale.

Your only true control over the other party is prior to the closing, so take advantage of all your contractual rights to make sure that you get exactly what you are supposed to receive.

6. Money Problems

"Do you have change for a twenty?"
"Sure. Two fives do?"
"Yeah. Two fives are fine."
"Say, can you lend me a twenty?"

Not a good way to start out a deal, but in reality many real estate transactions fall into the **nothing down** category. In my book *Cashless Investing*, (Playboy Press, 1982) and the later edition, *$1,000 Down Can Make You Rich* (Prentice Hall, 1985), I discuss many different techniques of acquiring property without putting up any (of your own) cash. Sellers who shy away from creative deals offered to them, or buyers who do not believe it is possible to buy and sell real estate and make a profit—even though the buyers never spend any of their own money—will never truly succeed in the real estate game. Exchanges are another form of cashless investing.

There will be times, however, when cash is essential and a part of the contract. It might be that you are the party to get cash, and the other party shows up with excuses that the mortgage he was expecting, or the brother-in-law who was to invest with him, has yet to show up.

Other money problems come in the forms of who is to pay for what. This question comes up from time to time with inspections, and repairs the inspections indicate are required.

In any event, the last-minute rush for money by either party can throw a closing in a tailspin.

The Best Tactic Is Last-Minute Urgency

If you are short of funds and need to extend the closing, but the other party has not been cooperative, you may have no choice but to spring your urgency at the closing table. If this is the case you would not want to do it with a personal confrontation.

"Good afternoon, gentlemen," your closing agent would begin, "Mr. Cummings will be late, as he is flying in from Montevideo, Uruguay. Can I get you some coffee?"

Three hours later the phone rings . . . static. After being cut off several times the message comes through. "Well, as you obviously gathered," the closing agent continues, "Mr. Cummings's aircraft apparently has crashed somewhere between Brasilia and Cayenne. Good thing his mobile phone is still working. We will have to reschedule for, let me see [looking at the appointment book] for the same day next month."

Okay, okay, so that is extreme. But in desperate cases you have to call on desperate means. Only make sure that your plane did crash somewhere south of Cayenne, or come up with a more plausible story. Just don't be there, and don't be available for communication. Arguments are not possible if you cannot communicate with the person.

7. Renegotiation Time

This is one of the toughest games to play, but many buyers do it very well, and they wait until the last moment to spring a new contract on the table.

The scenario is something like this. You and Theo have entered into an agreement to exchange your 200 acres for Theo's shopping center. Everything seems to have gone okay. The inspections have been over with no objections, the title is checked, and now is closing time.

Everything starts out fine. People even start to sign the documents, and Theo, who is to pay you an additional $100,000 to match the equity in the exchange, brings out his cashier's check (or at least it looks like a cashier's check) for $100,000.

Then, just about the same moment you are starting to daydream about how you are going to spend some of that money, Theo's lawyer points to something in one of the documents and in a surprised and slightly squeaky voice, stammers something startling to Theo. He turns to the table and says, "Excuse us for a few minutes, I need to speak with Theo in private," and they depart—leaving the whole room to sweat out what turns into an hour-and-a-half wait. On their return, they are relaxed. The lawyer politely suggests that there has been an error made with the title and that under these circumstances he cannot advise his client to close . . . unless there are some minor changes made in the agreement.

"What changes?" everyone wonders. Someone asks and then everyone gasps. "Reduce the price by $500,000? Why, why that's impossible."

Not impossible of course, nothing is impossible, and given the right circumstances you can be put over the barrel by someone like Theo and his lawyer.

You can avoid this scenario by making sure that all documents have gone through pre-closing approvals by both sides. There is no reason for any surprises at the closing; when it does happen, it is always because of sloppy closing agents who did not do their job properly. Mind you, there can be problems, but the time for them to be noticed is not at the closing table when **you might have run out of time.** You need to close **now,** or be in deep trouble.

Check with your closing agent or lawyer a couple of weeks prior to the closing, and make sure that everything is ready and that both he and the lawyer or agent for the other party are in agreement as to the forms and documents for the closing.

The smoothest closings are where the parties do not meet at the closing table. Each party comes in and executes what he needs to sign or give up, and then the other party does the same. You can become a drinking or social pal to the other party another day; the closing day is not the time.

The 4 Critical Self-Protective Steps

1. Make sure that all preclosing conditions are met.
2. Cross every T.
3. Live up to your end of the deal.
4. Open a file labeled "To sue or not to sue."

So, this is what defensive planning at its best boils down to. Dig the foxholes and batten down the hatches. All this might sound like a negative thought process, but to paraphrase the words of President Lyndon B. Johnson, "better them than us."

Make Sure That All Preclosing Conditions Are Met

Start with the first critical step. This sounds easy, but there will be times when meeting all the preclosing conditions on time can be downright hard to do. Remember, you are dependent on what other people do and on their timetables. Your needs are not their priority, so you must make sure that proper scheduling of whatever it is that **you have to do** is properly accomplished.

To make sure that you do all that is needed, you should review the contract and make a note of everything that is a preclosing condition. Some of these "to be done" events will be under your direct control, others under the control of the other party. It is likely that some of the things that need to be accomplished prior to closing will depend on an action by you to start something the other party must do, such as, deliver a survey, or provide an inventory . . . delay this and you run the risk of setting off a new set of negotiations that can end up with a busted deal, or a deal that is not what you had hoped for. Remember, one side of the deal will have a tighter timetable than the other. If you are the side with the short fuse, you had best make sure that nothing allows the other side to light it. So it goes for having every T crossed.

Cross Every T

This concerns the multitude of approvals that are apt to be a part of any exchange, or most real estate transactions, for that matter. Your rights, their rights, everyone has something that needs to be checked and approved. Did you approve on time? Did you send notice by the proper date and to the exact address as stated in the contract? Or did you make a phone call and think that was good enough? It might be okay, and the other side just might forgive you for making a little mistake. But then, perhaps they won't.

Make a checklist of the things to do as soon as the contract has been fully executed by both parties. It is important that you list everything and not just what you must do, because critical tasks that you must do may depend on the other party's giving you documents or other information. One delay can start a domino effect of other postponements, and the contract closing can be jeopardized.

Sample Preclosing Contract Checklist

```
First-party checklist between
Bates as first party and Jones as second party
Date of Contract—March 3, 1993
```

To Be Done	Deadline	Date Done
Order termite inspection		March 4
Order roof inspection		March 4
Order general inspection		March 4
Deliver survey to second party	March 7	March 5
Deliver inventory to second party	March 7	March 6
Receive following documents:		
First mortgage on his property	March 7	March 7
Second mortgage on his property	March 7	March 7
All leases	March 7	March 7
Contracts of employment	March 7	March 7
His inventory	March 7	March 7
Review reports on:		
Termite inspection		March 10
Roof inspection		March 10
General inspection		March 10
Approve:		
Termite inspection	March 12	March 10

Roof inspection	March 12	March 11
General inspection	March 12	March 12
Inventory	March 12	March 12
First mortgage	March 12	March 12
Second mortgage	March 12	March 12
Leases	March 12	March 12
Contracts of employment	March 12	incomplete

```
Get approvals from second party on:
    Inspections of first property       March 12       March 12
    Survey                              March 12       March 12
    Inventory                           March 12       March 12


Preclosing conference                   March 26       delay
Date of closing                         March 31       delay
```

Problems encountered: Did not get full list of employment conracts and on request second party indicated that the CPA had another file that contained them and was in South America for three weeks and no one could find them. Closing to be rescheduled later.

Live Up to Your End of the Deal

You still want the property, don't you? Nothing has changed your mind about that, so why delay or become a wrench in the gears of a smooth closing?

With a checklist such as the one shown, you should be able to get everything together that you need to give to the other party, and you can stay on top of those items you need to get from the other party, outside advisers, or inspectors.

Open a File Labeled "To Sue or Not to Sue"

The ultimate can of worms, called legal action, is the very last thing you want to get involved with. However, it should be one of the first things that you defend against or plan for, depending on the point of view and what occurs with the other party.

The question: What must you have done wrong to have a lawsuit brought against you? Answer: Nothing.

We live in a world and society where we can bring legal action against someone on a whim, or in an attempt to bring about a delay. In real estate transactions of all kinds, there can be potential problems, which may result in one or more of your contractual rights being breached. The other party can delay the closing to the point where you lose financing, and cannot close without getting more expensive money; or the other side may remove items that you thought were included in the inventory you approved; or, worst of all, the other side may elect not to show up at the closing at all.

Everything pertaining to the transaction that transpires between the date you first see the property and the date of any potential legal action, whether initiated by you or the other party, should be well documented. You might need any of the following documents to defend yourself or provide proof of your claims.

What If You Have to Sue?

Where Legal Problems Can Arise

The property package. This is the property offering you have so carefully labored over. Is everything stated in that package correct? Could any misrepresentations or outdated information have accidentally been put into the package? To prevent this from happening, you should continually review all your property material and make sure none of those flowery words that describe your property are untruths.

A sound, truthful property presentation, a property package that points out the facts, is a good defense against claims of misrepresentation.

The broker's offering. This is often different from your property package, and may be a listing service form or the broker's own version of your property package. Your broker is your agent, and if he misrepresents the property, the end result can be a broken contract.

Just as you would want to make sure your own property package is correct, review in detail the material the broker sends out to prospects. I have seen many printer's errors occur that were not the fault of the broker, and often are undetected by the broker (sloppy review of his own listings), which become gross misrepresentations. This form of laziness can come back to haunt you.

If you have been the victim of any kind of broker misrepresentation, you may have a good reason to seek damages from the broker. You surely would have cause to break the contract if that was what was in mind. Keep all the forms and listings the brokers give you. When you have important questions to be answered prior to entering into a contract or later, put the questions in writing and make sure the broker responds to them in writing.

Property representations. This covers all property representations, not just those from the other party or the broker. Documents you request as a part of the ultimate approval process may not be the full representation of what you have requested. Surveys can be old and not show important changes in the site plan of the property or encroachments onto that or a neighboring property.

When you get documents or give them to the other party, study them thoroughly to be sure that they are complete and up to date. It is possible that the other party pulled out an old set of leases for the property you are about to receive title to, which greatly distorts the facts of the current leases. Check termination dates on all leases to be sure they are the latest ones. Always get estoppel letters from tenants to verify that the lease shown is in fact the lease in effect and that there are no other terms or conditions that would modify the leases.

Review property inventory lists very carefully. Do not just look at the list; go to the property and match and check off items. This is a lot of work, but one or two items missing per room in a 200-room hotel can add up to big bucks.

Warranties implied or stated. Implied warranties are the ones that can come back to haunt you, so be very careful about what is said about the property or mechanical items on the property. Stated warranties should be understood before they are stated or written down in the contract as they can have a connotation beyond what you thought them to be.

When you are told things about the conditions of the property and the state of repair of electrical or mechanical items such as machines, appliances, etc., be sure that you also put these statements in writing. If the broker or principal says, "and everything is in great shape, and like-new working order," then put that in the contract and expect the other party to live up to that warranty.

Inspections of property timely made and approved. A rushed inspection can be a problem, because things can be missed or repairs understated. If you were the cause of the delay, and you were unwilling to relax the terms of the contract to allow for additional time for the inspections, which, by virtue of being rushed, missed a major problem that surfaced later, then a legal problem may be about to come to the boil.

Do not let simple things create problems. Get your inspections ordered and make sure they are timely made. In anticipation of possible delays by the other party, make sure you have a provision in your contract that accounts for such events:

> In the event either party causes a delay in the delivery of documents or instruments they are to make to the other party, or delays access to the property they are to give up for inspections, and because of that delay the other party cannot meet the deadline for approval of the documents, instruments, or inspections, then the deadline will be automatically lengthened by the delay plus two days.

Let your lawyer draft a phrase that fits your situation exactly, but the idea is to provide for extensions to deadlines you have to meet that are thwarted by the other party through no fault of yours.

Complete agreement on who pays for the repairs. Nothing can be more frustrating than to show up at the closing table thinking that the $23,500 of repairs to the roof (that the building inspections had indicated were needed) are going to be covered by the damage provisions in the contract, only to find that the other party has had another inspection made that indicated only $2,000 in minor repairs are needed (but you are just finding out about it).

Agreement on results of inspections. You must get agreement on the results of inspections as soon as you have them made. If the other party disagrees with the findings of your inspector, the other party should (and most contracts provide for this) have the right to have his own inspection, to see if he is being taken over the barrel. After all, you would want that right if you were on the other side of the problem. If there is a conflict, it should be settled well before the closing date, when all the time has run out and fuses are lit.

Full disclosure of the items requested. This is often the major problem with large properties. Less than full disclosure can be by design or accident, depending on the amount of material and information that has to be delivered. You may not realize things are lacking until a later problem comes up. Unfortunately, this kind of problem often does not show itself until after the closing . . . sometimes years after the closing.

Your best defense when delivering items is to put together all that you honestly believe is required, and to get an acceptance that the other party has received everything they have requested. When you are the other party, you had best make sure that you have everything before approving it.

Title problems. When you acquire property, it is a good idea to obtain title insurance at the same time. If you have title insurance that has no exclusions (or no important exclusions), then when you pass the title to another person you can be relatively sure that you will not have potential title difficulties that can give rise to legal actions later on.

If the other party in a transaction does not have title insurance, or there are exclusions in his old policy that leave loopholes in the title, your lawyer or title closing agent should make absolutely sure that there are no potential dangers in your taking title to the property.

Your best defense in this is to make sure that you are dealing with competent closing agents. Some title transfers take place between the parties. Without having title thoroughly checked, your new property might be a pig in a poke.

Communications between the parties. Conversation between the principals can be the prelude to a busted contract. Things are said that turn out not to be true. As a principal, it is best to avoid any encounter with the other principal at all, or to keep the conversation to the business at hand, and limit it to answering questions that you absolutely know the answer to. If you do not know the answer, simply say, "My agent will get that for you," then make sure he does.

Any important communications between parties should be through their agents or in writing. Keep all this documentation, as it may become extra evidence that you were told something that turned out to be untrue, or that you did tell the other party the facts, even though they now claim you did not.

Parol evidence. "Parol evidence" means something spoken that is "extra" to the written contract, and often comes in the form of an added promise to do something not covered in the contract. For example, the two principals are talking while the inspections are made, and the owner of the building being inspected says, "In addition to any repairs I'll have the roof cleaned and painted." The roofing inspector is there, as are several other people. In most situations, the party that ends up with this house will not expect the roof to be cleaned and painted.

The best thing you can do about parol evidence is to follow up such statements with a letter to the subject party, with a copy to the agent or closing agent. In that letter, you would make reference to the conversation and the statements or promises made. If your memo goes unchallenged, then you should press for the parol evidence to be a modification to the original agreement.

Follow-Up After the Closing

You should be watchful of all that was promised and warranted to you when you acquired the property. If there are problems, or if things turn out not to be as promised or warranted, then go back to the other party and seek remedy.

Maintain a posture of building a good reputation in the investment community by being prompt with payments due from you, and give credit to those who helped you or played a part in the successful acquisition of this property.

Reward Your Team Members

Your team members should be especially rewarded with thanks for a job well done. This was, after all, just one in what you hope will be a long list of successful closed real estate transactions.

Taking Positive Steps for Positive Gains

Throughout this book I have stressed that setting and working toward your goals is an essential part of attaining success. In this final chapter, I want to delve a little deeper into the importance of developing a positive attitude as your primary focus for both success and happiness.

What You See Is What You Get

Your perception of what success means will govern your setting of priorities, which in turn will direct your energies. If you attempt to establish goals tied to your understanding of what **your success** should be, and are confused or see contradictions between success and happiness, your goals will not be in tune with reality and you will be frustrated, because you will attain neither your goals nor success. You need to define success in your own terms as it relates to your concept of happiness.

Getting Your Head Screwed On Right

Most people view their success from someone else's point of view. We listen to our friends and peers and image models. We believe, or at least envy, what they say and do and how they live. In the fantasy world of film and video, we develop a concept as to what other people consider success and happiness, and see ourselves in their shoes.

When it comes time to set our own targets for the future, we formulate plans to reach desired goals selected not because we have carefully analyzed what will truly make us happy, but because we need to achieve what others will recognize as a success.

The usual tendency is to reach for the moon without first climbing to the top of a building.

Pressure to "succeed" comes at us from every quadrant. If it isn't a family member shoving us along, it is a friend; or our own inner explosion of embarrassment at having remained stagnant. Without being willing to admit it, we become our own worst enemy. The self becomes a most destructive force when frustration and disappointment enter the picture. We are capable of becoming miserable and can live in fear of everything, without acknowledging that it is the

254

self that is keeping us in the miserable state we are in. Without knowing why, we blame everyone and everything for our failure, exonerating ourselves all the while.

Becoming a Superperson

Most people ramble about with no clear purpose. They either cannot find a job they like and keep looking, going through job after job, never satisfied, or they stick to a job they hate because they are afraid to venture away from the comfortable familiarity of surroundings they cannot stand. A superperson is someone who recognizes that he or she can control his/her own motivating force and take positive steps to activate this force.

As a superperson, you will be able to change the way you think, act, and tackle the future. You will begin to attract a different kind of person to you. They will be other superpeople, and together you will reinforce each other and build on the force that is generated in this kind of environment.

A superperson knows that above all, there must be the drive to attain inner happiness, that to achieve success without that kind of happiness is an empty vault, no matter how many jewels it contains.

Health is the ultimate goal that most people ignore while they have it; no matter how much "success" they get, they would, one day, trade it all for good health. But superpeople know that the secret to complete happiness is setting a high priority on health. There is every benefit to having a clear mind and a healthy body, because these are positive elements that provide a glow. This glow is a beacon that lights from within and shines brightest within the happiest.

You have seen those people. The truly happy ones. You envy their smiles and laughter and feel their happiness, despite the fact that they appear to have less than you do. But they are not living in utopia; they have problems and frustrations like everyone else, only they deal with them, they overcome them because of their own self-confidence. They recognize and accept that there can be no ultimate success without some failure, and no final happiness without some hurt and pain. That is, after all, the reality of life.

Why Superpeople Succeed in Real Estate

First of all, superpeople succeed at almost anything they do. They succeed in their own mind without needing to have an outside opinion of their level of success. This is a key element to happiness. In the business world, the drive to have more or do more than someone else can be all-consuming. People attack their job, their personal lives, and their social activities in a driving attempt to demonstrate their success: by getting more, having more, showing off more, doing more. That is not a measure of real success; it is, however, a criterion for greed. Superpeople rise above that and recognize that simply having more or doing more is relative to your own circumstances. No matter how much you have there is bound to be someone else who has more, and to try to win that contest is a no-win situation. There is no substitute to being able to sleep soundly at night, and if you are bound and determined to have more, do more, and own more, the sad truth is you will also need more—but it will not come. You can easily be rich but not happy. Or, as a superperson you can be happily rich.

Discover the Dynamics of Success

If you decide right now to deal out everything negative that touches your life, your tomorrow will be brighter and clearer, and your future is destined to be a happier one. By taking a pass on everything negative, you let in the positive. Your vision of yourself and of other people around you improves, because you stop looking for excuses and focus on areas of strength. There is no reason ever to think, "How can I overcome my faults?" because that is a negative process. Instead concentrate on "How can I build on my strengths?"

If you are wondering how in the world does this have anything to do with success in using real estate exchanges, then I have not done my job thus far. Developing a positive outlook on life and your own niche in this world has everything to do with real estate exchanges. It has, in fact, everything to do with anything you want to do . . . if somewhere in the back of your mind you hope to connect your version of success with a real version of what happiness is and will be for you.

Energize for Success

There is an electrical energy force that flows through the body when you decide to accept only the positive elements around you. You stop complaining, and you become more patient with genuine problems. You avoid or brush off people who do complain, and who are constantly finding reasons for their own problems or excuses for their failures. You do not need that; you do not want to associate with those losers, even though you might have had a tinge of that yourself in your recent past.

Charged with this positive flow, you change from a follower to a leader and feel good about yourself. You are able to see a total picture and at the same time know that to paint any picture requires more than one brushstroke. This is a process of building according to a pattern that may exist only in your mind, and even as it goes down on the canvas it is not discernible by others; but you see it all the time. You know how it will turn out, even if there are slight changes in midstream. You flow because you are charged with the confidence that your goal is attainable, and that you are doing what is necessary to get there, step by step.

The dynamics of this are so wonderful that once you attain this you will never be the same person again. The irony is that, though this state is simply gained, it is rarely found because many people are frightened at the prospect that their success depends on no one but themselves. These people are scared to death that if left to their own devices they will fail, and that failure is a measure of worthlessness. They are wrong. Failure is not a measure of worthlessness.

Stop Worrying About Failure—Use It

Let me tell you that failure is not the opposite of success; failure is a part of the driving force that allows you to build and discover where your strengths really are. Failure is simply practice that has yet to be perfected. Failure is just a trial run that leads you to success.

Successful businesspeople know that being right does not require you to be absolutely right all the time. The best decision maker is one who knows how to make decisions, and often, a mediocre quick decision is far better than a wonderful decision that comes too late. Every successful investor knows that making some mistakes is part of the game, as long as negative mistakes are removed from their act.

Never fear failure; embrace it, learn from it. Get all your failure out of your system, because that opens up the door for success. Follow my checklist for success and I guarantee you a better tomorrow.

The 7 Steps to Success and Happiness

1. Remove everything negative from your life.
2. Recognize failure as a learning tool for success.
3. Strive for a balance of health and happiness in your goals and plans.
4. Develop a clear image of yourself 10 years from now.
5. Formulate the intermediate goals that must be attained for you to complete the total painting.
6. Implement a plan that moves you and those who are a part of your life toward the highest goal.
7. Know that the only person you really have to outdo is yourself.

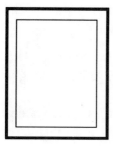 **Forms**

Contained in this section are all the forms used in this book. They are provided here so that you can make copies of them for your own use.

How to Find Taxable Gain

a. Mortgage seller is relieved of $_____

b. Cash or other boot seller gets   _____

    _____

1. Sales price $_____
2. **Less** expenses of sale   _____

    _____

3. Amount realized on sale $_____
4. **Less** basis (current adjusted basis)   _____
5. Taxable gain $_____

    =============

Annual Adjustments to Basis

1. Basis at beginning of the year $_____
2. Improvements made (not repairs or maintainence)

_____   _____

_____   _____

_____   _____

_____   _____

_____   _____

_____   _____

_____   _____

Total $_____

Less depreciation taken   _____

New basis $_____

Installment Sales Calculation

1. Sale price $_____

    Less expenses of sale   _____

    Less basis in property   _____

2. Gain on sale $_____

3. Mortgage the seller is relieved of $_____

4. Adjusted basis at day of closing $_____

5. Amount existing mortgage exceeds basis $_____
    (Line 3 less Line 4)
    (if Line 4 is more than Line 3 enter 0)

6. Contract price (combination of following) $_____

    a. Cash, boot, or mortgages $_____

    b. Mortgage over basis $_____

7. Calculate gross profit ratio. Divide Line 2,
    the gain on the sale, by Line 6,
    the contract price   _____

8. Expressed as percentage (Line 7 x 100)   _____

9. Mortgage held by seller $_____

10. Total received at closing $_____
    (combination of following)

    a. Cash and boot $_____

    b. Mortgage over basis $_____

11. Gain received at closing $_____
    (Line 10 total x Line 7)

12. Amount of mortgage held by seller that $_____
    represents gain (Line 9 x Line 7)

1034 Residence-for-Residence Exchange

Adjusted sale price of old property

1. Sale price of old residence $_____
2. **Less** fix-up cost   _____
3. **Less** selling expenses   _____

4. Adjusted sale price $_____
                                                                    =========

Basis, old residence

5. Original cost $_____
6. **Plus** improvements made   _____
7. **Less** depreciation taken   _____

8. Basis of the old residence $_____
                                                                    =========

Realized gain

9. Sale price of old residence, Line 1 $_____
10. **Less** selling expenses   _____

11. Amount realized in the sale $_____
12. **Less** basis of old residence, Line 8   _____

13. Realized gain on old residence $_____
                                                                    =========

If new residence cost is less than Line 4

14. Adjusted sale price of old residence, Line 4 $_____
15. **Less** cost of new residence   _____

16. Gain recognized (taxable) from sale $_____
                                                                    =========

17. Total realized gain, Line 13 $_____
18. **Less** Line 16   _____

19. Gain not allocated to new property $_____
                                                                    =========

20. Cost of new residence, Line 15 $_____
21. **Less** gain not allocated, Line 19   _____

22. New basis of the new property $_____

If new residence cost is more than Line 4

23. Cost of new residence $_____
24. **Less** Line 13 (gain of old residence)   _____
25. Basis of the new residence $_____
                                                                    =========

1031 Exchange Tax Calculations

1. Mortgage you are relieved of $\qquad$ \$_____
2. **Less** debt on the property you assume _____
3. **Less** cash you paid to the other party _____
4. **Less** value of other boot you gave _____

5. Boot against which netting is permitted \$_____
   (cannot be less than 0)
6. **Plus** value of other boot you received _____
7. **Plus** cash you received _____

8. Boot received \$_____
   =========

Computation of realized gain

9. Value of 1031 qualified property you receive \$_____
10. **Plus** qualified deferred installments _____
11. **Plus** value of boot you receive _____
12. **Plus** cash received _____
13. **Plus** existing debt on your old property _____

14. Total consideration you received \$_____
15. **Less** adjusted basis of property you give _____
16. **Less** cash you pay to other party at closing _____
17 **Less** mortgages you assume at closing _____

18. Gain or loss realized \$_____
19. Gain recognized and taxable \$_____
    (lesser of Lines 8 and 18) _____

20. Gain not taxed because of the exchange \$_____
    (subtract Line 19 from greater, Line 8 or 18)
    =========

Two-Party Balance Board

	First Party	**Second Party**
Value of property given	$	$
Less existing mortgage		
	_____	_____
Equity		
Balance mortgage		
	_____	_____
Second equity		
Pays cash		
Gives paper		
Gives boot		
Gives other		
	_____	_____
Balance		
Gets cash		
Gets paper		
Gets boot		
Gets other		
	_____	_____
Balance		
Sweetener	_____	_____

Exchange Worksheet

	First Party	**Second Party**
Kind of property		
Value for exchange	$_____	$_____
Existing financing	$_____	$_____
Original purchase price	$_____	$_____
Additions made	$_____	$_____
Allowable selling cost	$_____	$_____
Depreciation taken	$_____	$_____
Mortgage held back to balance	$_____	$_____
Will pay this amount of cash	$_____	$_____
Will give this other boot	$_____	$_____
Basis in boot	$_____	$_____
Will give this other property	$_____	$_____
Basis in this other property	$_____	$_____
Will give this amount of paper	$_____	$_____
Basis in paper	$_____	$_____

Closed-Transaction Equity Record

Date closed:_____ Closing agent:_____

Property acquired: _____

Legal description: _____

Address:_____

Justified value of property taken $_____

Less

Mortgages assumed at closing* $_____

Secondary financing obtained* $_____

Market equity at closing $_____

How you obtained this property

Exchange of equity (your cost)   +$_____

Add cash paid   +$_____

Add boot paid   +$_____

Add bonus paid (your cost)   +$_____

Add other exchange given (your cost)   +$_____

Less total debt assumed   −$_____

Less other value you got   −$_____

Your real investment equity $_____

Other important information

Mortgage on your exchanged property $_____

List any other item, boot, or service you got in this
exchange and show real value. _____

_____

_____

*(attach details and copy of mortgages)

Calculation to Find New Basis

1. Adjusted basis of property given up in exchange $_____
2. **Plus** adjusted basis of boot given up   _____

     Total of basis for properties given up $_____

Add the following

3. Cash paid to the other party $_____
4. Mortgages you assume on new property $_____
5. Gain recognized (Line 19 of tax calculations) $_____

     Subtotal $_____
6. **Less** cash you received   _____
7. **Less** other taxable boot you received   _____
8. **Less** loss recognized   _____

9. Basis of all property received $_____
10. **Less** value of boot received   _____

11. New basis of 1031 qualified property $_____
     ============

Inspection Checklist   Date:_____

1. Property address: _____
    _____
2. Owner's name: _____
3. Owners motivation: _____
4. Legal description: _____
5. Date listed: _____
6. Salesman's name and phone: _____
7. Price: $_____ Mortgage amount: $ _____
8. Mortgage terms: _____
9. Describe property: _____
    _____
    _____
    _____
10. Present zoning and use: _____
    _____
11. Potential uses:_____
    _____
    _____
12. Problems with this property: _____
    _____
    _____
13. Did you like it or not? _____

Sample Preclosing Contract Checklist

First-party checklist between _____

Date of Contract _____

To Be Done	Deadline	Date Done
Order termite inspection	_____	_____
Order roof inspection	_____	_____
Order general inspection	_____	_____
Deliver survey to second party	_____	_____
Deliver inventory to second party	_____	_____
Receive following documents:		
First mortgage on his property	_____	_____
Second mortgage on his propety	_____	_____
All leases	_____	_____
Contracts of employment	_____	_____
His inventory	_____	_____
Review reports on:		
Termite inspection	_____	_____
Roof inspection	_____	_____
General inspection	_____	_____
Approve:		
Termite inspection	_____	_____
Roof inspection	_____	_____
General inspection	_____	_____
Inventory	_____	_____
First mortgage	_____	_____
Second mortgage	_____	_____
Leases	_____	_____
Contracts of employment	_____	
Get approvals from second party on:		
Inspections of first property	_____	_____
Survey	_____	_____
Inventory	_____	_____
Preclosing conference	_____	_____
Date of closing	_____	_____

Problems encountered: _____

_____

_____

Index